SQUARES IN CONTEMPORARY ARCHITECTURE

PAOLO FAVOLE

SQUARES
IN CONTEMPORARY
ARCHITECTURE

WAANDERS PUBLISHERS
ARCHITECTURA & NATURA PRESS

© 1995 Federico Motta Editore S.p.A., Milan
© 1995 English translation: Leslie A. Ray
Artistic and literary property reserved for all countries
Any reproduction, even partial, is forbidden.

First Italian edition: 1995, published by
Federico Motta Editore S.p.A.
Milan, 1995
Original title:
Piazze nell' Architetture contemporanea

Editorial Manager: Federica Motta
Editor: Mariacristina Nasoni

Editorial coordinating of the profile section and iconographical research:
Giovanna D'Amia
Profile editing assistant: Anna Vaghi

English version published by
Architectura & Natura Press
Leliegracht 44
1015 DH Amsterdam
The Netherlands

ISBN 90 71570 58 4

Translation: Leslie A. Ray
Text editing: H.J. Scheepmaker

Distributed in the English language market by
Idea Books
Nieuwe Herengracht 11
1011 RK Amsterdam
The Netherlands

SUMMARY

PHOTOGRAPHIC REFERENCES

11: Takahashi Architect & Associates
14: Stefano Topuntoli
15 top: Yasuhiro Ishimoto
15 bottom: Kallmann McKillen & Wood Architects Inc.
18 top: Giuseppe Patanè
18 bottom: Paolo Favole
19: Panstudio - Bologna
22 top: Peter Walker and Partners
22 bottom: Paolo Favole
23: Richard Bryant - Arcaid
26: Dubi Tai
27: West 8 Landscape Architects
28: Fondation Le Corbusier - Paris
30: Mario Brunati
31: Fondation Le Corbusier - Paris
32: Fondation Le Corbusier - Paris
33: Fondation Le Corbusier - Paris
34: Fondation Le Corbusier - Paris
35: Mario Brunati
36: Aalto Archive - Helsinki
37: Paolo Favole
38: Paolo Favole
39: Giovanna Gandini
40: Paolo Favole
42 top: Paolo Favole
42 bottom: Paolo Favole
43 top: Paolo Favole
43 bottom: Paolo Favole
44: Institut d'Aménagement et d'Urbanisme de la Région Parisienne (I.A.U.R.P. - Paris)
45: Institut d'Aménagement et d'Urbanisme de la Région Parisienne (I.A.U.R.P. - Paris)
46: Paolo Favole
47 left: Paolo Favole
47 right: Paolo Favole
48 top: Institut d'Aménagement et d'Urbanisme de la Région Parisienne (I.A.U.R.P. - Paris)
50 top: Ponti Archive - Milan
50 bottom: Ponti Archive - Milan
52: Urbano Pierini
54: Federico Brunetti
55: Urbano Pierini
56: Ezra Stoller
57: Richard Meier
58: Peter Cook
59: Arup Associates - London
60 top: Studio Purini-Thermes
60 bottom: Studio Purini-Thermes
62 top: Paolo Favole
62 bottom: Studio Purini-Thermes
63: Studio Purini-Thermes
64: Constantinos Ignatiadis
66 top: Andréas Heym
66 bottom: Giovanna Gandini
67: Giovanna Gandini
68: Paolo Portoghesi and Associates, Rome
69: Paolo Portoghesi and Associates, Rome
70: Paolo Portoghesi and Associates, Rome
71: Paolo Portoghesi and Associates, Rome
72: Charles W. Moore
74: Yukio Futagawa
75: Yasuhiro Ishimoto
76: Norman McGrath

77: Charles W. Moore
78: Norman McGrath
79: Norman McGrath
80: Grazia Neri
81: Grazia Neri
82: Studio Podrecca - Vienna
84: Archivio Lotus, Biblioteca Poletti - Modena
85: Archivio Lotus, Biblioteca Poletti - Modena
86: Studio Podrecca - Vienna
87: Studio Podrecca - Vienna
88 top: Studio Podrecca - Vienna
88 bottom: Studio Podrecca - Vienna
89: Studio Podrecca - Vienna
90: D. Gale
91: Studio Podrecca - Vienna
92: Helge Bofinger
93: Helge Bofinger
94: Antonio Cortina
96: Foto Arte Cespa, Cefalù
97: Archivio Lotus, Biblioteca Poletti - Modena
98: Juhani Pallasmaa
100: Alessandro Anselmi
102: Municipality of Athens
103: Municipality of Athens
104: Municipality of Athens
105: Municipality of Athens
106: Moshe Atzman
107: Moshe Atzman
108 top: N. Folberg
108 bottom: Shlomo Aronson
109: N. Folberg
110: Studio Franco Zagari
111: Studio Franco Zagari
112: Tom Bernard
114 top: Mark Cohn
114 bottom: Mark Cohn
115 top: Tom Bernard
115 bottom: Tom Bernard
116: Matt Wargo
117: Matt Wargo
118: Alessandro Anselmi
120: Avraham Hay
122: Andreas Heym
123: Rheinisches Bildarchiv, Cologne
124: Lourdes Jancana
125: Lourdes Jancana
126: Studio Pica Ciamarra, Naples
127 top: Studio Pica Ciamarra, Naples
127 bottom: Studio Pica Ciamarra, Naples
128: Michel Moch
129: Espaço Niemeyer-Turin
130: Espaço Niemeyer-Turin
131: Espaço Niemeyer-Turin
132: Espaço Niemeyer-Turin
133: Espaço Niemeyer-Turin
134: Espaço Niemeyer-Turin
135: Michel Moch
136: Ermanno Casasco
137: Ermanno Casasco
138: Ron Green
139: Ron Green - Shin Koyama
140: Andrew Lautman
141: Paul Friedberg

142 top: Ron Green - Simon Scott
142 bottom: Ron Green - Ural Talgat
143 top: Kleinhout Photography
143 bottom: Kleinhout Photography
144: Gerald Campbell
145: Gerald Campbell
146: S. Koshimuzu
147 top: Dixi Carrillo
147 bottom: Alan Ward
149: Art on File
150: Consorzio 'S. Satta' - Nuoro
152: Archivio Jaca Book, Milan
154: Ermanno Casasco
155: Ermanno Casasco
156: Archivio Arte Contemporanea Crispolti, Rome
157 top: Archivio Arte Contemporanea Crispolti, Rome
157 bottom: Archivio Arte Contemporanea Crispolti, Rome
158: Studio Pomodoro, Milan
159: Studio Pomodoro, Milan
160: Studio Pomodoro, Milan
161: Studio Pomodoro, Milan
162: Gottfried Böhm
164: Renzo Piano Building Workshop - Genoa
165: Paolo Favole
166: Giovanna Gandini
167: Paolo Favole
168: Paolo Favole
169 top: Archivio Lotus, Biblioteca Poletti - Modena
169 bottom: Giovanna Gandini
170: Paolo Favole
171: Paolo Favole
172: Giovanna Gandini
173: Giovanna Gandini
174: Giovanna Gandini
175 top: Giovanna Gandini
175 bottom: Studio Favole
176: Giovanna Gandini
177: Giovanna Gandini
178: Giovanna Gandini
179: Giovanna Gandini
180: Paolo Favole
181: Paolo Favole
182: Paolo Favole
183: Paolo Favole
184: Massimiliano Prina
185: Massimiliano Prina
186: cb foto, Barcelona
187: Freixes-Miranda, Barcelona
188: Studio Pericas i Bosch, Barcelona
189: Studio Pericas i Bosch, Barcelona
190 top: Bach and Mora
190 bottom: Bach and Mora
192: Gottfried Böhm
194 top: Barbara Caretta
194 bottom: Gottfried Böhm
196 top: Barbara Caretta
196 bottom: Barbara Caretta
200 top: foto Diade
200 bottom: foto Diade
203: foto Diade
206 top left: foto Diade
206 top right: Federico Brunetti
206 bottom: foto Diade

INTRODUCTION

The following authors and their projects are discussed in this chapter:

Alvar Aalto:
Steel House in Helsinki

Emilio Ambasz:
The Plaza Mayor in Salamanca and Houston
Center Plaza in Houston

Alessandro Anselmi:
The Piazza Roncas in Aosta

Various Authors:
Strada Novissima, at the Biennale of Architecture in Venice, 1980

Various Authors:
The Plaza Mayor de Parets dels Valls in Barcelona

Luigi Caccia Dominioni:
The Piazza Santo Sepolcro in Bologna

Guido Canella and Antonio Acuto:
The Piazza della Repubblica in Aosta and Piazza del Municipio in Pioltello

Municipality of Bologna - Municipal Technical Office:
The Piazza del Nettuno in Bologna

Paolo Favole:
The Piazza Arese in Cesano Maderno, the Piazza Terragni in Lissone and the Piazza Sant'Antonio in Vimercate

Norman Foster:
Carré d'Art Square in Nîmes
Arata Isozaki:
Art Tower Mito in Ibaragi

Kallman, McKinnell & Wood:
Boston Center in Boston

Rob Krier:
Exerzierlatzes in Pirmasens

Philip Johnson:
Crystal Court in Minneapolis

Jean Paul Leanen:
The Place Royale in Brussels

Martellotti - Pascalino:
The Square in Nazzano

Adriano Mason, Vincenzo Pavan, Elena Galli-Giannini:
The Piazza d'Inverno in Aosta

Gustav Peichl (with Niki de Saint-Phalle):
Covering for the Art and Exhibition Building in Bonn

Arnaldo Pomodoro:
Project for the Porta Milano in Pavia

Franco Purini and Laura Thermes:
Project for the Archaeological Park in Aosta

Reinhard and Hofmeister, Corbett, Harrison and MacMurray, Hood and Fouilhoux Architects:
Rockefeller Center in New York

Gino Valle:
'Campiello' in the residential complex at La Giudecca in Venice

Claude Vasconi (with G. Pencrea):
Forum des Halles in Paris
Ugo Vietti:
The Square in Porto Rotondo

West 8 Landscape Architects (Adrian Geuze, Wim Kloosterboer, Jerry van Eijck, Paul van Beek, Erwin Bot, Cor Geluk, Huub Juurlink, Ineke Meijer):
The Schouwburgplein in Rotterdam

INTRODUCTION

This book is a reflection, from an architect's point of view, on the theme of the contemporary square, as a designed place.

The word 'square' brings to mind social, traditional and philosophical considerations. I wish, however, to deal with the subject from the specific disciplinary standpoint of architecture, in which the historical meaning of the term seems to belong to the collective cultural heritage: from the Greek world, gradually on through the Roman, medieval, Renaissance and baroque periods.

Forum is an enclosure, the same etymon as *raum* (room, space), *antrum* (cavern, room, primordial space). The court is also an enclosure, from the Greek *kortos*. The term 'piazza' (square), even if it derives from *platea* (open space, clearing), is always used to indicate a space surrounded by buildings, which delimit it and qualify it: other further distinctions do not set this basic fact in doubt.

In San Gimignano the road that leads from the Porta San Giovanni up to the centre, following the path of the Via Romea, shut in by the town walls, is pressed and flanked by continuous houses, between which the entrance to the side roads cannot be seen. The Piazza della Cisterna, at the top, is the natural widening of the road, with the same houses at its sides, with the same paving: a 'void' in which only the curb of a well stands out, and the towers looming above form the background.

There is no projecting building, for reference, be it the church or the town hall, the courthouse or the market. It is only the town square, and people meet there.

For a long time, squares were spaces enclosed by a continuous surround, and only from the late nineteenth century, with the progressive opening up of the curtain of buildings, does the term change meaning, blending with those of an open space, a clearing, a round island.

The Modern Movement, more attentive to other, more urgent questions, was for the most part indifferent to the theme of the square. The reasons for this lack of interest are many and intertwined: the decision to give preference to quarters composed of isolated, open-plan buildings, which broke with the traditional continuity of façades; or to residential projects in city suburbs, referring to the historic centre and traditional squares for public functions. In addition to this, we have the full-blown explosion in the growth in the number of cars.

The 'heart' of the city, instead of forming the core of a design programme, has remained merely a cultural reference. Squares have only been created as centres or pivotal points in the new towns, not in the suburban zones or in the large areas of urban expansion. What is more, the square seems to have become extraneous both to the urban construction framework and to planning culture.

In New York, among the skyscrapers, there are no squares, at least not in the traditional sense of the term. The dimensions of buildings seem to be in contrast with the pedestrian use of a square. A plaza was needed at the Rockefeller Center, and the architect obtained it by sinking it a floor below street level, restoring its human dimension and conferring an autonomous spatiality upon it. Thus, that small bowl has become a meeting place, where you can go skating on Sunday morning or lunch during your break from work. The buildings rising up from the sidewalk do not loom over the sunken space: the city of skyscrapers seems to begin at another level.

In the last thirty years, the square has once again become topical as a design theme, following the new-found attention devoted to quality of life. The number of competitions announced has increased (with thousands of participants) and building has begun again. The term, however, no longer has a single clearcut meaning: 'square' is now a word with a broad spectrum of meaning, indicating heterogeneous locations and design intentions.

In Paris, for the inauguration, in August 1990, of the Grande Arche at La Défense, the decoration of the surrounding squares, a series of clearings with an indefinite outline, was also completed. The children play around the lighting towers, in the north square, or else leap around on their skateboards on the track in the east square. But are these really squares? Probably not: they are only decorated clearings, technological landscapes on fields of stone. In the other spaces the passers-by move hastily, almost indifferent to the numerous sculptures which should make these spaces qualify as 'squares'.

The first condition for a place, today, to qualify as a square is pedestrianization: access, thoroughfare, use restricted to people. This choice is indispensable and of universal value: that the concept of a square coincides with that of a space exclusively for pedestrians. If necessary we can reinforce this statement with an empirical observation: there has been no need to restore or repave any square, or 'campo', in Venice. There are certain specific elements which distinguish the contemporary square from the historic one, separating regeneration or restoration projects from those intended to define 'new' squares. The latter are the result of the redesigning of deteriorated spaces, predominantly in the suburbs. There is nothing surprising in this: suburban areas sum up the contemporary city, the only urban form produced by our age. Leaving aside the marginal exceptions constituted by, for instance, the New Towns, suburbs are similar, if not identical, the world over: hard to distinguish, devoid of identity. They are closer to a car park than to a space conceived for people.

The objective of projects for a square, then, is to enhance the quality of a location: the positivist conception of the space as a void is replaced by the will to create a space with contents.

The traditional square had an endogenous function, defined in the process of its formation, as the servant of a building (the church square, the civic space annexed to the town hall, a square belonging to an important building), or else identified as having a specific use (a market for herbs, hay, shoes, etc.).

The contemporary square almost never has a specific function, nor does it depend, strictly speaking, on a building or monument. The purpose is still to constitute a place for meeting, coming together, and attraction, but the subject of the project is now the square in its own right. The place where the community gathered for a collective function (religious, commercial, political) is replaced by a space where single individuals act. Yet a space which is unified and qualified by a design.

The square as a meeting place today has many anomalous competitors, in all those spaces where the various collective functions and their rituals have been moved to. To give just a couple of examples, we need only mention stadiums, shopping centres, large multi-purpose buildings such as Philip Johnson's Crystal Court in Minneapolis, or the Évry-Ville Nouvelle civic centre near Paris.

Once we have established the distinction between the modern square and different spaces, understood as containers of collective functions, it is necessary to state that in the designing of squares a dialectic between the surround and the floor is performed, which is completely new historically.

Shiohiko Takahashi: port square (Kaiko Hiroba) in Yokohama

The project acts only upon the surround in creating new squares; in contrast, it is applied only to the floor, with reference to the context, in regenerating historic squares; or else to the floor without reference to the context, in the case of areas revived as squares.

A strange antinomy may be noted here: those who design new squares seem indifferent to the floor; likewise, those who design floors which are indifferent to the context do not concern themselves with creating a new surround.

Planning takes on different coordinates, depending on the specific case. In new squares, it is a question of shaping the surround and working on the contained space (as it is in the tradition of the square and how this is expressed in the language). The 'monument' to refer to is almost always lacking, but projects are distinguished according to their spatial morphology or the language used in the architecture of the surround. In the other cases the architect must work on the floor, conferring form, functions, landscape, scenery, graphics upon it, anything that can be used to determine a centripetal effect in relation to the context. Perhaps it is worthwhile, with respect to this theme, to consider the statement by William Morris, according to which even a stone placed in the middle of the desert is architecture. Unfortunately, few take advantage of the opportunity to extend the project beyond the floor, to the surrounding streets.

It seems, then, that of this exterior-interior dialectic, in which the contents of the architecture can be summed up structurally, only the exterior dimension remains.

If we examine the historic spaces of the city, we might state, for instance, that the 'campi' in Venice are interior spaces, that the Campo in Siena is a space within the surround (the imaginary 'tent'), which has the ring of the perimeter houses as its base, the Torre del Mangia as its 'pile'. Likewise, it is possible to state that St Peter's Square, in Rome, is conceived as an exterior, and the same applies to all newly designed squares.

In constructed squares, people can move within a spatial surround, the perimeter of which exhibits its own definition in relation to the space contained. In the case of floors, people can only move around the objects which form the decoration of the landscape. Brandi could have written: we are on the outside of an exterior.

Planning research is split up, therefore, and can go in various directions. For new squares it is focused on the quality to be attributed to the space; in other cases research aims to identify the various components which are to be synthesized in the project.

This research is very varied, and within it elements of local history, symbols, intellectual references may be found, or else sculptures, fountains, architectures, trees. The square is understood to be a place of synthesis, sometimes a place of excess or utopia.

Some elements seem to be especially highly charged in communicative terms, and recur in numerous projects: the ellipse used by Anselmi and Podrecca, in Tsukuba and Hong Kong; the compass used in Santa Severina, Cefalù, Brussels.

Symbols from astronomy are frequent, as are references to the heavens, to the sun and the moon; almost as though squares were a projection of the firmament. Again, the motivation for the design is sought in the *genius loci*, or in the designer's culture, in local traditions, in the land register layouts. The slow completion of historic squares permitted the accumulation of meanings and the classification of functions: there was no need for anything else. New contemporary squares have no historical stratification, neither have they the possibility of acquiring this over the course of time, because they are built in a short period and in one single operation. It is necessary to replace history with research into contents. We have an occurrence of what Heidegger states in *Die Kunst und der Raum*: 'Things not only belong to the place, they are the place.'

The absence of historical time and the occurrence of a new culture have eliminated public participation in the defining of projects. The architect and his client are now the only active protagonists in designing: they decide upon the site, the theme, and even upon the collective needs.

It seems that even interdisciplinary investigations, which the culture of assemblies and gatherings of the sixties and seventies considered indispensable in defining any public project, have disappeared: now we rely exclusively on the creative fantasy of the planner.

The relationship between the various artistic contributions is redefined and the architect maintains his coordinating role, while sculpture, painting, decoration, landscape art are all reduced to being single contributions, to be fitted within the general design. Architecture, which produces objects intended for use, tends to employ other activities as instruments, extending and exalting its own role in designing public spaces. The evolutions summarized above can be found in the same terms the world over. When local culture, or that of individual designers, does emerge, it does so only to a limited degree, in relation to certain particular solutions.

The purpose of this book is to create awareness of realized works (only briefly citing certain projects which were not completed); these works may or may not be agreed with, but they are nevertheless useful for developing a critical pathway, to indicate working methods and hypotheses, to constitute a useful (I hope) patrimony for reference for those who find themselves having to deal with a project for a square. For this reason, the projects are always viewed in their totality, and not divided into chapters for individual topics (typologies, *décor*, lighting, etc.). These orientations have suggested a key to interpretation and a criterion for choice and ordering. To begin with, only a few examples from the fifties and sixties have been cited, because projects from that period can by now be defined as 'historical', or in any case likened to a traditional conception of the square. After this, we examine the new squares, where the project concerns both the surround and the space contained within it: new squares, new surrounds, new scenarios.

There then follows an examination of projects which revive historic squares, where the floor is designed on the basis of the existing surround, with the exception of certain interesting cases which break with this policy. Finally, projects for floors which are indifferent to their context are considered. These are examined as attempts to create an interior landscape, which is shaped according to various criteria and methodologies, giving rise to differing typologies. To conclude, we examine squares built in anomalous locations - such as on the roof of a building or in a space in open countryside. These are understood to be an extreme interpretation of the project for a floor, without surround and context.

NEW SQUARES - NEW SCENARIOS - NEW SURROUNDS
Understood in the original meaning of the term, as empty spaces defined by a designed surround, new squares are perhaps the theme with the smallest number of examples. Indeed, the opportunity to build a square from scratch rarely presents itself. It does happen in the case of newly-founded cities (in the developing countries, because there no longer seem to be spaces for such initiatives in Europe and the United States), in the process of reconstruction of parts of cities (Berlin, Paris, London...), in the new housing developments for tourism, but above all in the old and new suburbs.

The designer's task is the 'historical' one: to give shape to the space through the surround and to qualify this as architecture. An example of this procedure is provided by the squares created in the sixties, in the New Towns, to counterbalance an open-plan urban framework with enclosed spaces, surrounded by buildings. They are, in a certain sense, 'historic' squares, and they also maintain this precise historical functional qualification: they are market squares, or, more specifically, shopping squares. They represent the only authentic realization of the rationalist approach to the 'heart of the city' theme.

We can count three extensively studied projects by masters of contemporary architecture among the squares of this first period: the church square and public spaces created by Aalto in Seinajoki, among buildings destined for civic use; the large square in Chandigarh by Le Corbusier, which still maintains a programmatic and poetic content, despite its extra-large dimensions; the transformation of a courtyard into a square, achieved by Gio Ponti in Eindhoven.

When designing, to place oneself within a tradition which has been consolidated historically by such prestigious results means architects must choose between expressing themselves with a contemporary language and adopting stylistic eclecticisms. The designers of floors without surrounds were not forced to make such a choice, as their experiences were totally innovative, without precise models to refer to. This choice is laden with unknowns, because it once again offers the comparison between architecture as investigation and architecture as scenography, a hedonism of form.

The search for a language seems to be more important than research into the type and functions of the square. The architects most committed to investigation, who express themselves through a contemporary language, seem to prefer systems with elementary geometry (square, rectangle), bordered by architectures defined by homogeneous buildings, the façades of which consist of the repetition of a modular element. This is the matrix for the projects by Meier, Pierini, Canella, Krier, Purini, to mention just a few.

Choices are formulated in two different levels of scale: on the large scale, the conformation of space; on the small scale, the module-unit to be used repetitively. The project develops between the 'large dimension' and work on the quality of the detail, where the image is sought, almost stimulated by the urgency - desire, necessity - to communicate with a sense of immediacy the perception of space in its unity. The surrounding buildings perform their role as backcloths. The spatial surround is contained in the low and continuous profile of the buildings, as though the vertical dimension, typical in the historical development of the square, had been lost. Even architectural and functional projections are contained within the common profile, and the meticulous work on the façades tends to make the design of the surrounds appear like a set design, independent of what is behind.

Projects which concern themselves with the container seem to neglect the floor, which is drawn synthetically, indeed summarily, almost as though architects are not devoting all the attention that would be considered indispensable for a floor with a pre-existing surround, or without a surround.

Some designers define the surround with buildings of which the Cartesian structure is underlined: the simplified (and rational) essence of the specifics of contemporary architecture. Pierini's project, in Monza, arranges buildings around a sistem consisting of two squares (civic and religious) and a large courtyard. The buildings' intentionally repetitive modular grid is evident, and the eloquence of the surround is entrusted to this. The sculpture by Arnaldo Pomodoro, which projects from the paving like a structured landscape, enriches the civic floor with shapes abounding in defined symbolic references.

Meier's choice for Twin Parks in New York is similar; a double space obtained inside three groups of buildings (in an alternate-internal position in relation to a street), almost defining two court-squares. The simple parallelepipeds of the seven-storey buildings only exhibit their own structural grid in the alternation between pilaster and window and between beam and window. The communicative strength of the surround is entrusted to the repetition of this design on all the surfaces. Only one of the floors is designed: twenty-five trees are arranged in a corner area, organized in rows of five, while the rest of the paving is developed using low terraces, with a design independent from that of the buildings. A sculpture-totem projects from this.

As an obvious historical reference, Meier sites two towers at diametrically opposed corners, each dominating one square, with the façades designed the same as the buildings. These are just an evocation, and not projections sublimated in their role as a 'pile' supporting a spatial 'tent' (as the bell tower in San Marco in Venice in relation to the square, or the tower looming over the Campo, in Siena, mentioned earlier).

In his design for Pioltello, which has not yet been completed, Canella uses an elementary, square system, in which two vertices are open, while in the other two the functional and architectural projections are located, conditioning the floor, which is organized along the connecting diagonal. A flight of steps descends from the circular hall positioned at one outer corner, qualifying the square as a place of assembly, a municipal exterior, annexed to the town hall. The method is analogous to the one used in the project for Aosta, where the steps inside the 'Forma Urbis' building dominate the Piazza della Repubblica through a large glass window.

The architecture of the two low town hall building sleeves is very simple. In the other two buildings, with three floors, Canella works on the contrast between smooth surfaces and very close-knit grids, through a design that becomes more condensed as you move slowly towards the centre (as in the case of the projects for Legnano and Peschiera Borromeo). The two buildings continue, forming a half-square, a half-court homogeneous with the square, open towards the new residential quarter. Here too the concave vertex is resolved by inserting a convex volume.

Krier has developed a project for a new municipal square for Pirmasens, in the Saar, opting for a horseshoe shape opposite the existing building, joined at the ends to two lodges. The whole of the new complex, with three floors, is designed using a single module, consisting of a portico and two loggias, one on top of the other. The designer's sensitivity suggests an immediate - albeit not a usual - reading of the system, and a façade module that is extremely communicative, due to the evident historical evocation. Completely without a rear, it emphasizes a role of continuous backcloth. It is a Post-Modernist reminiscence - or temptation - that can be read as being transfigured by the simplification of the design or by the communicative strength of the sequence of images: a radicalized interpretation of the criteria summarized above, to which the great quality of the project is entrusted.

The result is an Elizabethan theatre of large dimensions, a vast *plaza de toros*, or an open-air circus with boxes. At the centre, covering the vents of the underground car park, Krier has placed a circular turret with a number of graduated storeys, the only decorative element of the floor, which is reminiscent both of San Pietro in Montorio in Roma and the towers of Aldo Rossi. Thus the axiality that the horseshoe-shape scheme suggests towards the existing building is contradicted by a pivot, around which the new building rotates, underlining the importance of the square in its own right, rather than its function. Perhaps the most significant example of the new squares, new scenarios, new surrounds created is the work by Franco Purini and Laura Thermes for Gibellina. It is a very elongated rectangular *agorà*, with the ends slightly rotated. The module of the lateral façades consists of architectural theatre 'wings', a wall with apertures and doors arching up into a concave cornice, concluding the space vertically.

The design paradigms are made extreme.

The system is a simple rectangle, but so lengthened as to be interpreted as a street. The façades by Meier, Krier and the others tend to become wings, making themselves independent from the buildings they cover. Here we would only need to remove the constructions to reduce the surround to real theatre wings, against which buildings may - perhaps - be leant in the future. A potential, destined to remain such, for a surround, where the choice of materials and colour proves finally to be important. The square does not have a definite function, it is only available public space, bounded by an architecture which is only rendered eloquent by means of its disciplinary instruments.

Work on the floor is reduced to a minimum: the design of the paving is simple and the only decorative elements are concentrated in the building that forms the head of the scheme. There are no sculptures, if we exclude the 'Neo-Gothic Neo-Ruin' by Nando Vigo, inserted as a 'lay pulpit' which echoes the other 'Neo-Ruins' spread around the area. The project for the square is all the more important if contrasted with the dismal, to say the least, building and town planning framework (despite the declared intention of creating a model housing development, employing the stars of international architecture), where often questionable 'pieces' by famous authors are set, out of their element. Finally, we should perhaps perceive the homogeneity between the Purini-Thermes project for Gibellina and that for Aosta, where the square is closed off by a 'great mask': again wings, pure spatial definition and separation from the surrounding buildings. Two indications emerge: the square understood as a closed space and a place distinct from the building framework in which it is located, and the project entirely entrusted to the disciplinary instruments of architecture.

Other examples, such as the small square of Les Halles, in Paris, can be related back to the same thread. This square, defined on its four sides by new terraced glasshouses, is arranged over three storeys and cadenced by white posts. Again recourse is made to an elementary geometrical system, the square, and to a repetitive façade module. The complete transparency achieves a continuity between the exterior and the interior, with the multi-coloured shopping centre visible through the large glass windows. Consequently, the square-space looks more like a cavaedium/lighting well, the opposite mould of the perimeter buildings, than the patio of convergence.

The courtyard at the centre of the district designed by Gino Valle at La Giudecca, called 'campiello' (small square) following Venetian tradition, is also square in shape. The quality of this small suburban space, empty and rarely frequented, is entrusted to the design of the façades, an unstable, refined balance between historical citation and innovation.

The Meringplatz, in Berlin, has a central role in the reconstruction of the city. A circular shape has been chosen for the plan, defined by low buildings, at the centre of a residential housing development, as the tradition of the Central European Modern Movement would have it. The vastness of the floor in relation to the perimeter, however, makes it impossible to qualify the enclosed space as an 'interior', as it should be, consistent with the layout.

A separate chapter is devoted to covered squares, which are rather rare, and have remained for the most part at the design stage.

One example is the civic centre of Glenrothes New Town in Scotland, contained within a mega-glasshouse. It is functional, but difficult to define as architecture; the opportunity to revive the British and Belgian tradition of the large glasshouses, which found expression in the Crystal Palace, has been missed here.

A winter square has been designed for Aosta by Adriano Mason, Vincenzo Pavan and Elena Galli-Giannini, in accordance with the Post-Modern lexicon. It is a cube, closed on three sides and open on the fourth, with an iron and glass façade, which is continued in the pyramid-shaped roof. Its shape recalls the covered courtyards of the town hall of Guastalla, or of Villa della Petraia, or even the small winter square created by Aalto in the Steel House in Helsinki.

The layout of Isozaki's square is completely autonomous. The system is still simple, but the surroundings are intentionally formed by buildings with different weights, shapes and façades; these can be read volumetrically from the square, where the author freely expresses his own language.

The temptation to reiterate modules on a continuous perimeter wall is completely absent. In Tsukuba the floor, planned with great richness of design, seems to be predominant over everything else.

Art Tower Mito follows the same procedure, working in small dimensions. It is a montage of the scene in parts, where the buildings appear as volumes and there are neither repetitions nor continuities in the façades. Rising from the centre of the floor is a metal sculpture of superposed modules: a modern obelisk, recalling Brancusi's *Endless Column* in Turg-jiu, in Romania.

The square in Tsukuba repeats the same approach, accomplished on a vast scale. The surrounding buildings are different volumes, each autonomous and distinct, working around the volumetric compactness. The square floor is designed with a close-knit checked grid, which is very effective; the two-dimensionality of the system is interrupted in the centre by a three-dimensional piercing of the floor surface: a small square within a square (as with the Rockefeller Center in Manhattan), an explicit citing of the Capitol.

The square is a historically consolidated typology, images of which are powerfully embedded in collective culture. The call of memory, a complete parallel level of consciousness in the design approach, materializes in this extra plane, which emerges with its reduced dimensions from below ground, as a perspective image of the cultural foundations of the square. But the micro-capitol is broken in the corner by a rock-sculpture. So memory is not pure repetition, and overlaps, fits in, along with other stimuli (Land-art, Neo-Landscapism), like a return of the Michelangelo-esque 'unfinished' work, which in that corner assails the evocation of one of his completed works.

Isozaki's citation is a preliminary treatise to the examination of projects for new squares - new surrounds - new scenarios, created according

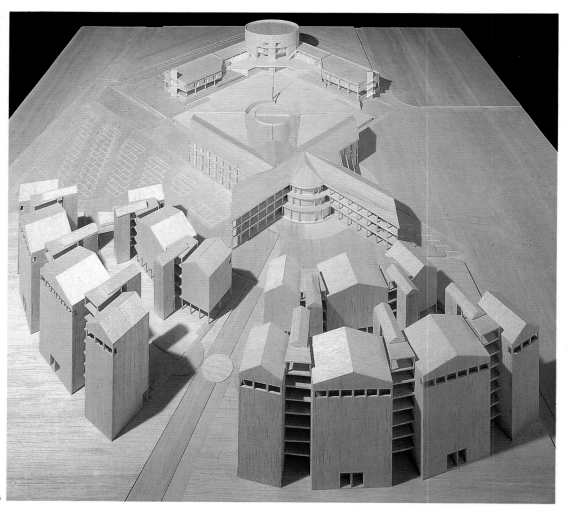

Guido Canella: project for the town hall square in Pioltello

to a stylistic language (which may become neo-eclectic).

In the suburbs of Paris, Bofill has created two squares, upon which a certain cultural gauchisme made it necessary to confer a monumentality comparable to that of the squares of the centre, in a sense redeeming their marginal location through imitative forms. Thus, on the model of Bath, the banlieue gained a Circus and a Crescent, which, as in the English town, are at the edges of the historic centre, but placed within a context where the construction of urban scenarios is continuous, in a model town of architecture and planning, between Baroque and Enlightenment. In the elementary imitative version in Paris, the façades are detached from the buildings they cover; they are neo-monumental, with all the schematisms of design that are proper to every eclecticism precisely portrayed in the columns and other decorative elements. It is doubtful whether the inhabitants of the suburbs, in their aspirations or in their collective imaginations, feel the need for a monumental square; in any case, this particular one is hardly inhabitable. The layout of this project is entirely due to the coming together of the aspirations of those commissioning the work and the architect's design approach.

The systematic replacement of study and creativity with the redesigning of works and languages from former times unfortunately reduced architecture to a surface, passing stylism off as commitment, decidedly the opposite tendency to the beliefs of those who understand the project as an investigation. In other words, it would be useless, in projects such as the

Opposite:
Arata Isozaki: Art Tower Mito in Abaragi
Below:
Kalmann, McKinnell & Wood Architects: Boston City Hall Plaza

one for Paris, to seek traces of Purini's 'wings', or something similar to Isozaki's reflections on memory.

Architecture, furthermore, can be understood as a spectacle in its own right. The Strada Novissima (Brand New Street) at the Venice Biennale of 1980 had the great merit of stimulating reflection on the urban scene, on the reconstruction of the continuity of buildings after the fragmentation executed by the Modern Movement. Yet the good intentions were suffocated by their representation in wood and *papier mâché* sets, which, like allegorical carnival floats, circulated gigantic forms, masks, disguises, in a climate of pluralistic hedonism, leading to the only possible outcome, absolute kitsch. Once the contents disappeared, the scene long remained, surviving the pavilions of the Biennale, which were quickly taken down.

We are now serving a heavy penalty to fit the crime: the liberation from eclecticism gave us the Modern Movement; the liberation from the 'inhibitions and limits' of the Modern Movement produced Post-Modernism (a definition that is now common, even though originally it had another meaning). The Post-Modern is a widespread attitude, because it has become the formal tradition of so-called yuppyism and a successful compositional formula. In this climate, and with an eclectic, Post-Modern approach, Portoghesi designed the square in Poggioreale, following methods probably exemplifying a precise 'philosophy'. The space is surrounded by a low terraced portico, on columns and caryatides, supporting a cornice painted in primary colours (a reference to the Greeks' usage?). At the centre a Neo-baroque stairway in red and white strips leads to the upper part of the portico, with metal ornamentation above it. This project is too far removed from the present author's cultural background, so an evaluation cannot be expressed here.

It is a redesigned 'Piazza d'Italia'. Besides, the Italian square is a wholly particular theme for contemporary culture: historical culture identifies the Italian square as the traditional prototype *par excellence*, and eclectic imitators regularly refer to it. Again it was Portoghesi who redesigned the plan of the Piazza Navona for Terracina, bordering it with complex architectures, where citings of Karl Marx Hof in Vienna also abound. In Africa, practically in the desert, Fakhoury created a copy of St Peter's Square with few variations; it even has a cathedral. It is a work the meaning of which seems clear - amazing, but also fascinating in its absurdity. On this theme, besides the interpretation of the Capitol by Isozaki already noted, mention must also be made of the paving of the Campo in Siena, reproduced outside the Boston Center (the residual trace of an imitative project that was not carried out), and also of Moore's 'Piazza d'Italia', which will be examined later.

The small square in Porto Rotondo was built in imitation of an Italian public square, confirming the fact that the need is felt for a square in every new tourist resort. In this case, the public spaces form a highly structured system on various levels, consisting of the main small square, open towards the port, near a secondary one with a flight of steps descending to water level from a garden and from the church square. The result is an artificial, neo-Mediterranean space: it is as though the houses looking out towards the sea from Portofino had been rearranged into a circle. The absence of any cultural intent is clear, and the result is a small set design, yet with a decidedly high degree of inhabitability.

THE 'HISTORIC' SQUARES

At least until the sixties, historic squares were abandoned to their destiny, often asphalted over and transformed into car parks. You need only look at a few photographs of squares, from the sixties too, to discover zebra crossings and other signs painted on the ground, cars parked everywhere, chaotic traffic circulation, disorientated passers-by.

It is a *décor* that is as compatible with the myth (and the economic requirements) of what was identified then as progress, as it is contradictory to the building context and its history.

Only a recent, slow gaining of awareness has led to the progressive closing-off of many historic squares to vehicle traffic and to their return to their original uses. This tendency has spread from the Central European area, where the wholesale 'in style' reconstruction of squares destroyed by the last world war (according to criteria that are certainly questionable but effective nonetheless) has entailed the reconstruction of the original conditions of pedestrian use.

Thus, during the last twenty years, we have witnessed numerous pedestrianization schemes, with consequent projects for the adaptation of paving and preparation of 'ornamental' works.

The design, or redesign, of floors for the reviving of historic squares is a specific contemporary approach to planning, and is applied only in old, or in any case traditional, urban contexts. Almost all the schemes of this type can be related back to a homogeneous methodology, of a historical-semiotic type; this is founded on a historical and structural study of the site, which then develops into planning schemes using the materials and forms suggested by tradition. A widespread desire to plan in a manner that is suitable for the context seems, in general, to be gaining ground.

This approach has led to very interesting results, yet without any reference to the original paving and the original ornaments, of which only very few examples remain; none of them are in the squares that have been redesigned in recent years.

The floors of historic squares are almost always without design, almost extraneous to the interests of the planners, who prefer to concentrate on ornamentation schemes: fountains, obelisks, statues, positioned in such a way as to form important spatial 'focuses'. After the completion of the Campo in Siena, which, in accordance with a special law, was paved simultaneously with the execution of the surround, the only significant paving design was by Michelangelo for the Capitol: a pre-contemporary situation, because there he found himself working in a partially defined space, to be completed and made unitary once again.

To repave and decorate historic squares is, then, to give a contemporary interpretation of a presumed real or potential original layout: a reading, or re-reading, is given of sites; perhaps history had no need of this, since in many cases the square was conceived and defined in its totality, and it was enough to pedestrianize it, even without designing the paving.

Architects, to use a 'Saussurian' distinction G. Baird used to refer to architecture, all seem to use the same language with different words. Their stimuli and suggestions for design planning come from common sources; from urban history first of all, such as the old lies of roads or the positions of old demolished buildings. The buildings surrounding the square are reinterpreted from the design standpoint, or else by identifying their entrances as thresholds between the private space and the public square. Again, cues are taken from civil history, from the memory of people or events, from the culture of the site, with its signs and symbols, from the pre-existing natural setting, including water courses, terraces, embankments, from the orientation of the sun. To identify all these elements, planning is preceded by historical research aimed at defining the formation of the square. Building techniques and materials are chosen, giving preference to those which appear, rightly or wrongly, to contain historical reference, such as porphyry, shingle, gneiss, tiles; a sort of latent stylism or mannerism while emerges from all this. As these projects are planned around historical analysis, the survey becomes all the more critical in terms of interpretation and use, because the *koinè*, the common language, can guarantee, in its own right, good quality results on the purely formal level.

Just as the range of methods of approach and design choices is limited, so the variety of examples of application is wide. Wishing to summarize this variety, according to definitions which are doomed to be schematic and not exhaustive, it ranges from the geometrical minimalism inspired by the location (Artés), to traditional historical minimalism (squares in Gracia), to 'archiculture' (Podrecca), to representative graphic play (Roca), to cultural and symbolic abstraction (Anselmi), to cite just a few. Projects that are decidedly explosive, such as those of Ambasz and Buren, lie outside these methodologies.

Many of the principles briefly summed up above can be identified in the project for the small square in Artés: simple, immediately communicative, yet loaded with deliberation. The paving, a rectangle and a circle, partially overlapping, occupies the position of an old buried water tank. On one side the plan of an old demolished church is reproduced, and outside the bastion the lie of the old path out through the walls is revived. Definitely a rare formal result, the product of a full application of historic and semiotic criteria.

The projects for the small squares in the Gracia quarter of Barcelona use the same method, but with completely different results. In the absence of historical and local references, the scheme for pedestrianization and return to public use is applied using few elements: pavements, short rows of trees, one or two simple central perspectives, all derived from the Spanish tradition. The same elements are used for each square in a different assortment, with extremely varied but very homogeneous results.

In this category, Podrecca's works by are exemplary; he carries out his projects in areas that were formerly Venetian (Cormons, Pirano) and Austrian (Salzburg), rich in the traditions of ornamentation of civic spaces. The project-related preparation of the three works cited is homogeneous: each scheme is organized around the dominant factor identified in the analysis of the site's physical structure. The ellipse of Pirano recalls the form and centrality of the buried circular port; in Salzburg the circular channel, the gutter stone for rainwater, is the representation and reminder of the underlying canal; in Cormons, the paving design is a metaphorical projection, simplified and allusive, of the façades of the perimeter buildings. In each case, a theme chosen as a key to interpretation of the location becomes a founding part of the project.

Natural materials, slight differences in level (a hollowed gutter, convex ellipse), essential elements of ornamentation, are used in accomplishing these projects: the monolithic red stone fountain, or the lamp posts so evocative of Venetian poles, or again the minute, sudden decorations obtained by variations in materials or levels (recalling the work on stone by Carlo Scarpa, who was active in the same region). The whole thing develops through passages of half-tones, barely hinted-at chiaroscuros, vibrations of light or colour in the paving, or else the positioning of an isolated object as an element of spatial aggregation.

Podrecca states that 'archi-culture', studies on the historical components of the location, on the visual axes, are elements of the project and not graphic exercises. The regeneration of the square, its return to civil use, occurs as though the threads of research were tied back into the project, with simplicity and balance; it occurs at a level - always mysterious and indefinable - where inventive capacity takes the initial materials into the realm of poetry. Podrecca gives the historical and structural interpretation of the site an extreme meaning as the matrix of a project, realized through a contemporary language - a language which, through the choice of materials, aims to be a continuation of, and compatible with, the historical context.

Roca designs the paving by obtaining his guiding theme from the location and from the existing buildings. In Plaza Ambrosio Funes, in Córdoba in Argentina, the design using concentric circles and rays has an altar in the middle devoted to the Holy Spirit and is placed on a map of Argentina, with the Falklands-Malvinas islands in relief. Roca's most important project is the rebuilding of the pedestrianized squares and streets in the centre of Cordoba, where the designs of the façades are folded over onto the new paving, which has become a sort of pool, yet a pool in which only certain architectural projections are reflected. Or rather: their simplified image is reflected, in the naïf manner so typical of certain South American paintings (how different from, say, Podrecca's organization).

Roca's project is the radicalization of an elementary reasoning, perhaps not wholly original, which is intended to tie a setting to individual monuments; in this case these monuments are the true qualitative substance of the space, and the reason for its consequent pedestrianization. A further, fundamental component is to be found: the extension of the project and the pedestrianization beyond the bounds of the individual floor, to the system of surrounding streets and squares. This, then, is an attempt to root the scheme into the context or, alternatively, to attract people from the surrounding streets towards the square. The latter, probably, is an indispensable characteristic in paving schemes, and therefore of the public reappropriation of historic centres, which can be seen in the projects by Podrecca in Cormons, by Foster in Nîmes, and finally by myself in Cesano Maderno.

The solution hypothesized for the Piazza Arese in Cesano Maderno (part of a joint project, the competition winner) may be considered important above all from the methodological standpoint. The square has a pedestrian axis running through it, the first section of a route that continues beyond, and onto which the accesses to the houses connect. The space belonging to the Palazzo Arese and the miniature square of the chapel are recomposed on the large floor of the square, differentiated by the materials used. The paving penetrates through the entrance corridors and is reproduced in the courtyards, using the courtyard of the Palazzo Arese in particular as an interior square. An undulating outline of red porphyry serves to indicate the old terraced edge of the river Seveso, upon which the square was built. There are no ornamental elements, if we exclude those projecting from the structure of the project, which serve to differentiate its parts.

The project for Lissone is even more elaborately structured. Here, the task was to pedestrianize the square (with an underground car park), redesign the base of the demolished buildings, create wings to screen off the out-of-scale buildings constructed between the fifties and sixties, and restore dimension to the space in front of the former town hall of Terragni, with a lean-to that repeats its rationalist modulations (a new portico, following the example of those for the Lombard civic squares or markets).

The paving design is differentiated in terms of functions: the whole space is used as an open-air museum of sculpture, complementary to the Premio Lissone art gallery inside the Terragni building. Here too, the whole design stretches to the access roads, where graphic and lit signs attracting people to the square are also located.

In Nîmes, Foster has created an extended layout, in which the façade of the Carré d'Art organizes full and empty spaces the opposite way round

Opposite:
Giuseppe Patanè (with G. Taverna and N. Tozzi): Monument to the Fallen and to Peace in Santa Severina

Below:
Ground plan of the project for the arrangement of the area

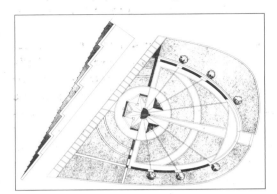

Below:
Norman Foster: view of the square between the Maison Carrée and the Carré d'Art in Nîmes

to those of the Maison Carrée. The space between the two buildings (though intersected by the city's inner link road) is completely repaved homogeneously, almost emphasizing that it aspires towards the unattainable, to be a wholly pedestrian square, lying between Roman and contemporary architecture. Once again, the paving is continued into the access roads.

Many other projects can be plotted on the same line. Of these, the project by J.P. Laenen for the Royal Palace of Brussels is worthy of mention, the demonstration of an extremely simplified way of applying the method. The square is rectangular, with an equestrian statue in the centre; the paving design has a regular, mondirectional grid, along the perspective axes and squared at the corners. Four rhombus-shaped strips connect the street axes and the palace, and in the centre, around the statue, there is a Compass design. This project, then, is the clear result of the assembly of certain basic 'phonemes' of the language.

Anselmi's project for Santa Severina can be considered in its own right for the organization and also for the final result. The space, originally a street of the old centre that was wider than average, was only transformed into a square through design. Historical, cadastral and natural references are therefore lacking: the research is wholly intellectual, in the most positive meaning of the term. The project is built on the axis connecting the gates of the church and the castle, and on the north-south polar axis. Their intersection, an arbitrary point in the geometry of the site, becomes the centre of an elongated ellipse, the purpose of which is to restore the unity of the space. This unity is confirmed by the concentric arches designed in the paving. It is an extremely conceptualized scheme, leading almost naturally to the use of numerous symbolic designs, contained in small circles at the intersections of the lines of design.

Towards the castle, the square opens up into a green space and, with the same mastery he employs for the other parts, Anselmi creates an Italian-style garden, where the flower beds are transformed into undulating stone benches. In general, it is a result that shows great clarity in its overall choices and great refinement in the details. This is an exemplary project, where problems of compatibility with pre-existing elements involved in the qualification of the space simply do not exist.

In contrast, two examples of projects in Bologna may be typical of possibly contradictory results in applying the method described above. Following a design by L. Caccia Dominioni, the Piazza Santo Sepolcro has been repaved starting from a low location, where, in the medieval urban symbology, the church of the Holy Sepulchre, facing onto the square, formed a relationship with the nearby temple of San Giovanni in Monte, positioned on an embankment and representing Golgotha. The square is therefore a point of arrival, to stop and sit, an expanse that constitutes the square of a complex of churches, placed in a scheme of streets which descends by degrees at that point, following the contours. Now repaved, the square is intersected by paths cutting across it diagonally in various directions, connecting the streets leading into it. These paths emphasize the square's dynamic role, a movement, a non-standing, which is contrary to the structure and the history of the square.

The project for the repaving of the Piazza del Nettuno has rediscovered a medieval layout, which is diagonal with respect to today's square. Instead of limiting itself to simple citation, the entire reconstruction has been carried out along the new axes, with a chequered paving system which exceeds its own role, groundlessly invading the whole space, generating stairways and triangular connecting paths. In synthesis: a scheme taken up from the history of the site becomes the cumbersome protagonist, and distracts from the composition of the square, formulated

in a later era on other axes and with different criteria.

Set in contrast to the planning methods examined so far, this is an autonomous, unrestrained, three-dimensional approach to a square's floor, where the surround is used merely as a modular reference and container, with its historical and architectural relevance removed. It is the effect of projects for floors without context seeping back into historic squares.

The proposal by Ambasz for the Plaza Mayor in Salamanca, which was not realized, and Buren's plan for the courtyard of the Palais Royal in Paris, are examples of this method. In both cases there is an attempt to occupy the space with landscapes of repeated elements, organized around a geometrical supporting grid. This expedient is relied upon by designers committed to a borderline work, on the boundary between sculpture and architecture. Incapable of resolving the floor as a large stretch of canvas, with a gesture or a sign, they are nevertheless always yoked to the design scheme of the pre-existing buildings.

The figuratively charged central space becomes the protagonist, and the perimeter - which is also so important - is reduced to being a frame, supporting the invisible threads of the mail, or filigree, of the modulation.

Integral to this type of work are the references to contemporary figurative experience which are to be sought firstly in the avant-garde programmed art of the sixties, though these are different for the two projects cited.

Ambasz shatters the paving with a close-knit grid, as in the project designed for Houston. His repetitive module is a parallelepiped, with its

View of the paving scheme of the Piazza del Nettuno in Bologna

dimensions based on a submultiple of the portico of the square, a checked design broken up at the centre by a sunken bowl: a square within a square, as in Tsukuba or at the Rockefeller Center. The vast space occupied by the bar tables, by the paths for students and inhabitants, is totally expropriated and replaced by sculpture-paving for contemplation purposes, running along the porticoes. Only the central bowl remains as a space to stop and sit (provided anyone is interested in going there). A similar result is achieved in Place des Vosges, after its transformation from Place Royale to Square, with the enclosed garden occupying the square's floor.

Buren has achieved a complex operation, projecting the modulation of the columns of the porticoes onto the floor and placing a new column, his repetitive module, at each vertex. The result is the occupation of the court-square with an ordered forest of columns, cut at different heights and painted with black and white bands: the ruins of a huge hypostyle hall stand unroofed, or covered only by the sky. The grid is graphically revealed on the paving by pedestrian crossings and by small multi-coloured lights, as though on an airport runway. Every choice is made in contrast with the context: broken columns parallel to complete ones, painted rather than in natural stone, lighting from below rather than natural. The plan of the square recalls the weaving black and white circles designed by Molnar, Rossi, Talmann and Yvaral, or the avant-garde Op-Art, of which the chromatic choice is also reminiscent. This raised structure could, in retrospect, many years after that experience, be the first great sculptural work of programmed art; it is the reliefs of Debourg, or the geometrical landscapes by Vecker and others, shaped on an urban scale. And, looking at the columns, how can Max Bill's designs, with their strips of colour, not spring to mind? Yet the use of tiny, evocative lights, drawn from advertising, or from juke-boxes, suggests a Pop-Art interpretation, and the overall result could also be interpreted in this light: the evocative quality of the work entrusted to the magnification of the object, obtained in this case through repetition to the bound of possibility, rather than through Oldenburg-style out-of-scale enlargement. Visitors and the inquisitive stand at the edges, rarely penetrating into this landscape of columns, whereas they ought to be playing amongst them.

Which is what children do, reading the square as an original space for enjoyment. The embarrassment which is created by the incompatibility with the old building remains: Buren has intentionally conferred a sense of the unfinished, of the provisional, on his arrangement, prompting visitors to wonder: 'When are they going to take it down?'

NEW SQUARES - NEW LANDSCAPES

Most contemporary squares come into existence in places which are already urbanized. They are the result of schemes to convert sites which are degraded, or unused, or residual, almost always located in the outskirts. Over recent decades, administrators' and planners' attentions have been focused on improving the urban design of these zones, while at the same time providing places for gathering and association. This is an attention which the Modern Movement had not shared. Though the considerable recent efforts have produced interesting results, these are not in proportion to the enormous need for conversion of the suburbs. In the final analysis, however, the examples accomplished provide an important record: instruction in this area in the schools of architecture has become gradually more attentive to this, and it can reasonably be hoped that in the future there will be a progressive dissemination of the culture of public spaces in planning. The consequence of building squares to fit into pre-existing contexts, even though they are for the most part devoid

of quality and evocative elements, is that designers become indifferent to the setting: the quality of the square is sought in the interior space, rather than in the relationships with the pre-existing. Furthermore, no precise, predetermined function exists, be this the space belonging to a church, to a town hall or to a market. The site must find even its own justification within itself, becoming a place of attraction and convergence, to the extent that most of the contemporary squares designed for a specific function are spaces of modest quality. Architects work on these floors without surround seeking form, function, message, in marginal and formless locations which are to be transformed into poles of attraction, abounding in images and meaning. The key to interpreting these projects, albeit in their multiplicity of approaches, is the search for a landscape 'within' the square's floor. Whether this is achieved using sculptures, trees, architectures, objects of design or technology or historical materials, they are always landscapes. But, if the phrase quoted from Morris above is valid, it must be agreed that here architecture becomes the ordering element for the various professional and artistic contributions, and that it enriches itself with new expressive possibilities, acquiring the value of a method of designing the urban landscape. It is hoped that this method acquired may also become a point of reference or a yardstick of judgement and comparison for 'traditional' architecture projects. Consistent with the observations summarized above, the order according to which the floors of squares are reviewed below is derived from the landscape typology created.

LANDSCAPE WITH SCULPTURE

The simplest way of conferring identity on a site, a floor, is to place a sculpture there, a generator of spatial aggregation, a natural reference point for users. This is the age-old procedure for transforming an indistinct site into a space: with a menhir, a stone, a cross, a memorial, even a simple tree; a large number of place-names have even resulted from this. The use of sculpture to this end is historically established in the designing of squares. We need only think of the Marc'Aurelio in the Capitol, the Horses in Piacenza (even more significant for being added in a later period), the statues in the Places Royales, the fountains in St. Peter's. Yet all these cases are centres or spatial focuses, referring to the surround. In the floors of contemporary squares, however, the aim is to create a square, or to resolve an anonymous space, without a surround, with a sculpture. Hence the greater meaningfulness of projects where the work becomes like an element of the landscape, or a primitive stone positioned to mark a place.

Arnaldo Pomodoro is the author of metal works with smooth, shiny shells, with cracks opening up in them to reveal a complex, tortured interior. His are totem-sculptures, totally indifferent to their context, and so can be and are used in different squares, in different locations; when they are repeated (as is the case of the three cylinders of Porta Milano in Pavia) or combined, they are by themselves capable of creating an evocative scene even in bland contexts (as in the Gregotti project in Copenhagen).

An abstract sculpture, almost a suffering metal bush, is placed in the centre of Mariannenplatz, in the Kreuzberg district of Berlin, where the Wall used to pass through. In the new Paris quarter of La Défense too, certain squares are only qualified by works of sculpture. Located within this line of thought is the most complete project by Nivola, in Nuora, which creates the landscape of the floor using actual fragments of landscape: rocks deposited with no apparent order, an abridged citation of the rocky Sardinian countryside, brought into the square, into town. It is a group of large menhirs, for which the contemporary reference points could be the works by the Japanese landscape artists, particularly the gardens of Kobe. The square in Nuoro is a project placed in opposition to the context of old houses of the historic centre, with the paving designed only through different delimited areas of stone, from which the benches also emerge. The figurative and thematic sculpture of the square is reduced to very small works, hidden between the rocks: sculpture within sculpture, or rather, sculpture generated by stone. The poetic attitude here is the same as the sketch of the monument to the US flag, or other of Nivola's works, where the image seems to be struggling to emerge from the stone. This work is a great example of Land-Art, the artistic current that uses natural and humble materials to design landscapes of primitive fascination on the ground; the method has considerable potential (as yet little exploited) for the qualification of floors. The procedure in reverse is where a sculpture-landscape becomes a place of aggregation, that is to say, a floor or a square. This is the case with Santa Severina; here, on a loop of road outside the centre, Patanè has created a complex monument, and this has become a meeting place, a municipal floor. The project displays two different qualities: an 'internal' one and an 'external' one. The internal one is bounded by the semi-ellipse formed by six segments of seats with portholes inserted and with a rim designed on the ground, completing its shape. On the larger semi-axis there is a triangular avenue, the tip of which points north, while the lesser axis, which serves as a container for the land behind, is in the shape of a harpoon and points east. A half-octagon, consisting of three full and two empty elements, concludes the perimeter of the 'interior'.

Positioned at the centre of the system and consisting of two semi-circumferences with different radii, is a fountain of two basins, the smaller on top. The central avenue wedges into the fountain. The 'exterior' consists of the triangle of land wedged between the boundary stairway and the 'interior'. Underlining the overall characteristic of natural space, the land has been modelled with low circular walls, which allude to the geographical parallels.

LANDSCAPE WITH TREES

A simple way of enhancing the quality of the floor is to arrange trees aligned in rows within bordered areas: the most elementary of landscapes. This method uses natural elements according to geometrical rules, with the trees as sculptures, according to a post-Enlightenment formula: the relationship between architecture and nature becomes the simple key to the project.

This is the case with the squares in Neve Zedek and the University of Tel Aviv, where the design is a squared paving system with trees inserted, arranged regularly: a primary interpretation of the formation of landscape iwithin the floor. What is more, the scheme in Neve Zedek is enriched by the designing of small waterworks, a reminder of Islamic architecture.

A similar arrangement is used for Place Arras, in Nîmes, where a fountain with two long, narrow channels is placed between two rows of trees; these channels are modelled on those of the Alhambra in Granada, again recalling the Islamic use of water.

THE LANDSCAPE ON THE PAVING

In Catanzaro, Zagari has made meaningful use of a design by Vasarely, enlarging it and extending it beyond the square. It is an anomalous déplacement, but the close-knit weaving of the Op-Art design seems to

adapt itself well to the new location and, according to methods similar to those of carpets which reproduce famous paintings, it suggests a design formula where the grid unifying the territory is the moduled weaving of the original design.

Of great importance is Anselmi's project for Piazza Roncas in Aosta, where the search for an interior landscape to qualify the square coincides with the chosen figurative theme: the metaphor of the landscape of Aosta.

In a very elongated rectangular context, the basis of the new design is a thin longitudinal cut, ordering the regular grid designed perpendicularly in the paving. One line is a channel-fountain (the river Dora), and resting on this is a procession of irregular three-dimensional triangles (the Alps) projecting from the plane; drawn on the latter are the Moon and the Sun. In the middle stands an ordered comb of columns, a metaphor for the city of Aosta, with the regular *insulae* of its Roman structure. It is a masterpiece of intelligence in its capacity to grasp the theme and of figurativeness in its synthesis of architecture, sculpture and Land-Art. Lastly, it is a work that totally invades the space: there will be no place in the square for anything except the enjoyment of the artificial landscape.

THE ENCLOSED FLOOR

In some cases designers make embankments emerge from the floor, as elements of the constructed landscape, generating a three-dimensional spatial surround with their massive proportions and continuity. This process can be compared with one which is sometimes used for gardens: three-dimensionality is conferred on a plane that has natural continuity by, so to speak, raising its edges.

In the large-scale arrangement of the Porte de la Villette in Paris, Huet defines the triangular square with two earth ramparts, a reminder of the ancient walls, and uses another 'rampart', the bridge of the raised metropolitan railway, as the third side. These grass embankments concentrate the design attention, while the central space is left empty, not paved, as the perspective axis between the Ledoux barrier and the grand canal. The writer has also used two embankments, to define the space of a square created inside a block in the historic centre of Vimercate: sloping lawns, leaving at the centre a narrow space, where water flows from a spring, a reminder of the irrigated flatland. The steps of an open-air theatre are set in an embankment, with the cavea dug out of the opposite rampart. Everything has been constructed, and under the lawn there is a row of exhibition studios for artists, opening towards the exterior onto a 'street of art'.

LANDSCAPE COMING FROM HISTORY

Venturi, Scott Brown and Associates are the authors of squares where the context is pre-existing, created on another scale or with another urban hypothesis, and therefore, far-removed or contradictory.

The project method employed is the 'implementation' of certain urban nodes, with the search for contents that are such as to render the site charged with meaning, which is to be translated into image. A meaning obtained from the history of the location, from its stratification, to be exhibited with absolute clarity.

It is the 'sense of place', according to the philosophy of Langer, from her article in *Landscape* of Autumn 1962; here, among other things, it is stated that 'a field is in a place, but culturally it is a place'.

Architecture becomes an instrument for representing an urban

Opposite:
Peter Walker and Partners: project for
the area of the Hotel Kempinski in
Munich

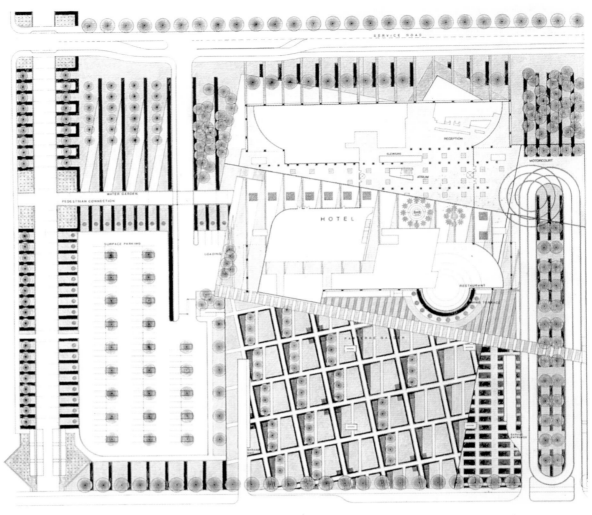

Below:
Paolo Favole: plastic model of the
project for the Piazza Sant'Antonio
in Vimercate

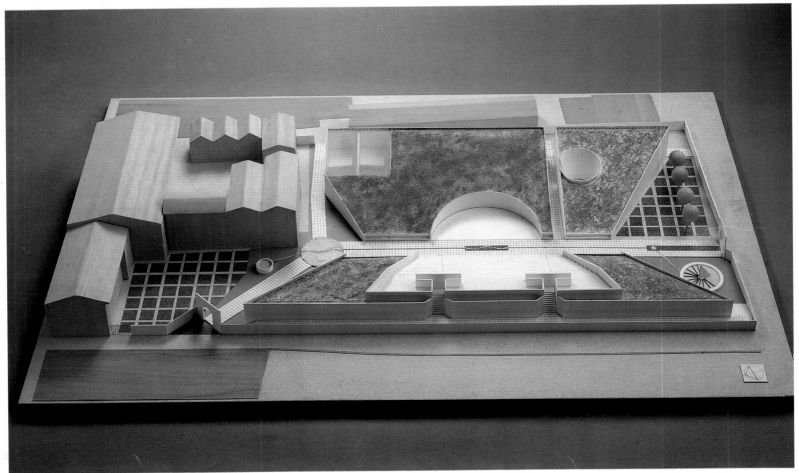

Gustav Peichl: Kunst und Ausstellungshalle in Bonn

philosophy, to express faith in the 'implementation' as a positive factor of transformation in a progressing city, which can be renewed as time goes by. It is hard to find contents and suggestions of urban history in the young United States: the two projects for Washington and Philadelphia propose the very plan of the city on a smaller scale as content.

Nothing is more typical, in Washington, than the grid plan, the one imposed on all the States by Jefferson's law; this law takes concrete shape in the very place it was formulated, personalized by the transgressive diagonal avenues. It is a historical model for the United States, since that plan, precisely because it was Washington's, has been considered charged with independent meaning and used in an identical manner for newly founded cities, such as Belo Horizonte in Brazil, or La Plata in Argentina.

Thus a residual area, qualified by the design of urban memory, has become a place of aggregation. In the two cases where Venturi, Scott Brown and Associates use the plan of the city as a model to mark the paving of the floor, the square is reduced to a two-dimensional plane, with simple design. The communication is entrusted to the graphic transfiguration of the plan, out of scale, without proportion between full and empty spaces, used as an abstract geometry with a powerful two-tone composition. The deciphering of the image and accentuated characterization make the space a distinct and identifiable place, albeit with vertical elements reduced to a minimum: a mini-Capitol in Washington, positioned in a refined interplay of perspectives and dimensions in relation to the real Capitol; in Philadelphia a statue positioned in the centre.

With the same method, the contents of Franklin Court are obtained from the history of the President and his house. They are memories echoed in a constructed garden, with the old houses suggested only by the subtle frameworks, which contain the same graphic meaning of the two two-dimensional squares in embryo form.

Those described are floors with simple landscape, yet highly charged with image, deriving from the historical content of the places. This is what Venturi had anticipated in *Complexity and Contradiction in Architecture*, stating that urban design should be fed by possible contents (even if occasional ones).

THE HIGH-TECH LANDSCAPE

In Naples, Pica Ciamarra has created a landscape which can be defined as high-tech, with three towers placed at the vertices of an equilateral triangle. The three towers are different, each one with a design making the most of its structural elements, with groupings of objects and forms that remind one of artificial satellites, or mysterious (and perhaps useless) machines: reminiscent of the sketches by Schöffer and the cybernetic tower in Liege and, above all, of the designs by another Neapolitan, Aldo Loris Rossi. One or two other precedents, however, could also be found, such as in the designs for the Pravda tower, or for the radio antenna, in thirties Moscow.

Those examined are obelisk-sculpture-towers, charged with meaning, not easily legible. Besides, to explain them would be like denouncing their communicative inadequacy; yet all this takes nothing away from the autonomy and originality of the project, which is the only one using high-tech elements to enhance the quality of the floor, with all the innovative and purposeful elements that this involves.

Certain squares at La Défense, around the Grande Arche, can again be read in a high-tech vein, but on a smaller scale. The space between the stairway that descends from the building and the external urban periphery is transformed into a square by a group of fanciful streetlamps; these are highly colourful, with designs overloaded with citations. They are clever because they are all useless and unlikely. In the same way, another group of cylindrical metal lamps, crowned by a thin steel ring, qualifies the square to the north. Both these landscapes are composed only of design elements and are repeated in totally empty and flat spaces.

THE LANDSCAPE OF ARCHITECTURE

Oscar Niemeyer works on large open spaces and, probably uniquely, proposes landscapes composed of architectural elements alone; these are sometimes arranged in spaces without precise boundaries, destined solely for pedestrian use. Niemeyer does not deal with the floor, does not design the paving, leaving it neutral. He freely arranges many low buildings on the area; these buildings are bonded to the terrain, modelled according to forms of pure invention, inherited from Ozenfant, Arp, or appearing from one of Le Corbusier's ribs.

When architecture is understood as being the creation of unique, unrepeatable objects, with a smooth and highly structured surround-chassis, the floor can qualify itself only by a free and masterly arrangement of objects on the territory, in a vast campus that becomes denser in the areas belonging to individual buildings. Paths are not marked out, fences do not exist, the context is indifferent and there is not even a reference to history, to tradition, to the *genius loci*.

The square is an absolute gesture: the artist-creator determines shapes and arrangement of the buildings, charging the whole thing with absoluteness, finally consigning it to public use and to the judgement of history, with boundless faith in his own qualities as a designer (as architect-demiurge?). Figurativeness is more important than any function, even if it sometimes creates meaningful symbolic forms, as in the cathedral in Brasilia: to use an old definition by Max Bill, a 'social academism', which is excellent formalism, and very South American.

In an artificial city such as Brasilia, where every arrangement of houses, public offices, hotels, is open-plan, the meeting place does not exist. The urban centre is the Rodoviaria (bus station). The square of the capital may only be the floor around the Parliament building, the terminating space of the city's large middle axis. It is a large bowl dug into the ground, closed off on one side by the Congress Building, the flat covering of which, accessible from the side embankments and from the large front ramp, is the second level of the square that faces onto the *esplanada*. An open composition, which is still subtended by a Cartesian grid, even if the double dome (straight and reversed) of the parliamentary halls and the double tower of the offices are arranged at the vertices of an irregular triangle based on a ponderal equilibrium. The vast square of Sao Paolo, on the other hand, is the paradigm of Niemeyer's poetics in its most advanced expressions: because of the vastness of the composition, the number of buildings, the freedom of forms. In Le Havre, the reconstructed city constitutes a continuous, repetitive, rigorous context, highly designed both in the road framework and in the arrangement of the buildings, in

the typology, in the colour of materials. It is a sort of spatial scenario, composed of wings, which are at the same time similar but different. To distinguish himself, Niemeyer places the square below ground level, creating a heart-shaped cutaway in the quadrangular block, with diagonal access, while on the opposite diagonal two irregularly truncated conical buildings house public activities. The commercial outlets are arranged on the outsides of the sunken level.

Summarizing, we have a sequence of choices: cutaway, diagonals, cones...all in contrast with the excessive urban rationalism of Perret, inspired by motivations similar to those of Wright, when he opted for a spiral for the Guggenheim Museum, to contrast with the parallelepipeds of the Manhattan skyscrapers. Lastly, in the lowered square, a giant hand holds out water, as a sign of life, in a fountain: one of Le Corbusier's themes, previously taken up by Niemeyer.

LANDSCAPE - SCENOGRAPHY

The square that Moore decorated with a backcloth and a floor, in a regenerated space in New Orleans, is totally constructed. The procedure used in this case is to take each component of the project to the extreme. Having set the attractiveness of the square as the objective, it is decided that this will be pursued by composing an astounding space-scenario: Moore's landscape is a real full-blown theatre set. To accomplish the new landscape, use is made of pieces of architecture, extracts from the most significant national history: Italy's. The result of the assemblage is a comfortable circular system, an authentic collage of images, the soundness and reliability of which are measured with the memory of the hurried American tourist. It is an Italian Piazza, in the form of Italian Graffiti, the quintessence of patchwork in architecture, where every component is challenged by changes of scale, intentionally inaccurate quotations, out-of-place colours. It is like putting a copy of the Venus de Milo, its size reduced because there is little space, colouring it red to make it stand out, and calling the whole thing a Greek, maybe archaeological garden. Moore's is an extremism that takes in Pop and Hyper-Realist tendencies, and as such is healthy, becoming the ridiculization of any residual Post-Modernism, the terminal point of this tendency. As the authoritative confirmation of the choices of other artists, such as Isozaki, Krier, Purini and many others, who at other times had been attracted by Post-Modern themes, only to gradually move away from them.

In conclusion, it is however appropriate to wonder how long a *décor* such as Moore's can last, beyond that of its own temporary provocation, since the phrases 'a place of excess' and 'a place of permanence' should be contradictory.

If it were the miniature theatre for a ballet, destined to last a few hours, it would be highly entertaining. Translated into the stable historical testimony of our age, Moore's landscape is, frankly, disquieting.

LANDSCAPE OF ARCHITECTURE AND NATURE

The numerous creations completed over a short period of time in Barcelona, all relating to unused or inactive spaces, to be revived for public use as gardens or squares, are the indication of a widespread tendency, even of a fashion. They are floors of vast dimensions, all to be invented for totally indifferent contexts, with the exception of the squares of Gracia, which interpret another condition. No function is defined a priori by the site and, therefore, each case takes in or multiplies the potential uses, becoming the centre of a context. Settings are introduced for stopping and sitting, for contemplation, paths for crossing or walking, spaces for play.

There is an attempt to create an 'interior landscape' through the combined presence of architectural and natural elements, that is, with real elements of landscape. The architecture manifests itself in the design of ordering grids of reference for the paving, elements of ornamentation, paths, streetlamps. These are grids of various types, linear, square, thickly or loosely woven, occupying the space with motivations making reference to architecture, to design, and not to history, to the cadastre, or to other forms of stratification. Grids that are broken, intersected, penetrated by natural elements arranged and marked out with forced 'naturalness': trees, hills, stretches of water... We are on the borderline between landscape design and the architecture of open spaces.

It is a delicate balance, due to the coexistence of environmental and naturalist culture with that of the architectural tradition, both represented by few elements, demonstrating possible cohabitation on the level of quality. The boundary between park, garden, square has become transient, perhaps reduced to a single dimension. There is no longer a constructed perimeter, the elements of composition and method are the same.

On the architecture side, all the elements which constitute a landscape are poured into projects: pergolas, cantilevers, footbridges, streetlamps, even the remains of pre-existing buildings, inasmuch as they are repeatable objects; or else they are used to support orientations, to form the unrepeatable skyline of the place. For this reason the coverings of the cantilever roofs in the Plaza Mayor de Parets dels Valls rise up like metal-mailed wings, or those in the Paisos Catalans square are arranged according to an informal design, with totally inventive liberty. The streetlamps are always the object of specific and refined design, charged with great figurative energy. Where possible, such as at the Clot park, the façades of a pre-existing building are used, reduced to wall-wings, with numerous closely repeated large windows. The whole thing is immersed cohesively in the artificial laguna of the new landscape, which has replaced the old building. In some cases, there is an attempt to give spatiality and new geometry to the square, with a lowering (at the Clot park and at the España Industrial) which, where it is reduced to a single centre (at Can Robacols), suffers as a result of the schematic simplification undergone by the models of reference we have cited several times previously.

On the landscape side, the trees are used as elements of architecture, in regular rows, in ordered sequences, following a grid which is sometimes designed in the paving. Both the architectural ornamental elements and the natural ones are powerfully charged figuratively, to the point of considerably reappraising the role of sculpture. Statues - which had a key position on the formation of squares - are now almost totally absent. Those described are systems with few reminiscences of the Catalan Modernist tradition. Perhaps the conception of the garden where natural and designed parts coexist is derived from Gaudí, but in contemporary experiences all easy imitations are avoided. And again, only a few traces from Miró can be found in some completely informal compositions, such as the garden of Villa Cecilia and that of the Besòs.

Thus every creation is a scenographic arrangement of great impact, and it is from this that the importance descends, for all the squares of Barcelona, of an extraordinary project of illumination, which is not comparable to that of any other similar experience. The light park is used by architects and specialist consultants; it is directed, as in the theatre, and the sites add a new face to the landscape of architecture and nature - the nocturnal one, when the transformation of elements gives the user enchanted gardens and squares.

NEW LANDSCAPE ARTISTS

One aspect of the US school that is particularly interesting and typical is that of the 'new Landscapists'. Starting with the slogan 'There are no more squares among the skyscrapers', they work on residual spaces, and if the project for new floors is in any case the search for an internal urban landscape, in the extreme phase it becomes the proposal for a pure extract of landscape. The architects interpret a spreading environmental awareness, representing it in an artificial key, with the addition of all the eclectic-consumerist temptations that 'Made-in-USA' culture allows. In these projects there is no souvenir of the American frontier landscape, with its large open spaces. The new landscapes are original inventions, compositions embodying a sort of naturalistic-botanical zoo, to be represented using any element available. The Neo-Landscapists are 'green', but unnatural. Their squares live out - and stage - the contradiction with the urban context; yet they, in turn, and with internal contradiction, are the product of complete artificiality.

These projects do not propose another reference to the site, they are never the reconstruction of pre-existing landscapes, sudden holes in the concrete to reveal what was there before. This is a renunciation, a cultural choice of great importance and meaning: neither history, nor *genius loci*, the communicative force is entirely entrusted to the archetypal value of the ex-natura elements used as materials. The work of the architect is expressed in the numerous variants of their composition.

Noguchi, in California Scenario, works on the boundary between architecture and sculpture, informally bonding blocks of stone, barren hills, a lawn, a wall-fountain. Into a garden, Halprin, the master of Environmental Design, in Levi's Plaza skilfully fits a complex geometrical pool, a landscape of rocks with water running through in all directions, likewise explicitly constructed. Beyond the reductive logic of green areas transplanted into the city, a highly figuratively charged composition is proposed. More simple, less complicated, are the many projects by Friedberg, who places pools of water at the centre of the square's floor, surrounded by rows of trees, designed and arranged according to Cartesian geometries, also in complex areas.

The work by Walker and his wife, Martha Schwartz, is of great interest; their project is formulated on highly varied grids of reference, weavings and plots that meet up in cuts and diagonals.

The compositions obtained thus are highly structured and, when read in plan, they call programmed art or certain works of geometrical Abstractism to mind. Very much an 'architect's' layout, so to speak, with excellent compositional results.

The Dutch group 'West 8', who have defined themselves as landscapists, are moving even further. So far they have developed projects for floors understood as amazing machines: steel paving, moving gardens, waterworks, light effects, unusual or innovative materials, all represented in designs of great graphic impact.

There remains, at the design stage, an avant-garde Kunstwollen, but only in the construction phase will it be possible to evaluate the feasibility of the designs, the cohesiveness of real spaces with the original schemes.

FLOORS WITHOUT CONTEXT

At the extreme stage of investigation, aiming at progressive detachment, the square, paradoxically, may even detach itself from the urban role and become a roof-garden, or a floor in open countryside.

In Bonn, on the roof of the House of Art and the Gustav Peichl Exhibitions, a square-garden-playing field comes into existence; it is accessible directly from the outside, up a long, straight stairway.

This is a full-blown landscape, consisting of the technical volumes of the building, designed for this purpose from the highly colourful sculptures of Niki de Saint-Phalle, with benches, shrubs, a fountain. The protagonists are the typical Peichl skylights. These are high and conical, half smooth elementary geometry, half technological game (large magician's hats, or space headgear); actually they are the traditional roofs of Medieval German towers, redesigned for the occasion.

A square on a roof no longer even has the limitation, albeit casual and indifferent, of the surround: the only boundary is the geometry of the building, with the edge of the roof forming the parapet. This too, the final limit, is lost when square-sites are created in the open countryside, as ends in their own right, the pure representation of a square. A place to reach, to seek, therefore a square-objective.

Campo del Sole, at Turo on Lake Trasimene, is a circular floor upon which column-sculptures are arranged in an open, spiral formation; their modest quality as individual objects is amply redeemed by that of the whole. The extreme situation seems to require a primitive form, chosen from among those which possess intrinsic and immediate communicative power. The reference returns to the fields of menhirs (Carnac, Stonehenge, Aalborg), or to the forests of columns of the great Roman ruins (Palmira, Gerasa): an evocative element that recalls the forest of columns that D'Annunzio wanted to lay at the Vittoriale, or the sculpture-labyrinth of concentric rings by Italo Manfredini, placed in the torrent of Castel di Lucio.

An empty, 'metafunctional' square is the one created at Nozzano by Martellotti and Pascalino, using simple geometry, as part of an architectural

landscape built in a wood. Kikar Levana Square, outside Tel Aviv, is a landscape of elementary forms on a square-shaped floor, composed by Karavan with his usual skill. It is an evocative field and belvedere, which is reminiscent of Indian astronomical observatories.

Aronson's belvedere for the walk from the Sherover Memorial to Jerusalem is another (private) square without context; it is a contemporary edition of the traditional church square-belvedere, such as those of the Monte Berico in Vicenza, or of San Luca, in Bologna.

SOME CONCLUSIONS

This summation of the various experiences of design and construction of squares suggests one or two critical considerations.

First of all, a primary requirement emerging for contemporary architecture, from all the projects, is to transmit individuality to locations, also, and above all, in the case of public spaces. In this sense, the qualitative and quantitative growth of experiences is certainly significant, in a pervasive process tending in many ways to assimilate the meaningful space of the square with that of the street, or the river, or the coastline.

The anxiety, the sense of impotence that habitually fills our visions of urban suburbs, or the areas at the edges of streets, can certainly find redemption in a planning culture of this type: the project as the aspiration to improve the everyday environment.

The categories proposed by Norberg Schultz for establishing the identity of a site - location, spatial configuration, structural characteristics - have been proven to be valid in the experiences examined. Yet we have noticed the expansion and improvement of the quality of the preliminary

Shlomo Aronson: Gabriel Sherover Promenade in Jerusalem

West 8: project for the Schouwburgplein in Rotterdam

investigations, before designing in a strict sense begins - investigations into which, without limitations, the complex and varied culture of the designers can flow. As Lynch points out, limited figurative representation generates fear, insecurity and difficulty of orientation in space. The new sites constituted by these squares, however, highlight the search for a powerful figurative charge and for motivations to compensate for the lack of certainty on the part of users. It is an approach perhaps in the style of 'magistri urbis', certainly amply justified by a concrete urgency. We can only regret, if anything, the project's limited power of action, in comparison with the dimensions of problems.

The great intelligence and the quality of the contributions by some architects must be acknowledged. This is the case with Isozaki, Anselmi, Karavan, Walter & Schwartz, but all those who have attempted the theme of the square have shown a powerful tendency and motivation towards innovative research, aiming above all to enhance the quality of the setting.

And if the square's floor is released from the context, it is now possible to augur that it regains possession of it, forcing architecture, as a current practice and usual method of approach, to confront public spaces. This is the desirable key to the interpretation of buildings and, without monuments, it could restore to houses their own original and historically consistent representative function.

Le Corbusier: sketch of the design for the Governor's Palace in Chandigarh

THE
MODERN
TRADITION

THE CHANDIGARH 'CAPITOL' (1950-1955)

If Rome was not built in a day, the same can be said of Chandigarh. The modern capital of the Punjab in India is in fact the result of a synchronic and cohesive planning operation, in which the most advanced positions of early fifties urban planning culture are reflected.

The reasons for the founding of Chandigarh date back to 1947, when, with the proclamation of independence from the British Empire, the Punjab state was divided up between India and Pakistan, the latter receiving the western territories and the ancient capital of Lahore. As there were no urban cores in the eastern area capable of taking on the role of capital, it was decided that a city of 500,000 inhabitants would be built from scratch.

The choice of location of Chandigarh - which owes its name to the Indian divinity Chandi, the god of the moon - was a fertile and temperate upland plain at the foot of the Himalayas, washed by the waters of the rivers Patiali Rao (to the west) and Sukhna Choe (to the east). The relative closeness to the Indian capital of Delhi (approximately 250 kilometres to the north-west) and the midway position between the two main towns of the region, Ambala and Simla, also guaranteed ease of access. Initially the urban planning was entrusted to the architects Albert Mayer, of US nationality, and Matthew Nowiczki, of Polish origin, who had formerly worked with Le Corbusier.

Reconciling the prerequisites of the Indian authorities - the forced subdivision of the region along traditional lines of social separation into classes and castes - with the Anglo-Saxon low-density model of housing development, the Mayer-Nowiczki plan involved an urban organization into residential sectors separated by spacious green areas. The public structures, which included an industrial zone, a railway station and a civic administrative centre, were to be located In the suburban belt.

Le Corbusier's involvement in the planning of Chandigarh dates from 1950, when, following the

Previous page:
The Parliament Building from the terrace of the Secretariat. Note the distinction between motor access and raised pedestrian walkways.

Below:
General ground plan of Chandigarh. 1. Parliament. 2. Secretariat. 3. Governor's Palace (later replaced by a Museum of Knowledge). 4. Court of Justice. 5. Fosse of Consideration. 6. Pools in front of the Museum of Knowledge. 7. Monument to the Open Hand

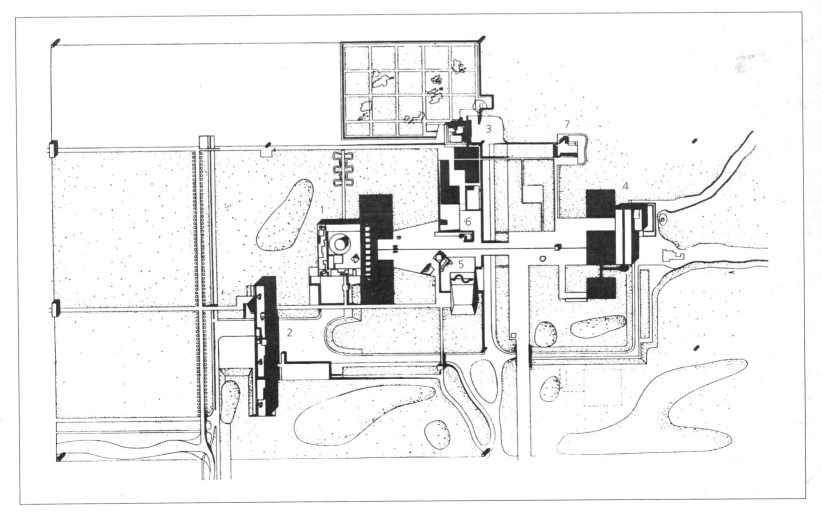

sudden death of Nowiczki, he was nominated government adviser for the construction of the new city. Though confirming the general layout of the first urbanization project, the Le Corbusier Plan, drawn up between February 1951 and May 1952, toned down its character of a garden city by completely reorganizing the road system. In line with the 'rule of the 7 Vs', which Le Corbusier theorized as a solution to urban circulation problems, Chandigarh's road layout is organized around an orthogonal grid, guaranteeing a strict separation between roads for fast through traffic (V1, V2, V3), roads reserved for local traffic (V4, V5, V6) and pedestrian walkways (V7).

The industrial zone and the university area are located at the two ends of the directrix for fast traffic which crosses the residential area in a south-east to north-west direction. The road axis perpendicular to this serves the vast commercial centre, which occupies the central position, at the north-east end of which is the administrative centre, allusively named the 'Capitol'.

Although the residential fabric, structured into sectors with population densities ranging between 5,000 and 25,000 inhabitants, fits within the checked grid generated by the road layout, it is separated from the fast traffic circulation. A system of parallel-running green bands guarantees each sector easy access to the garden areas and direct links with the pedestrian walkways.

Although the execution of the residential models and of the housing districts' facilities was entrusted mainly to a team of collaborators (among whom particular mention should be made of Pierre Jeanneret, Maxwell Fry and Jane Drew), the designing of the 'Capitol' was entirely directed by Le Corbusier and was completed in stages over the course of thirty years.

It is significant that the civic and administrative centre, intended to house the administrative functions of a new capital, was conceived - by the architect who perhaps more than any other refused the housing development models of the traditional city - in the terms of a huge urban square. This is even more significant if we consider that in Le Corbusier's previous architectural work, even if concerned with complete residential districts or urban plans, he had never developed the theme of the square. It was almost as though, in an 'artificial' capital such as Chandigarh, the conceptual unity implicitly guaranteed by the image of the square might save the functional unity of the city centre and underline the reciprocal relationships between individual buildings, despite the considerable distances between them.

The Parliament in a sketch by Le Corbusier. The hyperboloid outline of the Assembly Hall emerges from the prismatic block.

THE MODERN TRADITION

Sketch of the main façade of the Court of Justice, which is reflected in the large pool of water located beside the pedestrian enfilade. In the background, the monument to the Open Hand is visible to the left.

The spatial cohesion between the numerous episodes comprising the Chandigarh 'Capitol' is initially entrusted to a carefully calculated system of geometrical relations. The basic compositional principle is generated by the counterposing of two square-shapes (the 800-metre sides of these correspond to the lesser side of an urban residential sector), located on each side of the rectilinear axis connecting the 'Capitol' with the city. Delineated inside each of these larger squares, in an off-centre position, is a smaller square with a 400-metre side. Yet while to the west the double system of squares is made explicit by positioning obelisks at the corners, to the east the design is barely perceptible, frayed as it is at the edges by the irregular course of the river Sukhna Choe.

With a compositional methodology that is clearly of Purist influence, the formal control of such a vast surface is therefore entrusted to a subtended regulating scheme that only emerges onto the surface at irregular points.

The geometrical grid is thus defined, and in a certain sense it forms the scheme within which the architectural project fits (this is all the more necessary, considering that in Chandigarh's case the site is a homogeneous and undifferentiated plain). Yet transgressions of the rule are introduced into the actual arrangement of the buildings - transgressions which can only find justification in the 'poetic reasons' nestling in the designer's sensibilities and cultural background.

The individual building constructions that together form the Capitol are connected by a system of orthogonal axes which echo the road network around which the city is organized. Here too the surface walkways are rigidly separated from vehicle traffic, which is almost completely restricted to cuttings; the interstitial spaces generated by the road network are occupied alternatively by garden areas and by terraces with facilities on their various levels, for use for social activities.

The Parliament building and the Court of Justice are located one at each end of the central esplanade (the overall length of which reaches 400 metres), which meets with the walkway connecting with the city.

The Parliament, located indicatively in the middle of the smaller west square, is a square plan building, out of which emerges the hyperboloid volume projecting out the Assembly Hall, located inside the central core.

The main façade, facing south-east in the direction of the Court of Justice, has a monumental arcade with an enormous cornice above it, overlooking two rectangular pools positioned symmetrically at the sides of the entrance.

In the background, almost forming a backdrop to the Parliament Building - and connected to this via a covered bridge - stands the tall, massive Secretariat, whose lengthwise development follows the perimeter of the west square. The prismatic block of the building, amplified in the façade by the close-knit scheme of the *brises-soleil*, becomes animated plastically at the two 'ears' which circumscribe the pedestrian ramps placed on the outside.

The Court of Justice, which closes off the esplanade on the south-western side, is a rectangular construction concluded with an enormous two-pitch cantilever roof sloping towards the interior. The distinguishing feature of the entrance - this too facing onto large pools of water to amplify its monumental effect - is a hypostyle hall running the full breadth of the building, breaking up the latter's horizontal continuity. The façades of Chandigarh are in fact never barriers that delimit space; rather, they have depth, enabling the outside space to penetrate virtually inside the building.

Most of the spaces for social activities are located along the axis that forms a perpendicular intersection with the esplanade connecting the Parliament and the Court of Justice. This axis is slightly off-centre in relation to the directrix that connects with the city.

At the south-eastern end of this axis there is in fact a sunken square, significantly baptized the Fosse of Consideration, which contains some of the symbolic motifs that Le Corbusier held dear; one of the most noteworthy of these is the harmonic spiral which, like a monument, occupies the east side. A U-shaped ramp connects the Fosse with the Tower of Shadows, which stands on the north-east corner facing the Parliament. This is a covered, shaded structure, protected on three sides by walls serving as *brises-soleil* (only the northern side is completely open). With its decidedly north-south orientation, the Tower breaks deliberately with the Cartesian grid around which the whole composition is structured.

In a symmetrical position, beyond the esplanade, is the Monument to the Martyrs; this is a scalable sculpture consisting of a long rectilinear ramp that terminates in a high panoramic base, from where you can gaze out across the whole 'Capitol'.

Continuing in a north-easterly direction, a number of water pools are located at various levels. In Le Corbusier's original project these were to have reflected the image of the Governor's Palace, to be sited at the head of the whole complex; this was not constructed, however, and was replaced by the Museum of Knowledge.

The Open Hand of Chandigarh, the symbol of solidarity and reconciliation

THE MODERN TRADITION

Positioned off-centre with respect to the intersection of the two main axes, but in a position dominating the public spaces of the 'Capitol', is the monument to the Open Hand, a revolving sculpture made of enamelled and coloured sheet metal. Intended by Le Corbusier to 'receive the treasures created, to distribute them to the peoples of the world', the Open Hand is the symbol of post-colonial reconciliation and wisdom.

To complete the spatial configuration of the 'Capitol', a number of artificial hills were created, using the excavation materials from the digging of the foundations, and on these vegetation was planted. Some rows of trees, sometimes placed in a setback position to allow sheltered green spaces to form, were arranged along the boundaries to serve as visual screens.

The façade of the Parliament Building, reflected in the large pool in front

Universally considered the leading protagonist of the European Rationalist movement, **Charles Edouard Jeanneret** - known as Le Corbusier - was born in La Chaux-de-Fonds (in the canton of Neuchâtel, Switzerland) on 6 October 1887.

After gaining his diploma at the school of arts and crafts in his town of birth, he visited Italy (1907) and Eastern Europe on study trips; these trips, along with his apprenticeship at the Paris studio of August Perret and that of Peter Behrens in Berlin, proved fundamental in his development.

In 1917 he moved to Paris, where he made contact with avant-garde Post-Cubist artistic circles, founding the magazine *L'Esprit Nouveau* (in 1919, with Amédée Ozenfant).

In 1922, in association with his cousin Pierre Jeanneret, he created the architecture studio of Rue de Sèvres, an address to which he was to remain faithful for the rest of his life.

A relentless promoter of the radical renewal of contemporary architecture (from the pages of *Vers une architecture*, 1922, and *Urbanisme*, 1925), he designed the Esprit Nouveau Pavilion at the Exposition des Arts Décoratifs in Paris in 1925; this work constitutes a manifesto of his purified and functional language.

In 1928 he promoted the founding of the Congrès Internationaux d'Architecture Moderne (CIAM), which in 1933 issued the Athens Charter, long considered the basic text of modern urban planning.

Of his vast output prior to the Second World War, the following projects are the most memorable: the competition projects for the League of Nations Building in Geneva (1927) and the Palace of the Soviets in Moscow (1931); Villa Stein in Garches (1927) and Villa Savoye in Poissy (1929); the Cité de Réfuge (1929) and the Pavilion Suisse in the Cité Universitaire in Paris (1930).

After the war, Le Corbusier's theoretical and planning activities did not slow down; indeed - in works such as the Maisons Jaoul (1952) and the church at Ronchamp (1950-55) - he demonstrated an extraordinary capacity to overcome acquired positions and an openness towards new design horizons. The completion of a new scale of harmonic measures (the Modulor) forms the basis of projects such as the Unité d'Habitation in Marseilles (1946) and in Firminy (1960) or the Monastery of Sainte-Marie-de-la-Tourette in Eveux (1957).

Le Corbusier died in Cap Martin on 27 August 1965. The Foundation Le Corbusier was founded in 1968 to promote the study of his activities; its headquarters is in the Place du Docteur Blanche in Paris.

THREE MUNICIPAL SQUARES (1949-1976)

In the vast architectural production of Alvar Aalto it is perhaps not easy to identify a project for a square in the strict sense, as the formal characterization of an open-air autonomous public space.

If this is the case, it is certainly not due to any lack of attention on Aalto's part to the social dimension of civil life, but rather to the very close connection, established in his projects on an urban scale, between the architectural work and the area of aggregation associated with it. Perhaps on account of the specific environmental conditions of the Finnish context - ranging from the harsh climate to the low-density model of housing development - public buildings do in fact tend to jam all social life within themselves, absorbing the functions traditionally assigned to the municipal square. A case that is emblematic of this attitude is the project for the Säynätsalo town hall, developed for the competition by invitation of 1949, and completed in the early fifties.

Säynätsalo is a small centre on an island on Lake Päijänne, with a pattern of housing development consisting of single-family wooden dwellings arranged around the compact volume of the Enso-Gutzeit wood processing plant. The town hall too, standing on a rather steep ridge at the edge of the main road axis, is completely immersed in green.

A stringent distributional logic guides the building's functional organization in Alvar Aalto's project. Positioned around a central court, which presents itself ambiguously as a patio and as a municipal square, are two differentiated constructions: one with a U-shaped plan, for administrative and commercial activities, and a rectilinear wing enclosing the courtyard on the south side, used as a library.

The difference between the levels of the central court and the external street, made possible by the excavation work for the laying of the foundations, enables commercial activities - for which the ground floor of the U-shaped building is set aside - to be kept separate from the administrative

Opposite:
Säynätsalo: detail of the steps with planted greenery revealing the presence of the inner court. In the background, the strongly slanting outline of the council hall

activities. The latter take place on the upper floor and culminate, purposely with precise symbolism, in the council chamber, which acts as the head of the east wing. Access is gained to the central court via a stairway located to the east, in the interstitial space between the two constructions. The internal space serves as a garden and is surfaced partly with gravel and partly as lawn. A wooden pergola is positioned at the entrance. Parallel to the north end is a rectanglar fountain, in the waters of which a female figure, created by the Finnish sculptor Waino Aaltonen, is reflected. A flight of steps with planted greenery is located in a position symmetrical to the eastern access stairway; this constitutes the mediating element between the inner square and the natural surroundings.

A similar design organization is apparent in the plan of the Wolfsburg cultural centre, conceived for the 1958 competition and built between 1959 and 1962. Here too a complex functional mechanism - including a library, a small public university, a youth centre and various meeting halls - is structured around a square-courtyard at the level of the first floor, which is the designated location for public events. A simple broken line of skylights serves as wings for the staging of open-air performances, while the rhythm of the streetlamps intercalated into the south wing reproduces the perimeter cadence of an ancient agora.

The design of the civic centre in Seinäjoki appears much more complex. Seinäjoki is the town in central Finland that for more than twenty years Alvar Aalto has used as a laboratory to try out his urban design ideas. The present outline is in fact the result of the accumulation of a series of projects drawn up at different times for different occasions.

The first core area of construction comprises the church and the parish community house, located at the east end.

The church, designed for the 1952 competition and built in the years 1958-60, is a prismatic block with a trapezoid base, from which the broken outline of the roof emerges. The bell tower is separate and, with its large, rigid geometrical structure, provides the vertical balance for the whole complex.

The parish community centre, conceived in 1956, was built between 1964 and 1966. Its plan, with its upturned U-shape open towards the church, makes it possible to create a square-shaped space of gradually descending terraces in front of the latter; the concave nature of this space qualifies it as a closed square.

The Säynätsalo Civic Centre, immersed in vegetation

THE MODERN TRADITION

The square inside the Wolfsburg cultural centre

In the late fifties the decision to elevate Seinäjoki to the rank of a town created a compelling, more general need for a fully fledged civic centre, which resulted in the promoting of a second competition in 1959.

This too was won by Alvar Aalto, with a project that called for the construction of a system of public buildings (the town hall, a library and a theatre), ringing an esplanade oriented ideally towards the already constructed religious building.

The phased construction of this complex organism began the following decade with the building of the town hall, which forms the northern limit of the whole esplanade.

This is a low volume developing lengthwise, terminating to the east in a square prism on *pilotis* (the entrance hall); emerging from this is the oblique outline of the council hall situated on the upper floor. Here too, as in Säynätsalo, rows of terracing with planted vegetation serve as a linking element between the esplanade level and the raised level of the hall. Between 1963 and 1965 the municipal library was built opposite the town hall, along the southern edge of the square. Following a stylistic code that often recurs in Aalto's architectonic work, the library consists of an open, fan-shaped reading room, connected to a long wing to house offices and facilities.

The theatre building, outlined in 1968-69, intended to close off the esplanade to the west, was only built in the years 1984-87 by the studio that still bears the Finnish architect's name today.

Despite its complex evolution, the Seinäjoki civic centre appears today, its construction completed, as a unified and cohesive system.

This homogeneity is partly due to the repetition of certain formal devices - such as the 'fan-shape', or the tendency towards the multiplication of parallel lines - which create a kaleidoscopic image, the dynamism of which manages to tone down the fragmentary nature of individual constructions.

Yet the most cohesive element is undoubtedly the central esplanade, providing the focus for the main urban functions; it presents itself as the sum of all the public spaces belonging to individual buildings (the church square, the series of terraces giving direct access to the town hall, the meeting area outside the theatre). In fact a double system of squares is formed along the esplanade's longitudinal directrix; thus the civic centre is linked with the religious one, yet they are also differentiated.

Unfortunately, what Aalto intended to be one of the basic principles of the overall organization - the strict separation between pedestrian and vehicle circulation - was only partly achieved, as vehicles are allowed to cross at the junction between the two systems.

A leading protagonist among the architects of the second generation of the Modern Movement, **Alvar Aalto** was born in Kuortane - a village in central Finland - in 1898. After gaining his degree at the Polytechnic in Helsinki, he made study trips in Europe and opened a studio in Jyväskylä, adhering, albeit with his own highly individual style, to the Nordic classicism theorized by the Swedish architect Gunnar Asplund.

His 'conversion' to European Rationalism dates back to the late twenties (with his membership of CIAM in 1929) and the creation of works - such as the Viipuri Municipal Library and the Sanitarium at Paimio - which won him international recognition.

He was active in several fields, from urban planning to interior design (in 1935 he founded Artek, specializing in furniture production). In 1947, having been summoned to be visiting professor at the Massachusetts Institute of Technology, he designed the MIT Seniors' Dormitory in Cambridge, Mass.

Named head of the Finnish Technical Office for reconstruction, he prepared numerous projects on an urban scale (Helsinki, Seinäjoki, Jyväskylä, Rovaniemi), some of which were completed - following the architect's sudden death in 1976 - by the studio that still bears his name.

NEW TOWNS

The squares of the civic centres in new towns, generally devoid of quality urban design, are representative of the way of conceiving public space and towns that existed in Europe for about twenty years from the fifties onwards.

In various European nations, urban development was controlled by establishing new towns, yet differing objectives were being pursued.

In the countries of Eastern Europe, political ends, combined with national economic plans, were the *raison d'être* behind the newly founded towns. In contrast, in Great Britain, France and the Scandinavian countries, problems of overpopulation in the cities and social theories - according to which it is the city or town, as opposed to the surburban zone, that can guarantee a quality of life - led to the development of plans for the creation of new towns.

Present in all, however, is the idea of the centre as the 'heart' of the town. This theme is also proposed in the new housing schemes of Eastern Europe and in the new towns of Poland and Hungary. In the Soviet Union the expansion of Moscow was accomplished, for socio-political reasons, with the creation of large suburban districts, of which the square became the centre. The Ivanovskoe quarter, for example, is a large housing development for 60,000 inhabitants, intersected by two road axes; the service structures extend along these, converging on a centre marked by a compact building around a square.

NEW TOWNS IN GREAT BRITAIN

The New Towns Act has been the fundamental document of British urban planning from the Second World War onwards. The studies begun by Patrick Abercrombie in 1942 were the first organic attempt at controlling the development of certain large cities, particularly London. The United Kingdom was the first European nation to develop a plan for decongesting the metropolises: it is an obligatory point of reference for subsequent experiences.

The national act, promulgated in 1946, set as its objective the identification of models of urban development for application on a national scale. The response to the problem was the establishing of new towns: 'balanced towns', not bound by the logic of land rent, with a wide variety of functions: industries, shops, community and recreational facilities. The idea of setting up new towns fits into the English tradition, begun by Ebenezer Howard, of the garden city, examples of which are Letchworth - built in the early twentieth century - and Welwyn Garden City, founded in the years between the two world wars. The studies which led to the drafting of the New Towns Act were pushed ahead forcefully by the need to solve the problems of the conversion of the decaying urban fabric and overpopulation in the large cities, particularly London.

Three phases can be identified in the construction of the new towns in the first twenty years of application of the law.

The new towns of the first generation, established between 1946 and 1950, mainly responded to the need to decongest London and the large industrial centres. Indeed, eight of these new towns were located on the outskirts of London and two - Glenrothes and East Kilbride - near Edinburgh and Glasgow respectively. In the second phase, in the fifties, preference was given to the areas of industrial expansion of Wales and Scotland, building towns in the vicinity of mines to be enlarged or growing industrial poles. The third generation of plans for new towns was to deal with the problem of conversion of the core areas already in existence.

The newly founded towns were intended to achieve various objectives. Peterlee and Glenrothes were an attempt to bring the dispersed mining villages together into urban communities; Newton Aycliffe is the residential expansion of an industrial zone; East Kilbride and New Cumbernauld are Glasgow's outlets for decentralization.

The new towns in the outskirts of London differ from each other, although they have the aim of reducing the congestion of the metropolis in common: Hemel Hempstead is the expansion of an old urban core, while Basildon is an attempt to transform formless aggregations of scattered housing into an organic community. The urban form of new towns is generally irregular. They are planned for a

Previous page:
The clock tower and the presence of sculptural elements define the public spaces of the municipal square in Stevenage.

THE MODERN TRADITION

Above:
One of the pedestrian walkways leading to the covered square in the Glenrothes civic centre

Opposite:
Facilities for sitting and relaxing in one of the squares in the Albertslund civic centre

relatively low number of inhabitants, the typical dimensions being between 35,000 and 60,000. They are characterized by a 'coarse-grained structure' - according to Kevin Lynch's definition - that is, by the large scale of the main functions. Every town has just one civic centre, with the residential areas developing around it. The building density is low, and there is a preference for single-family dwellings with one or two floors above ground, surrounded by green spaces. The industrial zones are located near the major traffic axes and served by railways and road networks. The town centre is conceived as the 'heart' of the town: the pole of connection between the various functional sectors and the centre for public services. Shops, offices, cultural and health centres form the dynamic centre of the housing scheme.

In some cases the civic centre is organized around an open-air space. The square, generally closed off, bounded by buildings used for various purposes - prevalently commercial - is characterized as a space for social relations, for sitting and relaxing. Simple and essential, the elements of urban ornamentation mainly respond to the function for which they are intended.

One particular case is the civic centre in Cumbernauld, approximately ten kilometres from Glasgow. A large building complex, structured over several floors, houses multiple functions, both public and private. The compact structure is the extreme synthesis of the functions generally assigned to the civic centre. The open-air spaces - the square - and the covered ones - the buildings - are brought together in a single complex, designated to meet the community's requirements.

Stevenage is the first new town to be founded in accordance with the indications of the New Towns Act. It was a small urban core of approximately 6,000 inhabitants, to the north of London, and its favourable position - thanks to its vicinity to a highly structured road and rail network - prompted the decision to move the industries and inhabitants that were congesting the capital there.

Gordon Stephenson's designs for the Stevenage plan and those for a residential zone by a group of students belonging to the Architectural Association were founded on the concept that the town was to have a centre; this centre had the task of unifying the various quarters and establishing relations between them. This idea was proposed once again in the completed project. The railway runs through the urban core in a north-south direction.

The residential districts, organized around the principle of neighbourhood units, extend along the east side of the railway. The industrial pole is enclosed to the west by the axis for vehicle traffic and to the east by the railway line. The civic centre, exclusively for pedestrian use, is served by ample parking facilities and a bus station, as well as by the railway station.

The commercial centre is articulated along an axis of arches opening onto a square. This is rectangular in shape; the two short sides face onto the shopping street and the bus station respectively, the long sides are closed off by buildings for commercial activities. The public space is conceived as the 'heart' of social relations.

A tower, some trees and some benches designate the area intended for sitting and relaxing.

The square-based tower is produced by placing solid geometrical forms, such as the cube and the parallelepiped, on top of each other. The bodies are defined by a metal structure that only identifies the vertices. A clock occupies the topmost part of the tower.

Inherited from Rationalist and Metaphysical designs, the clock tower is therefore a 'light' structure, in dialogue with the façades of the buildings overlooking the square, whose geometrical cadence it seems to continue.

A footpath, raised with respect to the ground level of the square, divides the surface area into two parts: it is a separating element, but also a privileged standpoint for watching the performances that are put on occasionally.

A uniform floor of stone slabs connects the functional and decorative elements.

Crawley, a new town to the south of London, is judged to be the most successful venture of the plan.

A good road and rail network, in existence before the founding of the town, favoured the scheme's organic development.

The urban core has grown up around the civic centre.

A rail axis divides the built-up area into two parts; it is a branch line off the main north-south line, which brushes the town.

The industrial pole is concentrated to the north, bounded by the road arteries.

The residential districts, which possess a shopping centre and certain basic facilities, are connected to the civic centre by footpaths and axes for vehicle traffic, terminating in large car parks. The civic

Ground plan of Crawley civic centre

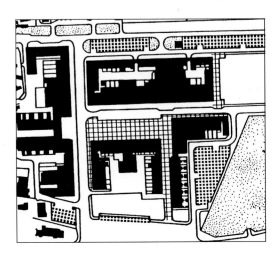

THE MODERN TRADITION

centre, pedestrian only, is structured around a rectangular-shaped square. The south and east sides are bounded by buildings, the other two by pedestrian walkways.

Facing onto the south side are a series of two-storey buildings with porticos; these form a sort of covered footpath for commercial use. The buildings differ according to the treatment of the façades, as though the wings of a stage. The west side is bordered by a single three-storey building. The simple form of the urban space is enlivened by multi-coloured paving, which generates two consecutive areas: one larger, rectangular in shape, and a smaller, square one.

The larger area occupies the west section of the square. The paving is composed of rectangular grey stone slabs, randomly alternated with black or white slabs designing ornamental geometrical motifs. A gazebo surrounded by benches, flower boxes and a fountain decorate the surface. The smaller area, made to stand out from the rest of the square by a few courses of porphyry blocks and by the clock tower, is the area designated for recreation. Indeed, the small, multi-coloured ceramic tiles reproduce chessboards and symbolic figures. Simple benches allow spectators to sit and watch the games.

East Kilbride, founded in 1947, lies ten kilometres from Glasgow. Built to decongest the large Scottish metropolis, it experienced rapid industrial development in just a few years. The direct consequence of this is the phenomenon of commuting, with people coming in daily to work from all over the Clyde valley.

In the first few years following its foundation, the town experienced exactly the same difficulties as the new towns on the outskirts of London: problem-ridden relations with the local authorities, obstacles in deconcentrating certain industries from Glasgow, the slowness of the procedures for approving the plan.

The urban core extends to the south of the main artery connecting with Glasgow and the railway. Two side roads off the important road axis intersect to the east of the civic centre. This is built in the barycentre of the urban core, which develops parallel to the main communication route with the metropolis. The civic centre occupies a triangular-shaped surface generated by the paths of the roads connecting it with the residential districts. For pedestrians only, it has car parks outside the buildings used for community facilities.

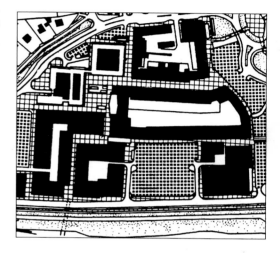

Ground plan of the East Kilbride civic centre

The centre possesses two squares: one inside the commercial structure, the other at the intersection of two pedestrian walkways.

The latter is rectangular in shape. The north and west sides are bordered by two interconnecting closed-block structures. Part of the east side is occupied by the commercial structure; the remainder opens onto the footpath. The south side is bounded by a pedestrian walkway that terminates in front of the shopping centre.

There are two-storey buildings facing onto the square; the ground floor of these buildings is porticoed.

The surface of the square is characterized as an area serving the commercial facilities. The paving consists of uniform, square-shaped stone slabs.

The expansion of a mine to the north of Edinburgh led to the founding of **Glenrothes** in 1948.

A slow and problem-ridden launch characterized the development of the scheme: not until 1955 did construction of the civic centre begin.

The urban core develops around the centre's community facilities.

The industrial areas were located in the southern suburb, in direct contact with the communication routes, and along a strip to the north, in between the residential districts. The housing is typically British: single-family houses surrounded by greenery.

A closed covered square was designed for the civic centre.

The theme of the winter square, created here to respond to the requirements imposed by the weather, has also been proposed in various towns, such as in the Agora in Évry, or more recently in the covered square in Aosta.

Peter Tinto has devised a steel and glass structure for this square. The choice of materials and the shape of the structure are linked ideally with the area's industrial vocation. The square is rectangular in shape, delimited on the two long sides by commercial buildings. It is completely pedestrian and is served by a bus station and ample parking.

The vertical connecting elements create a single multi-functional space, uniting the ground level of the square with the various floors of the building facing onto it.

The structure consists of steel supporting elements and glass covering panels. The roof is composed of four weatherings set against each other; the beams that support the transparent sheets are 'designed' with hexagonal holes. It is a covered space which is flooded with light and in dialogue with the surrounding setting.

SCANDINAVIAN NEW TOWNS

The planning of the post-war urban development of Scandinavian towns - the Copenhagen plan of 1947, the Stockholm master plan of 1952 and the Helsinki plan of 1948 - was based on radiocentric schemes. The industrial and demographic development of the capitals was regulated by the creation of satellite towns: the formation of autonomous cores was preferred to the construction of suburban zones.

The various Scandinavian experiences of the fifties have certain characteristics in common, which are implicit in the philosophy of new towns.

Great importance is attributed to the quality of the site: preference is given, where possible, to areas with an abundance of beautiful landscape, to offer the inhabitants the opportunity to discover the qualities of the town's relationship with nature.

The newly founded Scandinavian towns are conceived as autonomous developments, planned in accordance with the principles of neighbourhood units. A short distance from the capitals - between ten and 40 kilometres - they are served by an efficient rail and road network.

The new towns have a pyramid-like building structure: buildings with towers are erected around the civic centre, the two- or three-storey buildings in the outer zones. The industrial areas are located in the suburbs and connected directly both to the civic centre and to the road axes.

The road system, structured around roads designated for vehicle and pedestrian movement, is structured hierarchically according to directrices that link the districts with each other and with the centre.

The civic centre is always pedestrian and is served by ample parking facilities (in some cases underground). It is conceived as the base for social life: commercial, cultural, health, religious and sporting facilities are there to respond to community requirements. It is the heart of the town, according

Farsta: the square in the civic centre seen from the south

THE MODERN TRADITION

to the Post-Rationalist theories that apply the CIAM principles. In some Scandinavian new towns - such as Albertslund (Denmark), Farsta and Vällingby (Sweden) - the civic centre is articulated around a square.

The square constitutes the open-air urban space that is the 'living heart' of the community. It is usually an enclosed square, without projections to identify vertical axes. Often without architectural qualities, and with poor urban ornamentation, it is characterized and qualified by the functions that take place within it. It seems that the concern was with architecture rather than with design: the design schemes seem restricted to decoration or ornamentation.

Albertslund, 15 kilometres from the Danish capital, is the most significant example of the application of the Copenhagen urban plan of 1947, which envisaged the development of the city through the founding of 'satellites', linked to the main core in five directions by the railway converging on the city centre (the Five-Finger Plan).

The planning of the new town was entrusted to the architect Bredsdorff. The setting, which was quite flat and with little landscape beauty in this particular case, was modified by the construction of small hills, the planting of wooded areas, the creation of an artificial canal connected to a series of small lakes and waterfalls.

The residential development is concentrated to the north of the railway station, while to the south are the civic centre and a residential district. The decision to use types of housing that develop horizontally has given the urban outline a uniform appearance, without vertical projections.

The orthogonal grid road network is organized along directrices that connect districts up with each other and with the centre.

The pedestrian walkways branch out within each block and lead to the town centre.

The civic centre has been designed to cater for 8,000 inhabitants: inaugurated in 1965, it initially included prevalently commercial facilities. Expanded in successive phases and equipped with sporting, cultural, health and religious facilities, it now covers a surface area of 26 hectares.

The centre is exclusively for pedestrian use. There are large car parks to meet the users' requirements, both beside the commercial facilities and inside the residential districts.

The civic centre's structure, in orthogonal blocks, means that enclosed squares are formed. The largest of these is rectangular in shape, closed off to the west and the south by two- and three-storey buildings and flanked, on the remaining sides, by pedestrian walkways.

There are a number of shops facing onto the square, including a bookshop, a bank, a pharmacy and some municipal buildings.

The paving consists of rectangular stone slabs: two bands arranged at right angles to the uniform direction of the courses highlight a central zone, with benches and flower-beds.

Farsta, the satellite town to the south of Stockholm, is 15 kilometres from the capital. Built to cater for a population of 3,000 inhabitants, its civic centre covers nine hectares of surface area. The urban plan was entrusted to Sven Backström and Leif Reinius in 1957. The inauguration of the civic centre took place in 1960.

The underground railway runs through the town, dividing it into two practically symmetrical cores. The urban outline consists of groups of towered buildings, alternating with quarters of single-family dwellings.

The civic centre is located to the west of the railway, and is closed off to vehicle traffic. A system of footpaths links it to the residential districts. It includes large department stores, restaurants, cinemas, doctors' surgeries, buildings for worship and leisure.

The square, at the centre of the buildings of the civic centre, extends along an axis perpendicular to the underground railway's north-south trajectory. The shape is reminiscent of a very elongated ellipse, where the greater axis clearly predominates over the lesser one.

Four footpaths lead into the square, two from the north and two from the south, at right angles to the axial development of the area. The ends of the axis of the ellipse terminate in pedestrian walkways. To the north and south of the square - at the back of the buildings surrounding it - ample parking areas serve the whole civic centre.

The eastern end of the square looks onto the underground railway station. Here too, as in Vällingby, the public space is above the railway station. The square is bordered by two- or three-storey buildings, housing cinemas, restaurants, large department stores, doctors' surgeries, sports and religious centres.

An oval stretch of water, a group of four fountains and a few trees are aligned along the axis of the square.

Porphyry block paving links the various ornamental elements.

Vällingby, a new town 20 kilometres from Stockholm, was inaugurated in 1960. Markelius, Backström and Reinius were responsible for the urban plan.

The new town caters for 24,000 inhabitants and possesses a civic centre that is also capable of serving the inhabitants of the surrounding villages. The town consists of three nuclei along the railway, the preferred means of communicating with the capital.

The housing development is organized into districts directly connected to the civic centre, which is built in the central zone of the urban core. The residential districts are situated around the centre, and are rigidly distinguished on the basis of the types and densities of housing; the industrial poles are on the outskirts, near to the road arteries. The civic centre is built on a platform by the main station on the underground railway line. The area is linked to the residential districts by a highly structured system of footpaths; the arteries for vehicle traffic terminate in ample parking areas near the commercial, cultural, health and religious facilities.

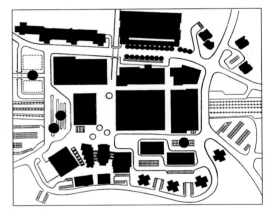

Ground plan of the Vällingby civic centre

The square of the civic centre is rectangular in shape; it is enclosed on its longer sides by two buildings with two floors above ground, a shopping centre and a multi-purpose structure respectively. The short sides open onto two pedestrian walkways.

The paving consists of porphyry blocks in two contrasting colours, which design large circles on the floor.

Four fountains embellish the large uniform surface; three are positioned at the vertices of an imaginary triangle along the south-west side of the square, and one along the north side. The circular white marble fountain pools reproduce the paving design.

VILLES NOUVELLES

Planning studies of the *villes nouvelles* in France began in the sixties, twenty years after the first British experiences.

In this period a series of interrelated phenomena - rapid demographic growth, immigration, the development of the service sector, economic expansion - generated problems of urban growth in some French cities, particularly in the Parisian region. The National Commission for Regional Planning deemed it necessary to plan the urban development of the large cities according to criteria common to the whole nation.

Using the experience of the United Kingdom and the Scandinavian countries as a basis, the Commission developed a national plan for the establishment of *villes nouvelles*. The newly founded towns were conceived as alternatives to the unrestrained growth of the suburbs of the large cities.

THE MODERN TRADITION

They achieved an objective which went beyond the simple need for new jobs and residential districts: they were to be integrated poles of expansion.

This view is all the more apparent if we restrict our field of observation to the Parisian region. The five *villes nouvelles* of the *bassin parisien* are situated along the capital's axes of development, within a range of 40 kilometres; they are large housing schemes of over 300,000 inhabitants.

Although they had common objectives, each of the bodies charged with the researching and planning of each *ville nouvelle*, known as 'missions', developed a programme based on specific requirements.

In Cergy-Pointoise - to the north-west of Paris along the Oise valley - and Évry and Tigery - to the south-east of Paris along the course of the Seine - the geography of the place determined the urban form, while in Trappes the economic activity of the zone restricted the layout of the town's productive areas.

In each scheme, the 'mission' devoted great attention to their research into the civic centre; this was conceived of as both an urban and a regional centre, at both an economic and an administrative level.

The centre is envisaged as the 'heart' of the town: a place with facilities to meet the community's requirements and to encourage the inhabitants to participate actively in town life, capable of fulfilling one of the main objectives: functional, economic and social integration. The idea of the 'urban heart', taken up from CIAM's theoretical principles, takes concrete shape in Évry, with the designing of a multi-functional megastructure: the Agora.

The 'Mission of study and organization' of the *ville nouvelle* of Évry, work on which began in 1966, was among the first to be instituted in France.

The objective indicated in the Development Scheme of the Parisian Region was the creation of an urban core that would be within easy reach of Paris and the bassin, capable of enhancing the quality of the zone. To this end, an area was identified 30 kilometres from Paris; it was connected with the capital by rail, along the south-east axis of urbanization identified by the regional plan, within the belt bounded to the west by the Autoroute A6 going south and to the east by the river Seine.

Évry is near Tigery Lieusant, a *ville nouvelle* situated on the opposite bank of the river. The role of Évry as the headquarters of the Prefecture of Essonne - the southern region of the *bassin parisien* - imposed the need for a network of communication with the rest of the region, and also for good access to the centre. These conditions, considered by the Commission to be fundamental, governed the urban form the *ville nouvelle* was to take.

The industrial areas are located near the access points to the town, near the bus station; the sports and leisure facilities along the course of the Seine. To the south of Évry, wooded and cultivated areas have been maintained, as an expression of the decision to place the town in direct contact with the countryside.

Located in the centre are a 'pole' of service activities, community facilities and one of the residential districts. The civic centre for pedestrian use is served by public transport and ample parking; it can be reached via three arteries connected directly to the autoroute and independent from the roads of the quarter. The residential sector of the centre is structured along two directrices, which intersect in the 'urban heart', leaving some free areas amid the branches of development, to be used as green zones and for future expansion. Along the axes the 'urban plots' are organized; these are integrated bands of footpaths and public transport, at the edges of which high-density buildings have been constructed. Leisure facilities have been located in the spaces left free from the 'urban plots'. The places which are characteristic of the 'heart' of the town are the Prefecture, the shopping centre and the Agora.

The Prefecture is a 50,000-square-metre complex that houses municipal and regional administrative structures. To the south stands the Agora, a multi-purpose centre directly connected to the shopping centre.

The Agora is a building with an integrated character, and the venue for the social functions necessary for the community; it is the meeting place where you can 'feel the heartbeat of the capital and the region'. The megastructure includes a covered square generated by the juxtaposition of various functional blocks. The square is irregular in shape: three sides, west, south and east, are perpendicular to each other and delimit a rectangular space which is closed off to the north by the corner of a building with a hexagonal plan.

Looking onto the south-west corner of the square is a small shopping centre, to the south-east are a café, a discothèque and a library; to the north is the structure for sports activities, the Hexagone. From the western side a pathway leads to the large shopping centre.

All the poles of the civic centre are linked by footpaths.

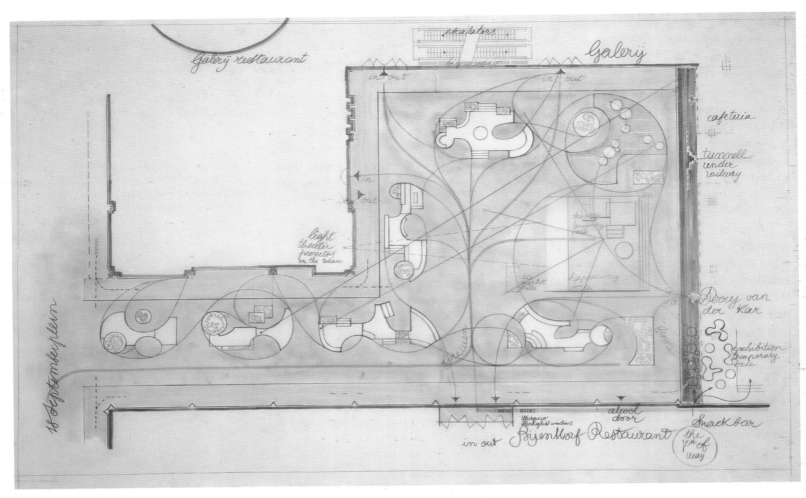

Above:
Study ground plan. A pool of water is located by the organ pipe sculpture facing the Piazza Galerij shopping centre.

Opposite:
Details of the 'dragons', a system of bench-sculptures created in collaboration with the sculptor Mario Negri

THE MODERN TRADITION

THE SQUARE IN EINDHOVEN (1967-1969)

The square in Eindhoven is an introverted space at the centre of a commercial block, closed in at the sides by the façades of the Bijenkorf department store to the east and the Piazza Galerij shopping centre to the west, and closed at the bottom by the Perry van der Kar sports shop.

A rectilinear axis connects it with the 18 Septemberplein, one of the city's most lively arteries.

Gio Ponti was initially called upon to design the façade of the new Bijenkorf department store, the internal organization of which had been planned by a different team of designers.

It should come as no surprise that the Italian architect agreed to create a surround that was totally independent from the intricate internal layout. During the sixties Gio Ponti was in fact developing his own theory of the façade as the 'skin of architecture', to which he assigned the task of determining the visual relationship with the urban space and the capacity to function as an attraction. 'Architecture is also useful (and very much so) to look at,' he in fact wrote in the pages of *Domus*.

Almost dematerialized by the absence of depth, the Bijenkorf façade has the appearance of a green ceramic reflecting band with 'diamond' tiles, measured by the rhythmic structure introduced with formal variations on the window motif.

As with many of Ponti's other works from the sixties (we need only think of the church of St Francis and the San Carlo Hospital in Milan), the openings are conceived, rather than to stand close to or for interior lighting, as 'self-lighting' surfaces, expressly devised for the nocturnal effect of the architecture. This stylistic code frequently recurs in the work of Gio Ponti, an architect with little inclination to make large spatial experiments (with the exception of the highly successful design of the Pirelli skyscraper), but an extremely capable decorator of surfaces.

The project for the square came about later, when - with the façade of the Bijenkorf by the architect Theo Boosten alongside the Piazza Galerij - the contrast between the two buildings was clear to all, and it was impossible to propose an access to the shopping arcades that was practically devoid of formal attractions. The only element able to enhance the quality of the exterior space was a large, stainless steel, organ pipe sculpture, which Frans Gast had successfully used to camouflage the stacks of the Piazza Galerij's heating system.

'Don't you realize the opportunities I represent?' Gio Ponti had written in the pages of *Domus*, allowing the square to speak in the first person. 'Don't you want to help me fill up with people? To attract people towards the seven doors that your façades, architects, open onto me?'

The first initiative taken in response to this was to close off the far north side by constructing the wing of the Perry van der Kar sports shop, using brightly coloured metal panels; these were devised to act like weathervanes, to attract the passers-by in the 18 Septemberplein. Immediately afterwards, two large bronze sculptures by Mario Negri were added; these were positioned opposite the entrance to the Bijenkorf department store.

However, the external space had to wait for Gio Ponti's 'archisculpturic' project (the definition is the author's) to endow it with figurative unity, so it could truly be called a square; this transformed the floor surface into a large bas-relief, peopled with fantasy figures.

Emerging from the silipol paving are five 'dragons' (two along the axis connecting with the 18 Septemberplein, three arranged in a 'C' formation inside the square court), an original system of bench-sculptures created in collaboration with sculptor Mario Negri. The perimeter outline consisting of curvilinear elements connected in various ways and the structuring of the figures on different levels allows them to serve several purposes, from steps to sit on to watch open-air performances, to flower-boxes.

Located at the centre of the space is a rectangular podium for theatrical performances and animation. The terrace of the Piazza Galerij has two projectors fitted - pointing respectively at the panelled façade of the Perry van der Kar and towards Frans Gast's metal stacks - for open-air light projections. 'A square' - Gio Ponti in fact argues, quoting Martin Gabriel Lederman, the inspirer of the 'performances' in Eindhoven - 'is what happens in a Square.'

Gio Ponti, one of the most famous personalities of the first period of modern architecture in Italy, was born in Milan in 1897 and graduated at the Politecnico in that city in 1921. Immediately afterwards, he opened a studio with Mino Fiocchi and Emilio Lancia, positioning himself within the Milanese Novecento current. From his enormous professional output - in association with Lancia (1926-33), with Antonio Fornaroli and Eugenio Soncini (1933-45), with Fornaroli and Alberto Rosselli (1952-76) - we must mention in particular the house-tower at the bastions of Porta Venezia (1932), the building for the Montecatini offices (1938-39) and the Pirelli skyscraper in Milan (1956). He was also prolific in the field of interior design, and collaborated energetically with the porcelain and ceramics manufacturers Richard-Ginori.

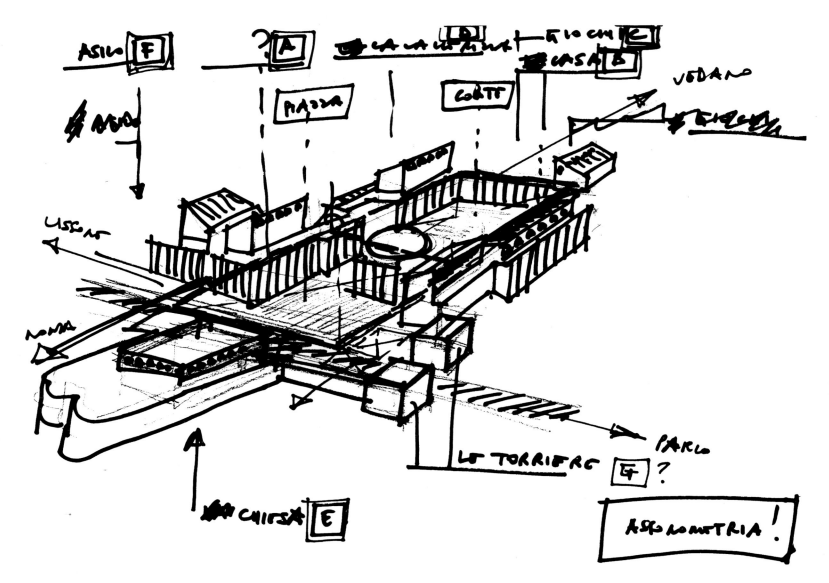

Urbano Pierini, axonometric sketch for the Piazza Ramazzotti, in Monza

NEW
SCENARIOS

THE PIAZZA RAMAZZOTTI IN MONZA (1977)

The Piazza Ramazzotti is the heart of a building complex constructed in the north suburbs of Monza, an important industrial centre as well as being a town of artistic interest in the province of Milan. The project, realized in an urban area lacking in planning and points of reference for the community, presents itself as a place of identification and cohesion for the social and building contexts.

Pierini's project envisages the creation of a compact building system incorporating the Via Ramazzotti, the road running through the large area affected by the plan. The series of open spaces is aligned along an axis perpendicular to the east-west direction of the Via Ramazzotti. Situated to the south of the street is the parish centre, designed by Pierini and the architect Marcello Pietrantoni, which is structured around the church square that opens towards the street. To the north is the commercial, residential and service sector complex, which extends around a municipal square - the Piazza Ramazzotti - and a large courtyard serving the residence. The courtyard is bounded to the north by a building for integrated functions, to the south by a circular-plan construction housing the reception facilities, to the east and west by the residence itself. The court communicates with the public square through a stairway which is open on the south side. The Piazza Ramazzotti lies between the street of the same name and the circular-plan building constituting the connecting element with the courtyard. It is bounded to the east and west by buildings characterized by their combining of different functions: commercial facilities are placed on the bottom two floors, on the third floor are the offices, while the upper floors are for residence. The constructions which look onto the square, different in terms of their types and functions, are made homogeneous by an arcade. The pillars of this arcade extend to the height of three floors, in a reinterpretation of the concept of giant order. The modular nature and the repetition of the compositional elements of the façades contribute to creating a unitary space.

The buildings are connected by footpaths, some of which are raised, such as the one that closes off the north side.

The paving of the municipal square and the courtyard is the traditional raised type, broken up by sandstone walkways which surround the sculptures and highlight the geometry of the space. Pebbles take the place of cobblestone in the passages under the arcade and coctile brick is used for the paths connecting the residential buildings. The set of sandstone sculptures, by Giò Pomodoro, is located in the centre of the Piazza Ramazzotti. It is a complex of evocative signs from the natural world, entitled *La Luna, il Sole e l'Albero* (The Moon, the Sun and the Tree). The work is articulated along an axis, parallel to the Via Ramazzotti, the ends of which are highlighted by the forms of the Sun and the Spiral Tree, while the centre is indicated by the *Moon* sculpture. The inscriptions engraved in the sculpture trace a didactic path, explaining the specific meaning of each work.

Urbano Pierini was born in 1931 in Milan, where he lives and works.

In 1957 he graduated in civil engineering at the Politecnico in Milan; from that year until 1960 he worked at Giovanni Muzio's studio. He was permanent assistant at the Institute of Building and Urban Planning of the Faculty of Engineering until 1969. Subsequently he worked in collaboration with the Study Centre of the Milanese Intermunicipal Plan and with a number of municipal administrations. He was responsible for completing the town planning schemes for Milan and Cremona. He promoted the creation of the first Italian Territorial Information System.

He is the author of essays and theoretical writings on the discipline of urban planning, on territorial analysis and on the methodology of town-planning schemes.

He is responsible for the projects for the industrial and administrative centres of a number of Italian and foreign companies. Among his most recent realizations are the new head office of the Banca d'Italia in Milan and, again in the same city, the Departments of Chemistry and Chemistry-Physics of the Faculty of Engineering.

Giò Pomodoro was born in Orciano di Pesaro in 1930. He has lived in Milan since 1954.

In 1956 he was invited to the Venice Biennale, where he exhibited a series of works using cast silver on cuttlebone, dedicated to the poet Ezra Pound.

In 1957 he began a collaboration with the magazine *Il Gesto*. In the same year he participated in the Nuclear Art exhibition at the Galleria San Fedele in Milan, where he met Bemporad, Dorazio, Novelli, Turcato, Tancredi, Penilli and Fontana, with whom, together with his brother Arnaldo, he organized the exhibitions of the Continuità group.

After a short while he split from the group, because of technical differences. His new direction of research is represented by the work called *Fluidità contrapposte* (Juxtaposed Fluidities).

In 1972 he began work on two cycles, *Gli Archi* (The Arches) and *Il Sole* (The Sun), working exclusively with marble and stone and creating large-scale works.

He has participated in numerous exhibitions, both in Italy and in the major European and American cities. On various occasions he has dealt with the relationship between architecture and sculpture, particularly in his works for public spaces, such as the fountain dedicated to Goethe in Frankfurt, the work *Luogo di Misure* (Place of Measurements) in the Piazza dei Signori in Verona, and the sculpture *Sole-aerospazio* (Sun-Aerospace) in the Piazza Adriano in Turin.

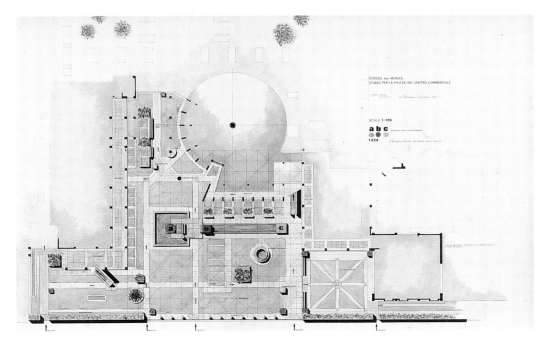

Previous page:
Giò Pomodoro's set of sculptures in the Piazza Ramazzotti with, in the foreground, the Tree Spiral

Opposite:
General layout plan of the project

TWIN PARKS NORTHEAST HOUSING PLAZA IN NEW YORK (1969-1974)

The quality of the Twin Parks residential complex, located in the eastern area of the Bronx, derives from an attention to urban space that is undoubtedly advanced, within that vein of architectural culture that latches on directly to the heritage of the Modern Movement. Against the logic of the isolated blocks which dominated the large-scale ventures of the sixties, Richard Meier's project in fact defined its programme as the integration of the new building within the surrounding urban framework, weaving the fabric of the blocks back together and respecting existing alignments. Consistent with these premises, a special emphasis was reserved for the organizing of the exterior space; this takes on the form of a zone with a public vocation, the centre of gravity for social relations between the quarter's inhabitants.

A semi-protected square is obtained in the interstitial space between two of the three buildings constituting the residential complex (all suspended on *pilotis* so as not to break up the continuity of the external space), at the point where the rectilinear axis of Grote Street converges. A geometrically based design with an abundance of elaborate structures is the qualifying element of the open space, which intentionally breaks up the rigid stereometry of the constructed blocks.

A colossal cement sculpture is located in the southern area, delimited by the C-shaped plan of one of the buildings; its combined rectilinear and curved outline offers various possibilities for sitting and relaxing. In the middle the vertical projection of a watchtower dominates the scene; this is a prismatic block partly softened by the chiaroscuro effect created by a series of horizontal flutes.

The northern area, in contrast, introduces a counterpoint to the artificiality of the composition: the paving of large cement slabs is interrupted by an island of planted greenery, allowing a small rocky hillock to emerge which suddenly introduces a natural element into the urban landscape.

Richard Meier was born in Newark, New Jersey, in 1934 and graduated in architecture at Cornell University in Ithaca. He worked in the studios of Skidmore, Owings and Merrill and in that of Marcel Breuer, before opening his own professional studio in New York (1963).

In 1969, with Peter Eisenman, John Heiduk, Michael Graves and Charles Gwathmey, he formed the Five Architects Group; they were committed to researching into the roots of modern architectonic language.

Meier has taught at the Cooper Union of New York, at the Universities of Harvard, Syracuse and Yale, and has received numerous architecture prizes, including the Pritzker Prize (1984) and the Gold Medal of the Royal Institute of British Architects (1989).

Of his best-known works, particular mention must be made of the Smith House in Connecticut (1965-67), the Douglas House in Michigan (1971-73), the Bronx Development Center in New York (1975-79), the Atheneum in New Harmony, Indiana (1975-79), the Protestant Seminary in Hartford, again in Connecticut (1978-981), the Museum of Decorative Arts in Frankfurt (1979-84), the High Museum of Art in Atlanta (1980-83) and the headquarters of 'Canal+' in Paris (1990-91). Among the projects he is currently developing are the town hall and library in The Hague, the Paul Getty Fine Arts Center in Los Angeles and the Museum of Contemporary Art in Barcelona.

Previous page:
The pedestrian square bordered by the residential buildings of Twin Parks

Opposite:
Ground plan of the square. Three different building volumes recompose the grid of the existing blocks and circumscribe the pedestrian space for sitting and relaxing.

THE BROADGATE COMPLEX IN LONDON (1982-1988)

In the extensive transformations carried out in the centre of London, 'the square', both as a centre of activity and as a project theme, seems to have remained extraneous to the interests of urban planners and architects.

The Broadgate Complex provides two exceptions to this; it is situated near Liverpool Street Station and occupies part of the block delimited to the south by Eldon Street, to the north by Whitecross Place, to the east by Finsbury Avenue and to the west by Wilson Street. The master plan, for which the Arup Associates studio was responsible, was developed in four construction phases.

The first part of the project, named '1 Finsbury Avenue', created between 1982 and 1984, consists of 2,500 square metres of surface area for use by the service sector. The structure is organized around a cavaedium covered by a transparent skylight, guaranteeing direct lighting to all levels. The last two floors, set back with respect to the plane of the façade, face onto broad terraces serving as hanging gardens. The project earned itself the *Financial Times* Award for Architecture in 1985. Another 25,000 square metres were completed during the second and third phases; these were to be used for a multi-purpose centre. Structures were created similar to those of '1 Finsbury Avenue', in that they were characterized by covered cavaedia and terraces on the top floors. The choice, due prevalently to contingent requirements, was also prompted by the desire to create private spaces with the characteristics of municipal squares. The fourth phase involved the construction of two open-air public spaces and a shopping centre.

A rectangular-shaped square, closed off on each side by buildings, communicates with Finsbury Avenue and Wilson Street via pedestrian walkways. The floor space at the centre of the area is lowered with respect to the kerb surrounding it, to which it is connected by steps. The edge of the square is at the same height as the road system outside and the second square. There are marble seats on the paved surface, in the shade of specially planted trees. A Hyperrealist set of sculptures by Segal reproduces figures of passers-by, who seem to invite you to make for the second square.

A circular plan building forms a diaphragm between the two squares. The second square is shaped like an amphitheatre. It is surrounded by a commercial structure with three floors overlooking the square and arcades gradually descending like a cavea towards the centre. The central platform was designed to allow for various uses, in imitation of the Rockefeller Center: in the winter it is intended to be used as a skating rink, while in the summer it is designed to host musical events. A number of sculptures by Richard Serra and Jacques Lipchitz have been placed in the passage connecting the square with Finsbury Avenue.

The Arup Associates studio was founded by **Ove Nyquist Arup** in 1963 to support the activities of Ove Arup and Partners, Consulting Engineers. Ove Arup's idea was to form a team of engineers, architects, specialists in acoustics, plant design and installation, structural experts, economists and foundations technicians, who would be capable of developing complete projects, the result of consistent architectonic choices, both functionally and technically.

In thirty years of activity, the studio has handled all types of building projects: residential buildings, sports facilities, theatres, concert halls, offices, schools, restructuring - being characterized by their specialization and the technical quality of the projects.

Previous page:
The large amphitheatre-shaped square, bounded by the shopping centre

Opposite:
Axonometry of the Broadgate Complex, which is articulated around two communicating pedestrian squares

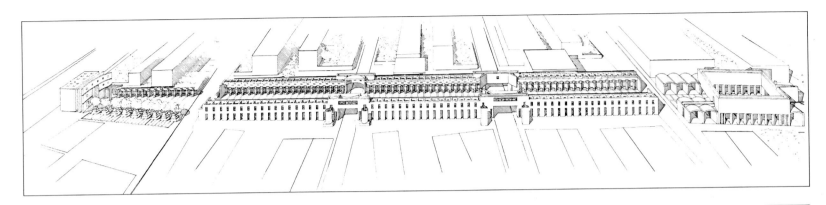

Above:
Drawing of a view of the new centre in Gibellina, consisting
of a sequence of five squares aligned along the east-west axis

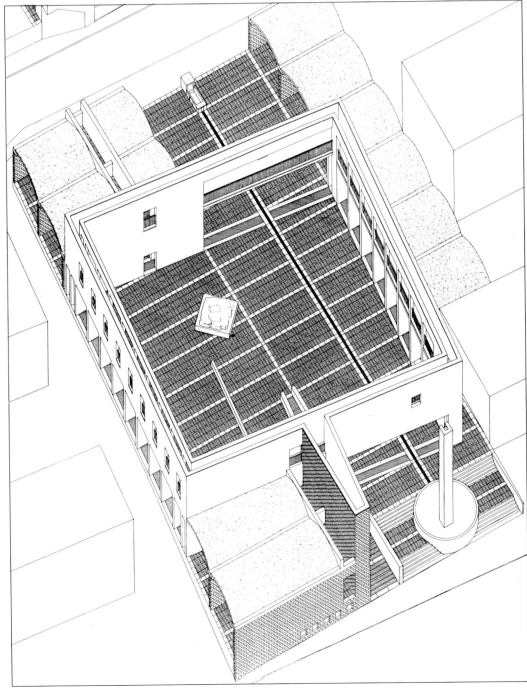

Opposite:
Axonometry of the project for the Piazza Portella della
Ginestra

THREE SQUARES IN GIBELLINA (1988-1991)

The total destruction of the historic provincial town of Gibellina, brought about by the earthquake in 1968, forced a general reconstruction plan to be drafted.

ISES, the public body set up to coordinate building operations in zones affected by earthquakes, identified an area for the new Gibellina 20 kilometres from the site of the old one, in the region of Salemi, near the Palermo-Mazara del Vallo motorway and the Salemi railway station. The new town, catering for 5,000 inhabitants, extends along the axis perpendicular to the railway, where the community facilities are located.

Along the sides of the axis are the residential areas, characterized by long rows of buildings. The overall result in urban planning terms is decidedly negative and the opportunity to realize a residential centre of an experimental nature has not been taken advantage of.

In the building fabric we find episodes of architecture and sculpture which are totally isolated from the context; yet at times (but only at times) these are praiseworthy, as is the case with Purini and Thermes' system of squares.

The report states that the project is part of an attempt at 'completion', to stitch together the heads of the rows of houses around an ordered 'room' space.

The study is linked to the proposals in O.M. Ungers' plan for the centre of Gibellina, the intention of which was to regain a relative complexity between the various sequences that bind the houses, roads and public spaces, which are often large and haphazard.

The squares in Gibellina constitute an example of the planning of a coordinated system of public spaces in Italy.

The strong design of Purini and Thermes' project is set against the building fabric of the new town and the traditional character of Sicilian squares. It is a system conceived to permit flexibility of use, a 'positive configuration', a structure conceived of as a factor of cohesion in the urban landscape.

The formal solution takes up certain compositional methods that are characteristic of Sicilian architecture, such as the temple peristyle, the monumentality of the Telamons, the geometrical grid plan of the newly established towns. The scheme is articulated as a series of aligned spaces, following the slope of the terrain along the east-west axis and separated by roads for vehicle traffic.

The project envisaged the construction of five squares: Rivolta Siciliana, Fasci dei Lavoratori, Monti di Gibellina, Autonomia Siciliana and Portella delle Ginestre. The first three have been completed.

Piazza Rivolta Siciliana. This square, 62 metres long, occupies a trapezoid-shaped space arranged on a slight incline. It is separated from the Piazza Fasci dei Lavoratori by the Via Colajanni. To the south it is bounded by a wall which fulfils various functions: it creates shade, it terminates the pedestrian walkway of the quarter and separates the square from the rows of public housing.

The wall stretches along the whole length of the south side, remaining at a constant height. It is divided up by seven wall septa, repeated modularly every 3.6 metres; each 'bay' has a 1.2-metre-wide interior aperture, flanked by two benches. The exterior of these wings is exposed cement, as are the coping and base of the internal frontage, while the middle area of the façade facing the square is covered with yellow tufa from Mazara.

A row of palms, positioned at regular intervals, winds along the opposite side. Each tree is surrounded by a base shaped like a stepped pyramid, made of Alcamo travertine, to be used as seating.

To the east the expanse is delimited by the façade of an 'open' building, acting as a monumental entrance to the system of squares. Access is gained through a tall portal, inside which a spring supplies a small channel that terminates, on the opposite side, in a fountain with a cylindrical basin. The water course irrigates the palm trees, taking advantage of the sloping terrain.

The paving consists of Alcamo travertine slabs, framed by square borders made from lava stone. An imitation ruin is used to conceal a pre-existing electrical mains distribution box. The ruin, a work by Nando Vigo, is a reminder of ancient Sicilian architecture.

Above:
The 'open' building of the *Piazza Rivolta Siciliana* was designed to provide the monumental entrance to the system of squares: the imitation ruin, a work by Nando Vigo, conceals a pre-existing electrical mains distribution box.

Opposite:
The perimeter arcade of the *Piazza Fasci dei Lavoratori* and the *Piazza Monti di Gibellina* has two pedestrian walkways running along it: one at the ground level of the two squares, the other at the impost level of the curvilinear 'trabeation'.

The raised pedestrian walkway inside the perimeter arcade. To the left: the extrados of the curved 'trabeation' that looks onto the square, covered with pieces of coloured ceramic

Piazza Fasci dei Lavoratori and **Piazza Monti di Gibellina**. Positioned in sequence, but separated from the Via Nunzio Nasi, these two squares are bounded to the north and south by a long arcade, which creates a large 150 x 24 metre enclosure. The repetition of shapes on the long sides of both squares and the size of the scheme generate an interior space which forms the project's philosophy and specificity. This is one of those cases where the authors have created the surround for the square and have done so in the simplest manner, by repeating identical elements.

The porticoed enclosure consists of prefabricated elements. Large hollow pilasters measuring 1.2 x 1.2 metres, arranged at a constant distance of 3.6 metres, are connected by a concave trabeation (with a radius of curvature of 1.8 metres). The different heights of the pilasters follow the difference in height of the terrain, making the upper outline horizontal. The long arcade has two pedestrian walkways running along it. The covered passage at ground level of the squares has benches and telephone booths fitted; the upper one, at the impost height of the 'trabeation', is a long panoramic axis, to which access is gained via the stairways at the ends of the Piazza Monti di Gibellina. The base of the portico is without a plaster finish, while the upper part is covered with yellow tufa from Mazara, as in the Piazza della Rivolta Siciliana. The extrados of the curved outline facing onto the inside of the square is covered with pieces of coloured ceramic.

The lavastone paving is in modules, with a regular 1.5 metre grid of Alcamo travertine.

As in the Piazza Rivolta Siciliana, small channels of water supplied by four fountains furrow the continuity of the floor level.

The Piazza Autonomia Siciliana, one of the squares not constructed, was conceived as the conclusion of the large porticoed enclosure. Indeed, the project envisages the repetition of the portico motif, while the existing squares are to be connected via a footbridge over the Via Ruggero VII.

The Piazza Portella delle Ginestre, located in a position mirroring the Piazza Rivolta Siciliana, is to form the western end of the system of squares. At the centre a portico with a raised walkway, conceived as a panoramic observation point, will delimit a space to be used to house a market. At the two heads there are to be some vaulted rooms, covered on the extrados with the same mosaic ceramic used in the vault of the arcade-enclosure, to be used to house the street vendors' stalls.

Vittorio Bitti and Mario Trimarchi collaborated on the project.

The Purini/Thermes Studio, founded in 1966, has directed its activities mainly at design experimentation, relating both to problems of urban planning and to questions of architectural language, and finding its identity in the reconciling of the heritage of Rationalism with the revival of historical themes. Of their projects, particular mention must be made of the following: the Pharmacist's House in Gibellina (1980-88), the residential complex for 65 dwellings in the suburbs of Naples (1983-88), the Chapel of Sant'Antonio da Padova in Poggioreale (1983-88). The studio created one of the façades of the 'Strada Novissima' at the Venice Biennale in 1970. In 1985 they won the Leone di Pietra for their project for the Ponte dell'Accademia.

Franco Purini was born in 1941 in Isola del Liri (Frosinone). He studied architecture in Rome with Maurizio Sacripanti and Ludovico Quaroni, with whom he graduated in 1971. He taught Architectural Composition in Reggio Calabria. He is currently full professor of Design and Surveying at the Faculty of Architecture in Rome.

Purini participated in the study centre and the editing of *Controspazio*, and is the author of various books, published both in Italy and abroad.

Laura Thermes was born in Rome in 1943, where she graduated in 1971. She works in the Department of Architecture and Analysis of the City at the Faculty of Architecture in Rome, and teaches Architectural Composition at the Faculty of Reggio Calabria.

She has held courses and seminars in Africa, the United States, Britain, Argentina and Brazil, and was a member of the editorial staff of *Controspazio*.

THE PLACE DES COLONNES IN CERGY-PONTOISE
(1980-1986)

Cergy-Pontoise in many ways constitutes a singular experience in the history of the *villes nouvelles* of the Paris suburbs.

The need for a considerable increase in housing, which had justified the founding of the new centre in the second half of the sixties, did not stop the planned development from keeping a vast area in the valley of the Oise free from construction. Thus, when in the early seventies a new sensitivity developed towards the qualitative aspects and the social implications of large housing developments inside the SGVN (General Secretariat for the Villes Nouvelles), Cergy-Pontoise could boast the availability of a vast natural park, a candidate to become the protagonist of a renewed urban identity.

On the threshold of the new decade, the urban planners Michel Jaouën and Bertrand Warnier perfected the idea of a contemporary garden with an axial vocation, capable of taking its place within the tradition of the large landscape schemes of the seventeenth and eighteenth centuries, which still define the shape of the Parisian Region (of which Versailles is only the most famous example). The choice of designer fell necessarily upon Dani Karavan, whose language, elementary yet full of symbolic allusions, guaranteed a result of controlled monumentality.

Conceived in 1980 and completed in stages over the years that followed, the project for the Axe Majeur of Cergy-Pontoise consists of a three-kilometre walkway, starting from the residential district of Cergy Saint-Christophe and terminating at the Carrefour de Ham on the opposite bank of the river Oise.

Its layout, stretching in a straight line with a northwest-southeast orientation, continues ideally towards the Ile de Chatou (so dear to the Impressionists), where it intersects the historic axis of the Champs-Elysées consisting of the Louvre-Tuileries-Place de l'Etoile-Arc de la Défense system.

Twelve stations are planned along the route. In Karavan's symbolic universe, twelve is in fact the number that marks the rhythm of man's life; it is the measure of time (the hours of the day and night) and of the cycle of the seasons (the months of the year). The first station is a round square, created inside the Place des Colonnes. Standing at its centre is a Belvedere Tower, the starting-point for the rectilinear promenade, which goes through the Orchard (a reminder of Cergy-Pontoise's rural past) and the Esplanade, finishing up in a terrace; here a colonnade (twelve columns) frames the view, dividing the landscape into vertical planes. There follows a slightly sloping terracing called the Garden of the Hills (interpreting the picturesque appearance of the surrounding landscape), which leads to a semicircular amphitheatre with a view over a scenic expanse of water. From here, a rectangular basin - conceived, in homage to the illusionist tradition of baroque gardens, in such a way that the water seems to lie on an oblique plane - connects the Seine with the waters of the Oise; these waters feed a reservoir in which lies the astronomic island (which the author intended to be a sort of 'poetic observatory'). Not far away, a pyramid emerging from the water, complete with wind organs, offers a final *son et lumière* spectacle, before the path terminates at the Ham motorway intersection.

Having defined the geographical coordinates within which the Axe Majeur fits, we can now move on to a detailed examination of the Place des Colonnes, the monumental head of the whole complex. The connecting point between the building fabric of Cergy Saint-Christophe and the natural valley of the Oise, this is the only element of the system to be conceived by 'four hands', those of Dani Karavan and Ricardo Bofill.

The decision to choose the Catalan architect for the creation of the constructed curtain with the Belvedere Tower in the background stems from his classically oriented language, considered by the initiative's promoters to be the most suitable type of backdrop to bring out the Neo-baroque atmosphere with which the whole of this landscape plan is infused. Bofill's project - which consists of a pair of court buildings with a vast hemicycle standing in front of them - is in fact clearly reminiscent of the French classicism of the seventeenth century, casually drawn from the court of the Sun King in Versailles or the grandiose colonnade at the entrance to the Louvre.

Large croisée windows mark a uniform rhythm in the white façades of the court buildings closing off the square on the northern side; these windows seem particularly inspired by Versailles.

In contrast, the Doric colonnade which, with its semicircular plan, delimits the square in the

Opposite:
The Place des Colonnes with the Belvedere Tower; in the background is Ricardo Bofill's vast residential hemicycle. The building, built using prefabricated panels, reproduces in colossal dimensions the classical colonnade of the Doric order, with entablature with metopes and triglyphs.

Below:
The beginning of the Axe Majeur at the base of the Tower; in the background are the court-style residential buildings which border the square on the north side. The circular ring emerging from the tamped earth surfacing is composed of 360 stone slabs and is an ideal representation of the earthly sphere.

NEW SCENARIOS

direction of the urban park, seems inspired by the Louvre. As in many other projects by Bofill, the elements of residential architecture (doors, windows, stair shells) are completely subordinate to the requirements of the classical order reduced to its essential components, with the rhythm of the columns and the entablature marked by the alternating of metopes and triglyphs. The whole scheme is constructed using a system of prefabricated concrete panels, while the 'voids' - the intercolumns, for instance - are rendered using homogeneous glass surfaces.

Within the Neo-classical frame shaped by Bofill's architecture, Dani Karavan's symbolic horizon unravels itself.

His circular square, which is located at the centre of the hemicycle inside a grass perimeter band, constitutes an ideal image of the earthly sphere. A ring in fact emerges from the tamped earth surfacing; this consists of 360 stone slabs (the 360 earthly degrees), each of which measures 36 centimetres. Standing at the centre of this is a square-plan Belvedere Tower inspired by the patricians' towers of the Italian medieval period; this too is proportioned according to the metric semiotics which regulates the whole composition (36 metres high, width 360 centimetres). It is slightly inclined towards the south-east, following the rectilinear lie of the Axe Majeur; the latter, clearly marking its way (it is paved with white stone slabs), heads in the direction of the Esplanade, through a passage between the perimeter buildings. An internal staircase means the tower can be scaled, and thus it is slowly transformed into a belvedere, which gradually guides you, as you ascend step by step, into the discovery of the successive stations of the axis, offering a different view at each stage.

Fitted at the top of the tower is a laser transmitter, which sends out a light ray that heads in a straight line towards the terminal at the Carrefour de Ham. Thus it is possible, even at night, to see the linear view that constitutes the synthetic image of the Axe Majeur at Cergy-Pontoise.

The residential hemicycle of the Place des Colonnes in a view from the Esplanade. The rectilinear lie of the Axe Majeur - originating at the foot of the Belvedere Tower - breaks up the continuity of the perimeter building curtain, opening up the view onto the vast expanse of the Oise valley.

Born in Barcelona in 1939, **Ricardo Bofill** studied at the School of Architecture of Geneva. In 1963, with a group of collaborators, he formed the well-known Taller de Arquitectura of Barcelona.

The Barrio Gaudí in Reus and the 'Walden 7' residential complex for the Catalan capital testify to the theoretical references that characterize the beginnings of his professional activities.

He gained first prize at the 1975 competition for the redesigning of the layout of the old market area of Les Halles in Paris, marking his passage to activity at international level.

His projects completed in various European countries - France, Spain, Belgium and Sweden - as well as in Algeria and the United States, are characterized by an architecture which reinterprets the monumental characteristics of classical

architecture, also in the low-cost residential building projects completed using prefabricated systems.

The son of a landscape engineer, **Dani Karavan** was born in 1930 in Tel Aviv. He embarked upon artistic studies in his city of birth (under the painters Avni, Stematsky, Streichman and Paul Levy), and then enrolled at the Bezalel Academy in Jerusalem. In 1956 he moved to Florence, in order to learn fresco technique.

From 1960 to 1973 he was active primarily as a scenographer, and was responsible for the sets for the Martha Graham Dance Company.

With his participation in the 38th Venice Biennale (1976) and in the exhibition Documenta 6 in Kassel (1977), he met with international success, earning him numerous commissions in

Europe and the United States. In particular, two Italian realizations - the temporary structures for Forte Belvedere in Florence and for the Castello dell'Imperatore in Prato (1978) - conditioned the subsequent course of his work, directing him towards minimal-concept sculpture that is highly charged with symbolism.

His interest in landscape and his monumental vocation have led Karavan into direct contact with architecture.

Of his recent projects, particular mention should be made of the following: the arrangement outside the Ludwig Museum in Cologne (1979-86), Kikar Levana (the White Square) in Tel Aviv (1977-88), the 'Path of Light' at the Olympic Park in Seoul (1987-88) and the entrance to the Shiba Hospital in Tel Hashomer (Israel 1992).

TWO SQUARES IN ITALY

SQUARE IN POGGIOREALE (1986-1988)

The opportunity to design an urban square which was not subordinate to the surrounding residential buildings presented itself in the mid-eighties, as part of a municipal initiative to convert the centre of Poggioreale.

The small Sicilian town, one of the centres most affected by the Belice earthquake, had in fact been experiencing a profound dichotomy between the old core, with an abundance of historical and environmental relics, but in considerable disarray, and the new town, built hurriedly due to practical necessity and completely without urban quality.

By 'digging down' into memories dating back to the period of Greek colonization, Paolo Portoghesi has organized the open space on the model of an 'agora', forcing it into a unitary design which is defined at its edges by an uninterrupted line of porticoes. The ground-plan organization, conceived as a white and grey stone grid, follows the slightly sloping course of the terrain; with a fan-shaped design, it is structured into four sectors at different levels, connected by concentric circular steps.

The side arcades, which border the square and act as connecting elements with the pre-existing buildings (including the church, built by Franco Purini), have an order of fluted columns made of centrifuged cement, with on top a sort of plaster trabeation with small oval windows. The progressive changes in level, following the variations in the level of the ground, introduce a counterpoint with a vaguely Oriental flavour into the classical citation; this is partly because of the curvilinear fittings, partly because of the gradually descending profile of the roofing.

The back end, which is the upper level, is closed off by a curvilinear wing consisting of a double order of colonnades. In the lower area there are closed rooms to be used for social activities (civic services, political parties' offices, etc.), while the area at the top is occupied by an open pergola facing onto the square. Here, embracing a suggestion from classical Greek architecture, some of the columns allow their anthropomorphic component to pour forth, changing into large caryatides created by the sculptor Paolo Borghi. Two curvilinear-flighted stairways act as connecting elements between the level of the pergola and the substructure of the square. Looming over all is the clock tower; this, with its tall parallelepipedal mass, lightened by a classical-style bell tower, presents itself as the symbolic reference on the town skyline.

The project, though formally autonomous, fits within a more general design for collective spaces; in this, provision is made - on the directrix of the square's symmetrical axis - for a public park and a swimming pool (currently in the process of being built).

Previous page:
The classical-style colonnade with the outline of the Poggioreale municipal tower

Opposite:
A view of the square from the clock tower. The side porticoes, which follow the slight slope of the terrain, circumscribe a fan-shaped space, paved with a white and grey stone checked design.

Previous page:
A 'caryatid' by Paolo Borghi looks out from the open pergola onto the square.

Opposite:
One of the pedestrian access points to the underground garage in the Tarquinia residential complex

Roberto Franchitti, Giancarlo Bertocchini, Pietro Brega, Salvo Lonardo and Stefania Tuzi collaborated on the project.

RESIDENTIAL COMPLEX IN TARQUINIA (1981-1987)

The 'poetics of listening' which Paolo Portoghesi has used to shape his architecture - that is, the willingness to embrace the manifold suggestions rooted in the memory of individual local sites - forces the designer towards a continual and gradual sharpening of perspectives. Starting with the building product, the attention progressively shifts to the organization of the urban surroundings, until it condenses itself in those residual open spaces - squares in particular - which are the favoured venue for social encounters.

Exemplifying this design approach is the low-cost social housing complex for the workers of ENEL (the National Electrical Energy Authority), built in the mid-eighties in the municipality of Tarquinia.

In conditions that were highly restrictive in terms of the choice of types and dimensions of dwellings, the organization of the project gave priority to the search for a powerful 'figurative quality', which would be capable, though without renouncing its own contemporary image, of emphasizing the bond with Tarquinia's traditions.

In fact the image of 'that haughty town, all built on precipices, protected by towers and by walls' (the quotation is from Vincenzo Cardarelli), was used as the stimulus to find the solution for the outline of the two juxtaposed constructions in which the residential function was to be concentrated. Here the typological duality between lines of dwelling houses and tower-shaped houses creates a powerful rhythmic cadence - measurable in the alternating between large arches and vertical septa - giving rise to a complex semantic plot where the initial idea of the town wall strays into the suggestion of the aqueducts which populate the Roman countryside, reclaiming the civil lesson of Vienna's Karl Marx Hof.

It is inevitable that such a decisive formal characterization of building façades accentuates the 'centrality' of the connecting space, conferring on it the identity of a pedestrian square - although this was extraneous to the client's requirements.

With a scheme wholly resolved on the floor level, the intermediate area - an elongated bowl - is forced to take on a formal characterization that is rich in evocations: an oval platform of stone, explicitly inspired by the Piazza Navona, stands out inside a perimeter frame of beige coctile brick with a fishbone formation. The analogy even extends to the details, involving the presence of a central fountain with a star-shaped plan (which was modelled on the Fontana dei Fiumi, but was not realized), and positioning two cylindrical elements - serving as the air intakes of the underground garage - in such a way as to evoke the lateral fountains of the Roman square.

The pedestrian entrances to the garage are semicircular, however, and located by the entrances to the residential buildings.

An architect and architectural historian - we need only mention his voluminous research into the Roman baroque (1966), the monographs on Guarino Guarini (1956) and Francesco Borromini (1967) - **Paolo Portoghesi** was born in Rome in 1931 and graduated in architecture in 1957. Ever since his youthful works (Casa Baldi in 1959), he has embarked upon a personal revision of the compositional and expressive modules of the 'modern tradition', which in the seventies prompted him to take up a clear position in favour of the Post-Modern movement. Known at international level for his theoretical and critical commitment (from *Le inibizioni dell'architettura moderna* of 1974 to the very successful *Dopo l'architettura moderna* of 1980) and for his energies devoted to planning activities (from the Royal Court of Amman to the Mosque in Rome), he has been editor-in-chief of certain campaigning magazines, such as *Controspazio* (from 1969 to 1983), *Eupalino* (from 1983) and *Materia* (from 1990).

He directed the Architecture section at the Venice Biennale, for which he prepared the Presence of the Past exhibition in 1980. He later took up the presidency of the organization (1983-92). He currently teaches history of architecture at the University of Rome.

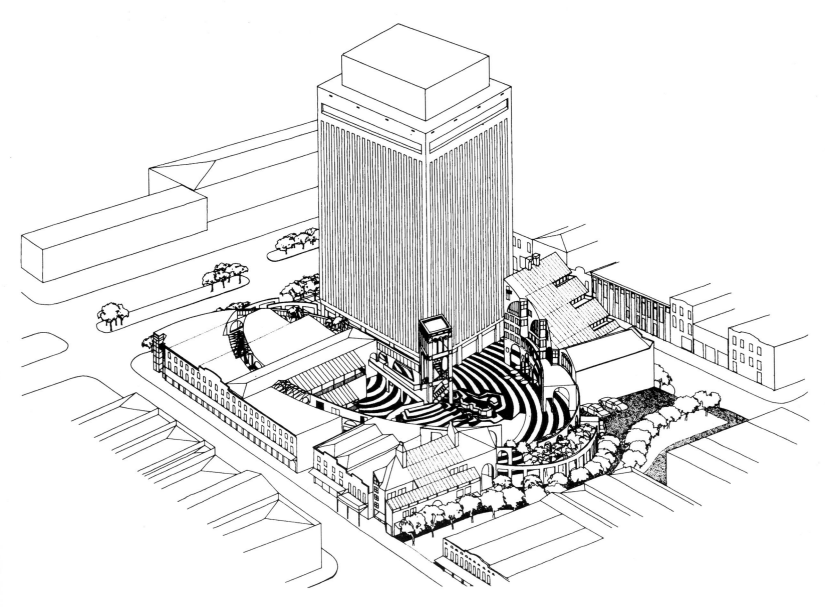

Charles Moore: competition project for the Piazza d'Italia in New Orleans

'PIAZZE D'ITALIA'

THE CIVIC CENTRE IN TSUKUBA (1979-1985)

Tsukuba is a newly founded urban centre built 60 kilometres from Tokyo to house the university institutes and research laboratories which were moved out of the capital. In 1978 the need to favour the residential development of this small town (which three years after the completion of works had barely attracted a quarter of the inhabitants planned) convinced the Japanese Housing Corporation to announce a competition by invitation for the creation of a civic centre equipped with recreational and commercial attractions. Arata Isozaki won the competition, with an urban project characterized by a scenographic plan abounding in evocative formal elements, based on an elliptic square which obviously echoes Michelangelo's Campidoglio.

Such specific use of the citation, one of the distinctive traits of Isozaki's design methodology, enables him specifically to characterize an urban space which would otherwise be without either historical memory or significant geographical peculiarities.

Located on the pedestrian walkway that intersects the town's road network in a north-south direction is a large rectangular square; this is closed off on two sides by buildings and bounded on the remaining sides by a double row of trees, which serve as screens for the buildings behind.

The paving design, which has a geometrical motif consisting of three overlapping and offset coloured grids, suggests a slipping and unstable effect, which is confirmed in the complex articulated structure of the perimeter building volumes. The east side is occupied by a large hotel; this comprises a tower housing the bedrooms, a parallelepipedal wing for the communal rooms (entrance hall, restaurant, coffee shops, etc.) and a cube-shaped volume in front, inclined and rotated with respect to the axis of the square, containing a hall reserved for banquets. On the frontal plane certain complex and differentiated compositional elements emerge (curvilinear bow-windows, broken-up frames, gable windows, etc.), while the regularly positioned bosses in the base area, set in contrast to the clear silvered surfaces of the wall above, offer a distorted new version of building models of the Renaissance tradition.

The concert hall on the south side is similarly conceived; its entrance volume is set forward, explicitly inspired by a classical pronaos. The assemblage of fragments and architectural forms from different sources seems to evoke a scenario of ruins; this becomes explicit in certain of Isozaki's sketches, where the Tsukuba civic centre is depicted following a hypothetical earthquake. A commercial gallery has been created below the rectangular square; this receives its light from large cylindrical skylights and looks onto the elliptic square, which is the episode in the project that stands out. Here too is a subtle intellectual conceit - the square, concave and not convex, is reversed with respect to Michelangelo's model - enabling Isozaki to make free and ironic use of the historical sources to which he refers.

The point of maximum spatial complexity is to be found at the 'waterfall' of steps which shatter the continuity of the ellipse, establishing communication between the different levels of the two squares.

Here elements taken from the natural universe (water, rocks, vegetation) break up the geometrical framework of the project by evoking metaphorically the site of a metamorphosis (for Isozaki, architecture is a metaphor-producing machine). At the centre, in a dominating position, is the statue of Daphne, changed into a tree to escape Apollo (by the Japanese sculptor Nagasawa).

Could this be a metaphor for the designing process?

Previous page:
Aerial view. Revealed inside the paving gridwork of the upper square, consisting of coloured overlapping and offset grids, is the elliptical square inspired by Michelangelo's Roman Campidoglio.

Below:
The tower of the hotel, with the unaligned cube of the banquet hall behind the naturalistic insertion of the tree of Daphne

Arata Isozaki, a leading personality in the panorama of Japanese architecture, was born in Oita in 1931 and graduated in architecture at the University of Tokyo in 1954. After a period of apprenticeship at Kenzo Tange's studio and brief membership of the Metabolist movement (an avant-garde current from the early sixties, which developed models of urban development centred on flexibly growing megastructures), he opened a professional studio in Tokyo, embarking upon a path of personal research that

in a few years enabled him to take on a definite physiognomy in the indistinct Post-Modern universe and to obtain international recognition.

Starting from the consideration that contemporary architecture can no longer exhibit a dogmatic and universal language (a consideration that is the subject of his book *The Dissolution of Architecture*, printed in 1975), Isozaki develops a 'theory of metaphorical manner', consisting in a free assemblage

of forms and elements taken from the historical traditions of architecture.

Only with this play on citations and metaphors, where on each occasion elements are decontextualized and take on different meanings, is it in fact possible in his view to give form to a powerfully symbolic architecture, capable of combatting the expressive poverty of the contemporary urban environment.

'PIAZZE D'ITALIA'

THE PIAZZA D'ITALIA IN NEW ORLEANS (1974-1979)

The Piazza d'Italia came about as a result of the collaboration between two different architecture studios, who had gained first and second place respectively in the competition by invitation announced in 1974. The theme of the project was the conversion of a deteriorating block in a central area, formerly occupied by the Lykes Building (a 22-floor building constructed in the sixties by the August Perez Associates studio of New Orleans) and by low industrial sheds dating back to the second half of the nineteenth century. This was to be used to house commercial structures and the headquarters of the Italian community in New Orleans.

The August Perez group had been the winners of the competition, with a project which envisaged a restructuring of the existing buildings; the project fitted in well with the directrices of the urban renovation plan promoted by the municipality. The Urban Innovations Group (UIG) from Los Angeles, directed by Charles Moore, had offered a solution structured around the powerful figurative capacity of the central square, devoting less interest to the perimeter building structures. Partly to combine the potential of the individual projects, partly to quell the polemics that the victory of a local studio had aroused within the American Institute of Architects, the jury therefore decided to complement Perez's winning project with the contribution by UIG for the organization of the exterior space.

Whereas the project presented in the competition has an elliptical square bounded by an arcade, with a fountain at the foot of a high tower covered with multi-coloured marble, Charles Moore's definitive solution takes account of the circular plan already suggested in Perez's project. Indeed, the paving shows a disk of concentric rings, made of slate and granite alternately; this disk expands

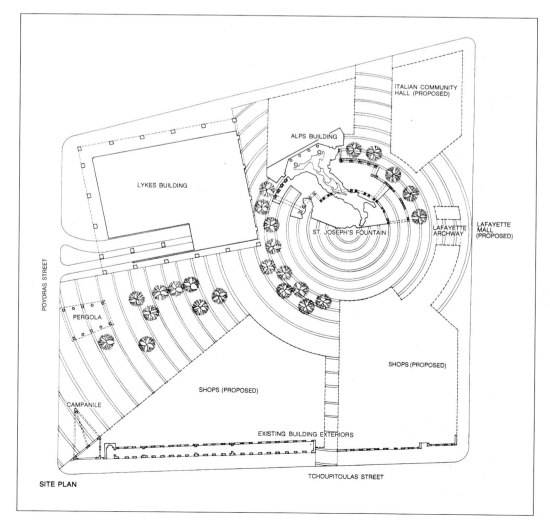

SITE PLAN

Previous page:
The porticoed wings provide the setting for St. Joseph's Fountain. With a taste for explicitly Post-Modern assemblage, the five architectonic orders that constitute the basic vocabulary of classical tradition are re-evoked here.

Opposite:
Ground plan of the Piazza d'Italia. The appearance of the episode of the fountain is announced by the concentric ringed paving that directs the attention towards the centre of gravity of the urban arrangement.

forcefully, spreading out to reach the lateral footpaths which connect the pedestrian square with the city's road network (to be specific, St. Peter's Street, Poydras Street, Tchoupitoulas Street and Lafayette Street).

The central core of the complex is occupied by a monumental fountain - St. Joseph's Fountain - shaped like a boot; this is of course a direct allusion to the Italian peninsula.

A terraced waterfall, made with an alternating play of slate, marble, shingle and reflective tiles, springs from walled wings that reevoke the Alpine chain. Three water courses (essentially the Po, the Arno and the Tiber) run inside it, pouring into two lateral pools, representing the Tyrrhenian and Adriatic Seas. At the geometrical centre of the floor design is a representation of Sicily (most of the Italian community in New Orleans are of Sicilian origin); this forms a terraced podium that can be used as a stand. The fountain is surrounded on the north side by a series of concentric arcades; with the typical freedom of manipulation that the whole Post-Modern experience is renowned for, these arcades represent the different architectonic orders of the classicists' world. For US culture, Italy is in fact the cradle of regulations regarding orders and is the centre of propulsion for their diffusion throughout the world. The Tuscan portico, placed astride the peninsula, consists of a row of columns enclosed in stainless steel, with a thin layer of water sliding continually down them.

The Doric portico, which stretches out by Sardinia, consists of a Serliana motif, its rhythm marked by steel semicolumns set on a tall base shown in section. Vertical fissures along the shafts of the columns reveal the presence of the water inside, before this gushes out from the metopes in the trabeation (ironically nicknamed 'wetopes') or jets from the two stone masks standing above the central arch.

Similar waterworks abound in the series of porticoes behind. The Ionic order, positioned to terminate the Adriatic Sea, has completely rounded columns with fluted shafts, with a steel capital and a cornice of disproportionate size. Both the Corinthian and Composite orders, occupying the rearmost position, include a procession of semicolumns with a high trabeation which has Latin inscriptions running across it.

Concluding the complex, close to the imaginary Alpine chain, a large 'niche' with a Serliana frontage is structured into a so-called delicatessen order, which is a free assemblage of elements taken from different orders. The theatrical opulence that has accompanied the whole operation reaches its peak, nodding allusively in the direction of the grandiose complex of the Fontana di Trevi in Rome.

With a taste for surprise borrowed from the urban precepts of Camillo Sitte (his *The Art of Building Cities* was widely read during the years of Post-Modern revanchisme), Moore wished to delay the

View of the fountain-boot alluding to the Italian peninsula

striking visual contact with the dominant symbolic element occupying the central core (St. Joseph's Fountain), by anticipating its presence with one or two 'signals' in decentralized positions. Placed at the entrance to the pedestrian walkway which connects the interior plaza with Poydras Street are a triangular bell tower and a pergola. The bell tower, standing on a base which again is triangular, has a stucco-covered metal structure, and is a visual reference point for motorists in Poydras Street. At night, the slender, grey-and-black painted structure is cancelled out, allowing the luminous plot of its neon lamps to emerge. The pergola appears in the guise of a classical temple, with a double colonnade tapering off in the direction of the internal plaza. On the opposite side, towards Lafayette Street, is a triumphal arch; this, of all the typological elements available in the classical repertoire, is the one that provides the best visual expression of invitation and promise.

Detail of the Doric order section of the porticoed wings. Vertical fissures along the shafts of the columns reveal the presence of water, which emerges in tiny jets from the 'wetopes' in the trabeation.

Charles Willard Moore was born in Michigan, where he graduated in architecture in 1947. He then travelled extensively on study trips, until, in 1955, he attended Princeton University, taking a doctorate in History of Art.

In the sixties, with Lyndon, Turnbull and Whitaker, he founded the MLTW studio in Berkeley and embarked upon didactic activities at Yale University. Since 1970 his numerous professional appointments have led him to work in collaboration with many others, as an associate of the Urban Innovations Group of Los Angeles and of Centerbrook Architects of Essex, and as partner in new studios, first in Essex (Charles W. Moore Associates, 1970-75) then in Santa Monica (Moore, Ruble, Yudell, from 1976) and in Austin, Texas (Charles Moore Architect, 1985-90, Moore/Anderson Architects, from 1991). Decorated with many international acknowledgements - of these, we must mention the gold medal of the American Institute of Architects in 1991 - he teaches at various universities in the United States.

Of his architectural creations, particular mention should be made of the following: the Sea Ranch residential complex in California, Kresge College in Santa Cruz, the Beverly Hills Civic Centre, the Fargo Episcopal Church, 'Nex Town' for the Disney Development Corporation in Florida, the museum of the Washington State Historical Society in Tacoma and the Tegel residential complex in Berlin.

NOTRE-DAME DE LA PAIX IN YAMOUSSOUKRO, IVORY COAST (1984)

Yamoussoukro, the birthplace of the President of the Côte d'Ivoire (Ivory Coast) Felix Houphouet-Boigny, became the country's capital in 1983, in accordance with a tradition that is common to many countries. It replaced Abidjan, a city with around two million inhabitants. This small village in the savannah was radically transformed by urban expansion. It was planned according to a grid scheme that is characteristic of newly founded cities, with buildings with imposing structures for prestige purposes.

President Houphouet-Boigny commissioned the architect Pierre Fakhoury to construct a religious building, entitled Notre-Dame de la Paix, to mark the 'rebirth of Christianity' in the country. The project is reminiscent of St Peter's in the Vatican. Fakhoury's intention was to establish a connection with the church-symbol of the Catholic faith, to provide visual expression of the unity between the people of the Ivory Coast and the universal church.

Notre-Dame was built in the suburbs of the capital on a large rectangular area; here a number of paved footpaths, linking up with the road axes that connect with the city, design geometrical motifs on the terrain: square-shapes, triangles, circular sectors carefully cultivated as lawns and bordered with hedges. The esplanade penetrates into the African savannah, accentuating the contrast between the imposing volume of the church and the finiteness of the designed spaces on one hand, and the immensity of the natural spaces on the other.

The religious complex consists of a circular-plan church, covered with a 90-metre diameter cupola and a colonnade, which is articulated into two semicircular arms, outstretched towards Yamoussoukro.

The colonnade encloses an elliptical space, the stone paved surface of which is broken up at the centre by the large figure of a dove, expressing the church's dedication to peace. The area thus delimited is a synthesis of a public square and a church square. It is in fact a place where it is possible to sit, rest, meditate, meet friends, assemble. The occasional use of this space, which was designed in accordance with concepts that are extraneous to African culture, expresses the intrinsic contradictions of the project. The square outside Notre-Dame de la Paix seems to be the transposition of the European concepts of urban planning and of a civic square into a place that is developing its own criteria for organizing public spaces.

Pierre Fakhoury, of Lebanese origin, graduated in 1971 at the Institut Supérieur d'Architecture St. Lue de Tournai in Belgium. He currently lives and works in Paris.

His projects have been realized both in France and in Africa.

Previous page:
Aerial view of Notre-Dame de la Paix. The spatial plan is explicitly inspired by the Basilica of St Peter in Rome.

Below:
The colonnade in front of the basilica

Boris Podrecca: view of the University Square in Salzburg

REVISITED SPACES

URBAN PROJECT IN CORDOBA (1979-1980)

Miguel Angel Roca's scheme for the urban fabric of Córdoba, Argentina's second city after Buenos Aires, lies outside the scale of a decorative operation, presenting itself as a general strategy for enhancing the value of the city's public space. The project's field of application has in fact not been restricted to the central area, though this has been generally redesigned, but has reached the areas at the margins of the city, working 'point by point', creating new squares and shaping modern cultural centres in old disused commercial structures. As regards the central area, the project's priority objective was to regain large pedestrian areas and to enhance the value of the open spaces; all this together with a strategy on a figurative level, to allow the inhabitants symbolically to reappropriate their own city.

The leitmotif of the paving organization, the uniform criterion of which includes the road network between the university and the new hospital, is to represent on the horizontal plane the sequence of buildings that form the compact body of the urban fabric - a representation which, depending on each specific case, may give preference to the street façade or offer a summarized image of the interior spatial layout. By the western end of the Alameda, the pedestrian walkway that runs through the city centre in an east-west direction, the university building is reflected in the street as though in a water course, outlining a 'carried-over shadow' that reproduces the two-storey frontage on the ground, inclined obliquely, with the large baroque portal standing out from the clock tower behind it. At the opposite end of the walkway, by the Chamber of Deputies, the visual representation of the buildings is in plan form. Here schematic lines enable the large hemicycle which provides the setting for the deliberations of the administrative apparatus to be perceived from the outside. Between the two buildings a close-knit grid of pedestrian spaces unravels, its quality enhanced by sequences of planted greenery and the widening of the street, to allow people to stop and rest, broken up by a small panoramic bridge positioned crosswise. A system of folding over similar to the one outside the university characterizes the solution adopted for the Plaza des Armas; this, due to the presence of the cathedral, is the city's most prestigious open space. Both the church and the adjoining porticoed building (the Cabildo) reflect the layouts of their façades on the ground, forming a filter zone between the pattern of buildings and the green space opposite.

The design proposal is different for the avenue perpendicular to the Alameda, which leads to the new hospital. Here the paving scheme has been abandoned in favour of an uninterrupted arcade, which acts as a kind of route, along which to travel to be allotted to the respective commercial activities. The theme of the urban project as the emblematic image of its own context is restated, albeit with variations to the motifs and dimensions, in the three newly designed squares encircling the city. The Plaza España, situated in a wealthy residential area at the western edge of the historic centre, has a geometrical design with differently inclined four-sided figures, depicting the double scheme which defines Córdoba's urban plan: the orthogonal grid dating back to when the city was founded, and the diagonals introduced in the nineteenth century.

The Plaza Italia, which occupies a triangular area in the northern suburban belt, proposes a representation of the province's orographic and hydrographic system, defining three hills furrowed by streams of water that flow into each other to form a central basin with an irregular perimeter. Finally, the Plazoleta Ambrosio Funes, located in a semicircular area to the west of the Plaza des Armas, has the appearance of a miniaturized image of the whole of Argentina: the outline of the South American country in fact emerges from the jagged-lined groove that breaks up the geometrical regularity of the blue and white stone radiocentric paving.

Image of the paving of the Plaza des Armas

Miguel Angel Roca was born in 1940 in Córdoba (Argentina). He studied architecture at the Universidad Nacional de Córdoba, where he graduated in 1965. In 1967 he gained a Master of Architecture degree at the University of Pennsylvania in Philadelphia, where he worked with Louis Kahn.

Since 1968 he has taught design at the University of Córdoba and from 1984 to 1989 he held a course at the University of Buenos Aires. He has participated in numerous architecture exhibitions, gaining international recognition. During his career he has won many prizes, including the Grand Prix at the International Biennial of Buenos Aires in 1991. His works are in Córdoba, in other Argentinian cities and in La Paz in Bolivia.

Previous page:
The western end of the pedestrian Alameda, alongside the old university

THREE URBAN PROJECTS

SALZBURG UNIVERSITY SQUARE (1986)

The University Square in Salzburg is in the city's historic centre, on the left bank of the Salzach river.

It is an elongated space, parallel to the course of the river, starting in the Sigmundplatz and terminating in a widened area. Typical Salzburg houses face onto it, including Mozart's birthplace; the broader area is dominated to the south by the university complex and by a church, built between 1696 and 1707 following a project by Fischer von Erlach, to the east by the Ritzer Arch, which communicates with the monumental complex of the cathedral.

The square is used daily as a venue for the herb market. The specific problem of the area was how to convert the space, while at the same time guaranteeing its traditional use and enhancing its architectural qualities.

Podrecca has been fortunate enough to be able to work in a space that is rich in qualities and history.

His scheme is 'soft': a paving of parallel strips, with a more close-knit design for the small central channel (a metaphor for the underground canal) and the parts adjacent to the houses. Here the details stand out, designed using a wealth of materials, freedom of forms and contained dimensions: with refinement and without a desire to be obtrusive. The historical components reemerge, and are taken as 'materials' for the project: the tradition of the ancient herb market, the corner well, the channel for the water, the stalls.

Boris Podrecca's intention was to revive the characteristics of the square by working mainly on the paving. The granite slabs are arranged transversally to the axis along which the square extends, and are broken up in the centre by a white marble drainage channel, which terminates in the middle of the Ritzer Arch. The design enhances the geometry of the space.

At the base of the façades of the buildings surrounding the square, the ground level is raised to form a pavement that serves as a connecting element between the different constructions.

The point where the University Square widens, by the church façade, is highlighted by a well over the waters of the Alm underground canal and by a sun-dial, the dial of which is designed on the stone steps surrounding the well.

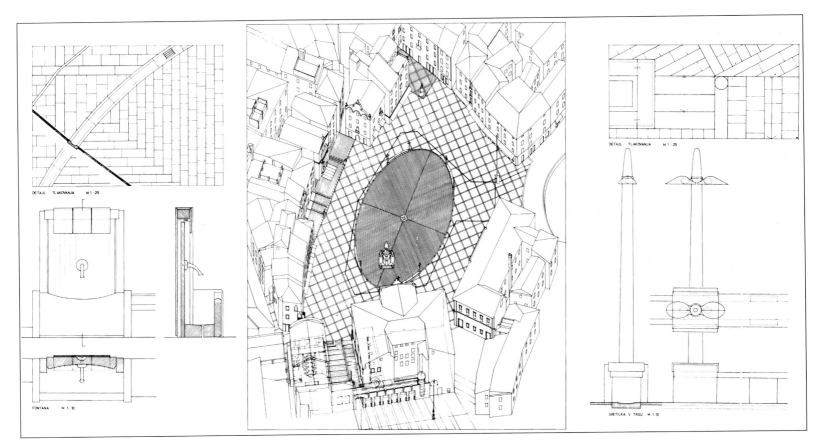

DETAJL TLAKOVANJA M 1:25

FONTANA M 1:10

DETAJL TLAKOVANJA M 1:25

SVETILKA V TRGU M 1:10

REVISITED SPACES

In front of the church by Fischer von Erlach there are two candelabrum street lamps with red marble bases. Podrecca intentionally avoided using spotlights, considering that this would have created a theatrical effect that was extraneous to the square's character.

G. Eibock and G. Luckner collaborated on the project.

THE PIAZZA GIUSEPPE TARTINI IN PIRANO (1986)

Pirano in Slovenia is a 'Venetian' historic centre a few kilometres from Trieste, on the coast of the Istrian peninsula. Representing the town centre is the Piazza Giuseppe Tartini, dedicated to the violinist and composer from Pirano who lived between the seventeenth and eighteenth centuries (1692-1770).

Until the nineteenth century, the vast irregularly trapezoidal surface was a port; it was later filled in by the Austrians, in order to obtain a square adjacent to the new port. For a long time it constituted a large void in the compact building fabric.

The so-called *mandracchio*, meaning 'the large mass of blocks', was in fact used as a car park before Boris Podrecca's venture.

The square is surrounded by important buildings, such as the Neo-classical church, the late-nineteenth-century Town Hall and Court buildings, and the Benecanka, a Venetian Gothic house from the fifteenth century: the project therefore concerns itself with a place that has an already consolidated surround.

The architect thought it necessary to give Pirano a public space to be used for cultural events, and also as a place for meeting, recreation and play for youngsters. The project is part of a series of proposals, involving the closure of the whole historic centre to traffic and intended to restore the original formation of the town. The middle of the square is highlighted by a large ellipse designed by the stone paving slabs.

This decision to use this system resulted from the analysis of the visual axes running through the square from the alleys of access, considering that the statue positioned on the Town Hall's axis of symmetry could not be moved.

The surface is slightly convex: at the centre is a typical sailors' compass design. At one of the focal points of the main axis is the monument by A. Dal Zotto, dedicated to Tartini and placed there in 1896. The perimeter of the ellipse is designed with a small channel to collect rainwater, and located around this are benches and street lamps to provide illumination.

As always, Podrecca's scheme works on two levels of scale. The general design is entrusted to the communicative strength of the white ellipse and Pirano's surrounding grey stone paving. The ellipse is the most unitary geometrical figure of those that can be inscribed within the irregular perimeter

Previous page:
Above:
Axonometry of the Piazza Giuseppe Tartini in Pirano, with construction details of the fountain and street lamps

Below:
The large, slightly convex ellipse that designs the new geometry of the space

View of the fountain and the spaces to sit in the square

of the square: a form that recalls the annular perimeter of the buried part. On the level of ornamental detail, Podrecca inserts a fountain composed of elementary volumes, sophisticated street lamps and a flight of steps; on the edge of this is a 'nautilus' made of red Verona marble, looking almost like a fossil recovered from the old port basin.

M. Vozlic and V. Vozlic collaborated on the project.

View of the Piazza XXIV Maggio in Cormons from the Parish church bell tower

REVISITED SPACES

THE PIAZZA XXIV MAGGIO IN CORMONS

Even a town like Cormons, small and far away from major inhabited centres, can have an important square: all that is needed is well-maintained buildings, a paving designed according to precise criteria and exclusively pedestrian use. Yet it is rare for a project such as the one for Cormons, simple as it is, to become exemplary.

The square is a simple elongated rectangular space that was already formed historically: the various urban quarters, with their different buildings, testify to this.

The west side comprises the Palazzo Locatelli and a wine retailer's. The front side is composed of small houses, traditional to Veneto culture, arranged along an undulating line, as though following the winding path of a stream. Similar houses compose the short sides; the north side is dominated by the tall bell tower, in a set-back position on the side of the parish church.

Podrecca's operation is simple: once the square is pedestrianized, he designs a paving system that repeats on the horizontal plane the design reinterpreted by the buildings facing onto it and chosen with a hierarchical criterion. He then matches together the different delineated areas with small ornamental interventions. Thus the north, south and east sides have simple paving, following the lie of the pre-existing streets, composed of parallel slabs arranged orthogonally with respect to the perimeter buildings. The paving outside the Palazzo Locatelli, on the other hand, extends for the whole length of the square with a fishbone pattern. The residual space in front of the wine retailer's is divided into delimited areas parallel to the building; there are five of these, the same number as the partitions of the façade, and the slabs are arranged orthogonally to the line of the latter. To the north the paving shows the bell tower projected down graphically, highlighted by a different arrangement of the stone slabs.

The boundary between the eastern end and the fishbone system is marked by a procession of street lamps, which are reminiscent of the columns that Venice placed in its state squares. The border between the fishbone and the area outside the wine retailer's is marked by a long white bench. Here a fountain, with a semi-spherical basin made of Verona marble and a bronze figure of a boy throwing stones, is aligned with the projection of the bell tower on the opposite side. The bronze figure is a work by Alfonso Canciani, a native of Cormons, who was trained at the Viennese school.

Remaining to be mentioned are some further details in the paving: one or two kerbstones and a broad door sill in front of the Palazzo Locatelli, a pavement along the outside of the wine retailer's, a winding route following the lie of the houses on the south side, a row of pilasters on the east side, a metaphor of the structure of a destroyed building.

Mirna Drabeni and Alexander Ostan collaborated on this project.

Boris Podrecca was born in Belgrade in 1940, and lived the years of his early youth in Trieste.

He studied at the Academy of Fine Arts in Vienna and frequented the university in the same city, graduating in architecture with Roland Rainer. After his degree he devoted himself simultaneously to professional and teaching activities. He currently has an architectural studio in Vienna, is full professor at the University of Stuttgart and director of the Planning Institute. He has been responsible for planning single-family housing in Munich and Vienna, reviving and restructuring historic buildings and fitting out exhibitions, and in recent years for the planning of public spaces.

Of his projects, particular mention must be made of the Institute of Neurophysics in the eighteenth-century Palais Starhemberg in Vienna (1979-82), the large Kika and Liener department stores in Wiener Neustadt, Linz, Salzburg and Klagenfurt (1984-89), the Kapellenwega residential complex in Vienna (1986-92), the projects for the Via dell'Indipendenza in Bologna and the Meidlinger Hauptstrasse in Vienna.

He has participated in numerous competitions, in some of which he has won prizes, such as for the 'Juzni Trg' square and hotel in Ljubljana (1989) and the Hauptverwaltung der Berliner Wasserbetriebe in Berlin (1993). His works have been displayed at various exhibitions in Europe and America.

Perspective drawing of the project

Above:
View of the plastic model of the project for the square

Opposite:
The semicircular amphitheatre in front of the medieval
tower of the Ledenhof

LEDENHOF SQUARE IN OSNABRÜCK (1976-1977)

The arrangement of the Ledenhof Square is one of the nodal schemes in the restructuring programme of the town centre undertaken by the municipality of Osnabrück in the mid-seventies. Located on the southern edge of the historic town, near the sports hall and the musical library, it acts as the head of the urban pedestrian walkway and presents itself as an element of interconnection between certain buildings of civic interest.

In the eastern zone stands the Ledenhof, a monumental complex consisting of a medieval tower and a Renaissance-style building, which is used today as a recreation centre. The northern and western limits of the space are occupied respectively by a home for the elderly and the Chamber of Commerce, located in a slightly set-back position beside the church and parish hall of St Catherine. Finally, to the south, behind the Neuer Graben, is an old late-baroque castle, housing an institute for higher education.

The object of Helge Bofinger's project, which satisfies the municipal requirement for an underground garage to hold six hundred cars, was to enhance the value of the pre-existing structures and to create a flexible space providing various possibilities for use, from walking to playing, from trading to the staging of entertainment. The result is a 'constructed square' generated by bringing together spaces which are functionally distinct, yet which all conform to a single design leitmotif: the representation of the different possible relations between architecture and nature.

The eastern zone, in front of the Ledenhof, is occupied by the forum, the space assigned for public events. A semicircular amphitheatre, partly with steps, partly housing a fountain, generates a triangular-plan space that converges towards the medieval tower of the Ledenhof.

Here there is an elongated pool, which has the appearance of the projection of the tower onto the ground. It is possible to ford this pool, as there are two circular 'floating islands'; concluding the pool is an artificial waterfall, a naturalistic insertion into the strictly architectonic context of the forum. Beside the pool, a flower bed, a pergola and a square-shaped 'Renaissance garden' (an example of nature adapted geometrically) present themselves as elements of transition towards the south-east wing, where the naturalistic aspect is accentuated.

At the southern end, opposite the late-baroque castle behind the Neuer Graben, is a row of trees arranged in a hemicycle, providing a backdrop for the pyramid-shaped fountain; this is situated in a slightly offset position in relation to the directrix of access to the forum.

Here is the start of a winding trail called the 'path of impressions', which connects a cylindrical brick kiosk with the rear entrance to the Ledenhof. The path crosses uneven lawns and paved knolls (an example of a natural form built artificially), finishing up at a turret overlooking the refreshment area to the north of the tower.

In the western zone of the square, beyond a play area protected by fan-shaped glass and iron gazebos, is the market area, consisting of low parallel pavilions immersed in greenery (an example of architecture penetrating within nature). Then, on the opposite side of a road allowing vehicle access to the market, the green of the square continues into the English-style garden (a representation of nature) connected to the parish hall of the church of St Catherine.

Figurative unity is obtained in this complex of differently structured spatial situations by using homogeneous materials to define the surfaces and the projecting volumes. The paved spaces have a brickwork fabric, broken up by sections of natural stone. The structures housing the facilities (the gazebos for playing, the marquee entrance to the market, the coverings of the vehicle entrances to the underground car park) are made of iron and glass and are reminiscent of the transparent glasshouses of nineteenth-century botanical gardens.

The design of the ornamental objects is also unitary (benches, transennae, lighting apparatus, etc.), while the alignments and angulations regulating the complex articulation of the space are determined by the basic geometries of the existing historic buildings. Thus the Ledenhof Square is not merely an element of urban connection and the covering for an underground garage, but becomes an instrument for interpreting the location and the architectures that are progressively stratified there.

Helge Bofinger was born in Szczcin (Poland) in 1940. She studied architecture at the Technical University of Braunschweig, where she graduated in 1968. With Margret Bofinger she launched a professional studio, first in Braunschweig (1969), then in Berlin (1974) and in Wiesbaden (1978).

She has taught in Dortmund, Venice, Amsterdam, Rotterdam, Buenos Aires and São Paolo, and has contributed to numerous architecture magazines, in Germany and abroad. She has co-written two publications: *Architecture in Germany* (1979) and *Young Architects in Europe* (1983).

Of her projects, we must mention in particular the 'Unité-habitation' in Göttingen (1972-74), the Museum of the Cinema in Frankfurt (1979-84), the Wilhelmstrasse residential complex in Berlin (1988-89) and the head office of the Commerzbank in Frankfurt (1991).

THE SQUARE IN ARTÉS (1982-1984)

The square in Artés, a small town in the Catalan hinterland, occupies a rectangular plateau (50 metres by 30) at the top of an upland plain, opening to reveal a panoramic view of the Pyrenees.

Along its longer sides, the square is bounded by two screens of stone and brick houses, by a castle (to the south), made unrecognizable by successive transformations, and by a ruined Romanic church (to the north), mined/undermined by the parish priest himself in 1914 to prevent his parishioners - who were fond of the church - from boycotting the new one. After losing its urban function, during the course of this century the old church square was occupied by two drinking-water storage tanks, which abruptly interrupted the visual continuity of the space, while the remains of the church escaped demolition only because they were the supporting structure for the sexton's house, leaning against the eastern apse.

In this context, the intention of Antonio Cortina's project is to allude to the different stratifications that have marked the history of the site, working principally at ground level; the floor of the square is understood as an interconnecting system representing all the fragments that have re-emerged onto the surface.

The area that was once occupied by the church has been transformed into a raised platform, a sort of open-air stage, with the chain of the Pyrenees as its backdrop.

The square grid paving in fact reproduces the series of bays into which the interior space was structured, while the basin traced on the eastern side corresponds to the encumbrance of the apse of an even older church, discovered during digging.

The square's broad esplanade, freed from the storage tanks, which have now been moved underground, has been treated like an 'interior', with paving consisting of parallel bands of concrete and stone fragments, with thin strips of Spanish travertine acting as spacers. On the base obtained thus, two different geometrical patterns extend like marble carpets: one is square, with a checked design achieved using parallel bands of travertine, the other circular, conceived as a graphic interpretation of the cycle of time and usable as a sun-dial. The geometrical dominant which the redesigned square summarizes is attenuated in the free space beyond the church; this provides an area of mediation, with the mountainous landscape opening out beyond the old walls. The memory of the old cemetery, once located on the terrace behind the religious building, is re-evoked by a grass enclosure with an undulating outline, and this connects up with the thick stone wall that forms the northern limit of the open space.

An old underground road, which was created as a secret escape route in the event that the fortified wall were besieged, has been reopened and restructured, and today forms a secondary entrance to the square.

The archaeological sensitivity that has characterized this project has also led to the creation of a museum of local history, located in the old sexton's house adjacent to the church.

Here in fact the pentagonal apse of the complex, dating back to the Romanic era, has been brought to light; the extrados of this apse, abounding in sculptural figurations, is the most important item in the collection. The adaptation into a museum has brought about a reorganization of the view downhill from the old residential building. This now has a broad glass surface, the proportions of which are marked rhythmically by a procession of columns with an S-shaped section.

Antonio Cortina was born in Manresa in 1950, and graduated in architecture at the ETSAB in Barcelona in 1973. During his stay at the university he spent long periods residing abroad to study (in Tel Aviv and Tübingen).

In 1974 he embarked upon professional activities; of his works, particular mention should be made of the enlargement of the Metallum factory (1978), the Pons House (1980), the project for Catalunya Square in Navas (1987) and the civic centre in Berga (1988).

In Artés, together with the square and museum described here, he also built the sports Pavilion (1981-84), the Town Hall (1986) and the Can Cruselles municipal park (1988).

He has taught at the ESTAB as professor responsible for Elements of Composition (1975) and Architectural Design (since 1980) and has been a member of the editorial team of the magazine *Annals*, intended to host the school's theoretical output.

Previous page:
General view of the square. In the background, by the bell tower, a raised platform reproduces the base of the old parish church.

THE COURTYARD OF STARS IN CEFALÙ (1984-1990)

'La Corte delle Stelle' (The Courtyard of Stars) is a court that has been revived as a square in the historic centre of Cefalù, inside what was once the Town Hall.

The town centre is characterized by a compact and uniform building fabric around a large road network of Greek origin. The only architectural projections, the Cathedral and the Fortress, lie outside the first core of construction.

The Comprehensive Planning Scheme for Samonà, approved in 1974, planned to increase the urban complexity of Cefalù. This intention is expressed, for example, in the proposal for the Piazza Duomo (Cathedral Square), where the aim is to create a system of squares isolated by a diaphragm of buildings, as the current organization is adjudged to be a residual area. In accordance with this philosophy, the Special Planning Scheme, drawn up by architects Culotta and Leone, envisaged the regeneration of the original Town Hall, formerly a hospital. The demolition of this building was begun in 1963, but was subsequently suspended.

Once the former Town Hall had been demolished, apart from the façade overlooking Corso Ruggero, it was planned for the area to be turned into an internal square on two levels, with an auditorium, obtained from the adjacent Church of Our Lady of the Annunciation, a multi-purpose hall and a bar/tea-room facing onto it.

As Panzanella wrote in his *Diario di Architettura*: 'To be a town, Cefalù needs what is commonly and synthetically defined as a "piazza" ... one or more squares, that is, a system of public places formed according to a complex scheme of relations, involving points of view of functions and facilities, along with formal, figurative and perspective points of view....' Thus Panzarella and Parlovecchio created a square on two levels, connecting on one side at the level of the Corso Ruggero and on the other at the level of the Via Costa. A kerb has been designed between the two levels to connect the two streets.

Access is gained to the lower level of the Corte delle Stelle through the fornices of the restored façade of the Town Hall. It is a small square, an interior courtyard the spatial matrix of which is a geometrical figure. The octagonal shape of the lower level of the Corte delle Stelle echoes the plan of the church of the monastery of St Catherine. The shingle and stone paving designs an eight-pointed star, oriented towards the cardinal points like a compass. This is one of the many representations with astronomical themes that characterize the repaving of squares. The kerb winds in a spiral around the star-shape, forming the perimeter of the octagonal space. Positioned symmetrically to the beginning of the flight of steps is a 'covered alleyway', similar to the many alleys of the historic fabric, going up from the Corso Ruggero to the Vicolo del Carmine and to the arcade of the multi-purpose hall.

The design is intended to unite the new with the existing, and this intention is also expressed through the repositioning and reinterpreting of forms and structures from the architecture of the location, giving to the town a new symbol in which to recognize itself. The site's structural unity is articulated in the functional differentiation of the spaces, obtained through the choice of various planimetric forms: an octagonal figure for the courtyard at the first level, an oval one for the multi-purpose hall, quadrangular for the second level of the square. The upper level is a silent, laconic rectangular space, delimited to the west by a wall perforated by six wide openings; these create a cut-out wing from which to observe the town. Ths space is surrounded with white plastered walls, reproducing a setting similar to a roofless room. The reading of the frontal views makes it possible to interpret the project as a 'box within a box'.

The windowed wings that delimit the upper level of the square move away from the perimeter wall (of the Corte delle Stelle) along the Vicolo Carmine Papa. Medlar and mandarin orange trees, typical essences of the region, have been planted in the cavity.

Previous page:
The distrinctive star motif of the Lower Courtyard

Below:
Ground plan of the square at the lower level

Marcello Panzarella was born in Cefalù in 1949. He graduated in architecture in 1973, and is a researcher at the Faculty of Architecture in Palermo.

He was deputy editor of the magazine *In Architettura*, founded in 1979 by Culotta with the aim of promoting a disciplinary debate on architectural projects in Sicily. In 1987 he participated in the XVII Triennale in Milan. He has published articles in *Casabella*, *Parametro* and *Progettare*. He is the author of *Diario di Architettura* (Cefalù, 1984), where he illustrates some of his projects for Cefalù.

In his professional activity he is responsible for planning on an urban scale and the design of public spaces. In 1990 he was invited to present his works as part of the initiative promoted by IN-ARCH 'Opera prima, generazioni a confronto' (First Work, Generations Compared).

ALEKSIN PIHA IN HELSINKI (1988)

In the centre of Helsinki, between Engel's monumental square and the Eliel Saarinen railway station, Juhani Pallasmaa has designed the transformation of a court inside a block into a square.

The 1988 study proposed the conversion of part of the area, between the Aleksanterinkatu and Mikonkatu streets, through restructuring the buildings of the block and modifying a service courtyard to make it into a covered public space for pedestrians.

Pallasmaa's solution echoes Aalto's theme of the covered courtyard of the Rautatalo (Steel House), this too built in the centre of Helsinki.

The buildings looking onto the square project long shadows, as some have eight storeys above ground, and this makes the place gloomy. This impression is accentuated by the predominance of the vertical development of the façades with respect to the reduced planimetric dimensions of the uncovered surface.

Pallasmaa's intention is to create a space renewed by light, with abundant optical and auditory sensations.

The square has an east-west axial development, and consists of two small quadrangular-shaped courtyards, each with 20-metre sides, connected by a rectilinear axis. Buildings for various uses close it off on each side; these differ according to their periods of construction and numbers of floors.

Two covered pedestrian walkways connect the court with Aleksanterinkatu Street and with the rest of the block respectively. A covered passage, for cars and pedestrians, leads from Mikonkatu Street to the east end of the public space, where the entrance to the underground car park is a 'colonnade', leading to the 'kingdom' of cars and to the 'kingdom' of pedestrians respectively.

The access ramp to the car park below the square is covered, to prevent the noise and car exhaust fumes from invading the public space. A teak cylinder, a triangular-based stainless steel prism and a square-based granite prism, about two metres tall and one metre apart, form the entrance to the square.

The choice of elementary forms and materials restates the concept of a monumental entrance in new terms. The 'colonnade' serves both as an element separating the common space from that reserved for pedestrians and as a sign of recognition of the pedestrian space.

The restructuring of the buildings looking onto the courtyard has meant that the ground floor has been allocated for public use, through the creation of a clothes shop, two restaurants, a café and a gymnasium. The entrance to the department stores is emphasized by a short stairway, with its curvilinear steps extending towards the centre of the courtyard. The areas for sitting are identified by tables in front of the café and the restaurants.

The façades bordering the small square are painted various colours: those to the south, generally in shade, are painted using warm colours, whereas those facing the north, generally well lit, have cold colours.

The careful chromatic study is linked ideally, as Pallasmaa has written in an essay, with the lively colours of the squares of the regions of the south, particularly in Mexican towns.

The façades of the buildings, treated in various ways, accentuate the scenographic effects of the small square.

A system of rainwater collection channels designs the frontages of the buildings. A circular white marble basin collects the water draining from the drips. The rhythmic tinkling of the water constantly invades the square even when it is not raining, through the gushing of a fountain in the marble basin.

Part of the square is covered with cantilever roofs. These are light, transparent structures, made of iron and glass, which create a new spatiality by establishing a new equilibrium for the relationship between the reduced base dimensions of the square and the vertical extent of the façades.

Concentric circles are designed in the porphyry block paving of the west court - the most tranquil part of the square - echoing the motif of the drops of water falling into the fountain basin. The porphyry blocks are arranged in parallel rows by the zones for vehicle traffic.

Two large circle arches designed on the ground ideally connect the pedestrian accesses.

Juhani Pallasmaa was born in 1936 in Hämeenlinna in Finland. He graduated at the Faculty of Architecture of the University of Helsinki, where he currently teaches.

Until 1963 he was involved with design and urban planning; now he runs an architecture studio in Helsinki, assisted by a large team of collaborators.

An art scholar and critic, he has written various articles and published numerous books, particularly on the relationship between philosophy, psychology and architecture.

He has been responsible for fitting out exhibitions - both in his own country and abroad - and for drawing up the catalogues for these, particularly in the years when he was Director of the Exhibitions Section of the Museum of Finnish Architecture - from 1968 to 1972 and from 1974 to 1978 - and Museum Director, from 1978 to 1983.

Of his numerous positions he has occupied within the university sphere in Finland and abroad, particular mention should be made of the two years - from 1972 to 1974 - when he was associate professor at the Haile Selassie I University in Addis Ababa.

Pallasmaa is an Honorary Member of the American Institute of Architecture, and also a Member of the International Committee of Architecture Critics and of the International Academy of Architecture.

Previous page:
General view of Aleksin Piha. In the foreground, to the left, the circular fountain which collects the water draining from the drips

THREE URBAN PROJECTS IN ATHENS

These projects concern the conversion of three squares within the urban fabric of the Greek capital, which time has consolidated. The studies, prepared both by freelance architects and by the Municipal Technical Office, all deal with the project theme in a similar way.

The natural element provided by the planting of trees is alternated with the 'constructed' element of the paving and the urban ornamentation, creating a multi-purpose space.

The simplicity of the schemes does not exclude in-depth investigation into ways of recreating areas for sitting and relaxing within the constructed fabric.

SEVASTI KARAKOSTA
THE PLATEIA KLAFTHMONOS (1980)

The Plateia Klafthmónos is near Stadiou Street, one of Athens' main axes, linking two of the city's most important squares, Omónia and Síntagma.

In 1973 a competition was announced for the organization of the square. It was won by the architect Sevasti Karakosta, who in 1980 was entrusted with the works management.

The project envisaged the construction of an underground car park and the arrangement of the square, with the creation of a lake and the planting of trees and plants typical of the area; there were to be paved passages where sculptures and marquees were to be placed, as specifically required by the competition announcement.

Requirements expressed by the municipality and economic problems brought about certain modifications to the initial project.

The architect Karakosta developed a further solution, which allowed the construction costs to

Previous page:
Aerial view of the Plateia Klafthmónos, conceived as a green lung in the heart of the city

Below:
The spaces with their facilities in the Plateia Metropoleos below the Great Metropolitan Church

be contained, while still conserving the fundamental characteristics of the initial project and those imposed by the competition.

The square occupies a quadrangular surface set on a slight slope. The paved pathways and stone terracing connect the level of the square with the level of the roads surrounding it. The footpaths design various geometrically shaped flower beds.

Marquees have been placed along the wider footpaths, to be used to display flowers and as places to sit down for the traditional coffee. A number of tall trees have been planted by the most sloping areas, while the flatter areas are covered with lawns and shrubs.

The small artificial lake which was also part of the second project has not been built, and a sculpture dedicated to 'National Reconciliation' has been placed in the area intended for this.

ALEXANDROS TOMBAZIS AND JOANNA PARASKEVOPOULOS
THE PLATEIA METROPOLEOS (1980)

The Plateia Metropoleos, to the north of the Plateia Síntagma, is dominated by the façade of the Great Metropolitan Church, a Neo-Byzantine religious building (1840-55), alongside which stands the Small Metropolitan, a church of smaller dimensions built in the eleventh century.

The square extends alongside Metropoleos Street; to the north, the south and the west it is surrounded by residential buildings. Before the scheme for restructuring it was used as a public car park.

Through the repaving and planting of trees in the area, the project proposes the revival of the characteristics of the municipal square.

In front of the façade of the Great Metropolitan, multi-colour paving has been created that seems to prolong the church square. A geometrical plot is designed by the porphyry and grey marble, within which there are alternating red and grey marble squares designed; these are inclined at 45 degrees with respect to the direction of the grid.

A number of trees have been planted at the ends of the paved area, creating 'wings' around the church, separating it from the residential buildings.

MUNICIPAL TECHNICAL OFFICE
THE PLATEIA SINTAGMA (1989-90)

The Plateia Síntagma, Constitution Square, is Athens' most important square. It occupies a quadrangular surface delimited by four important arteries, including Leoforos Amalias, which connects the square with the Acropolis. To the south, beyond the street, is the esplanade in front of the Royal Palace, erected in Neo-classical form by Gartner in the first half of the nineteenth

Plastic model of the Plateia Metropoleos

NEW FLOORS

century, as the residence of King Otto of Bavaria. Today it is the seat of Parliament.

The Municipal Technical Office was responsible for the project for restructuring the square in 1989-90, with the objective of converting the space while conserving the characteristics of the site. The area has been divided up into four sectors by two perpendicular pedestrian axes; these intersect in the centre of the square, where a fountain with a circular basin has been located.

The east-west axis, of larger dimensions, is aligned with the entrance to the Royal Palace, accentuating the monumentality of the façade. Tables have been placed along the north-south axis, partly covered by marquees and gazebos.

Different species of trees have been planted in the sectors bounded by the pedestrian axes. The paving is composed of grey marble slabs from Aliveri. Geometrical shapes are designed by the arrangement of alternating slabs, underlining the regularity of the space.

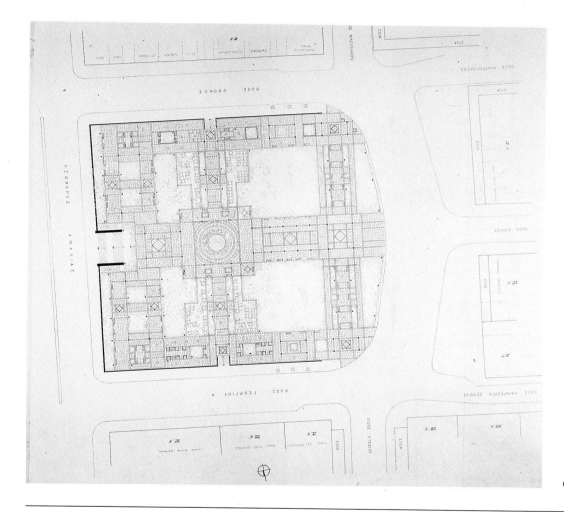

Ground plan of the Plateia Síntagma

Sevasti Karakosta was born in Athens in 1938. He graduated in architecture at the Athens Polytechnic in 1981. From 1968 to 1969 he was resident in Paris, where he worked with the architect George Kandylis on regional planning studies and urban design. For fifteen years, until 1986, he worked at the Ministry for Urban Regional Planning, where he was responsible for designing public spaces.

He has participated in numerous competitions, in the fields of both architectural design and urban planning. He has published his projects in architecture magazines, particularly those which have won competitions.

Alexandros Tombazis graduated in architecture at the Athens Polytechnic in 1962. After gaining his degree he formed a studio of associates. He has participated in numerous architecture competitions, both nationally and internationally. Since 1975 he has been involved in bioclimatic architecture. In 1991 he represented Greece at the Venice Biennale.

After her degree, gained at the Athens Polytechnic in 1969, **Joanna Paraskevopoulos** collaborated for seven years at the studio of the architect A. Tombazis. Since 1989 she has worked independently.

Antonia Markopoulou graduated in architecture at the Athens Polytechnic in 1970. From 1970 to 1988 she worked freelance, collaborating with various architecture studios and dealing with urban planning, architectural design and the planning of public spaces. She is currently working at the Building Constructions Office of the Athens Municipality.

After her degree in architecture gained at the Athens Polytechnic in 1979, **Eugenia Melambianaki** has been involved with architectural planning. Since 1985 she has worked at the Planning Office of Public Spaces of the Athens Municipality.

Nicola Peppas graduated in architecture at the Athens Polytechnic

in 1975. He worked freelance until 1987, dealing with the planning of residential housing. Since 1987 he has worked for the Athens Municipality in the Building Constructions Office.

After her degree, gained at the Athens Polytechnic in 1975, **Sofia Skanavis** worked freelance, dealing with architectural design, until 1984. From 1984 to 1989 she worked at the Athens Municipality in the Public Spaces Planning Office. She is currently the owner of an architecture studio operating both in Greece and abroad.

Elena Hatzigheorghiu graduated at the Ecole Spéciale d'Architecture in Paris in 1963. She has taught interior decoration at the ATO School in Athens. From 1985 to 1991 she worked at the Planning Office of Public Spaces of the Athens Municipality. Currently she collaborates with the ETO (Greek Tourist Centre) in the Marine Planning and Hotel Restoration Office.

UNIVERSITY ENTRANCE SQUARE IN TEL AVIV (1992)

University Entrance Square is an urban space mediating between the private zone of the university pole and the city. It terminates one of the widest road axes in Tel Aviv, at the point where this intersects University Street. These two broad avenues connect the zone with the sea and the city centre. The university campus has developed over an area of 600,000 square metres to the north of the city. The square, inaugurated in May 1992, is an addition to the already existing university structures to embellish the entrance. It was designed as a meeting place for students, as a multi-purpose space for the sale and exchange of books, as well as for theatrical performances and concerts. Atzmon himself wrote that he wished to reproduce the functions of Hyde Park in his design for an urban public space in Tel Aviv. For this square, the designer has chosen a square shape within a pre-existing polygonal space. The west side of the square is linked to University Street by a 'kerb' with a concave outline; this is a citation of the exedrae used to terminate perspectives, but without their spatial functions. A pedestrian walkway connects the north-west corner of the square with the 'Eric Mitchell' Students' Centre. The building, which is set back with respect to the edge of the square, consists of three blocks of different heights. The square is connected to the trapezoidal space delimited by the Centre by means of terracing, the profile of which reproduces the winding course of the ground's contours.

The 'Genia Schreiber' Art Gallery and the university entrance face onto the north-east side; the latter's position is emphasized by a marquee identical to the open portico on the south-east side. This structure separates the square from the gardens of the Athenaeum: the architect has thereby created the missing side of the square. The portico is conceived as a permanent structure for students to sell and exchange books.

The paving consists of concrete slabs of two colours; these design large squares arranged in orthogonal rows, bordering nine areas serving as lawns. Some of these stone slabs inserted into the paving system recall great scientific discoveries, including the formula for relativity.

Y. Moria and D. Sekely collaborated on the project.

Moshe Atzmon was born in June 1939 in what is today the state of Israel, where he currently lives and works.

He graduated in architecture in 1966, and for ten years collaborated with private studios.

In 1979 he began working with the Technical Department of the University of Tel Aviv, designing and building colleges, campuses, offices and structures for scientific faculties.

He has been responsible for designing urban landscapes and the layouts of public spaces.

Previous page:
View of the square within the urban context

Opposite:
The portico to the southeast

Above:
View of the northern side of Neve Zedek Plaza in Tel Aviv by night, bounded by the façade of the theatre. In the foreground, the partially concave flight of steps connecting the Suzanne Delal Dance Centre to the slightly raised level of the square

Opposite:
Aerial view of the project (bottom right) within the urban context. The sequence of constructed and open spaces comprises firstly a rectangular square, then the Neve Zedek Theatre (with its inverted U-shaped plan), the Neve Zedek Plaza and the Suzanne Delal Dance Centre.

THE NEVE ZEDEK PLAZA IN TEL AVIV (1989)

In 1883 a Jewish settlement named Neve Zedek was founded on the Jaffa sand dunes. The old urban core is now a district in the southern suburbs of Tel Aviv.

In the eighties the municipal authorities decided to regulate building projects in an attempt to conserve the settlement's historical characteristics. Subsequently an urban conversion plan was devised for the creation of a dance and theatre centre, to be located in two old buildings due to be restructured, with two squares between them. Elisha Rubin was responsible for the restructuring work, Shlomo Aronson for designing the public spaces.

The basic choice made was to close off the road between the two constructions to vehicle traffic and to make the garden belonging to one of the two buildings public. Thus alternate constructed surfaces and free spaces were generated, following the sequence, from north to south, of: square, the Neve Zedek Theatre, square, the Suzanna Delal Dance centre. The public spaces are therefore strictly dependent on the two buildings, which determine the former's uses and functions.

The project involved the reorganization of a peripheral area connecting the two buildings; the architectonic quality of this area is limited, the scheme culturally motivated.

The geometry of the paving grid and the order and dimensions of the public space, embellished by the arrangement of trees and small irrigation channels, make up a surface charged with image, where the modularity of the design contrasts with the formless fabric surrounding the project.

The Neve Zedek Plaza has a regular plan; it is bordered to the north by the façade of the theatre and to the south by the front of the dance centre. The lesser sides - to the east and west - join the pedestrian walkways that link the area with the road axes.

The entrances to the Neve Zedek Plaza, aligned along the longitudinal axis, are highlighted by a group of four date palms; these form the vertices of a square designed on the ground by the arrangement of marble slabs. The accesses to the two restructured buildings, again marked by pairs of palm trees, are at different heights. Indeed, a few semicircular steps connect the area outside the dance centre, standing at a lower level, with the square, while another flight of steps, this time rectilinear, ascend from the square to the theatre.

The space is organized by the symmetry with respect to the axis connecting the entrances to the entertainment centres. The rhythm of the central section is marked by the checked framework of the paving slabs; on both sides of this section are areas of citrus plants in a geometrical grid arrangement.

In his choice of paving materials and tree varieties, Shlomo Aronson has intentionally reproduced the characteristics of the Mediterranean landscape; the trees are used to emphasize the distinct purposes for which the space has been designed. Palms are positioned by the axes of access to the two buildings and the two squares, while citrus trees follow the geometrical grid of the paving. Each tree base has a white marble seam around it, and this in turn is surrounded by a blue ceramic tiled sunken gutter. The lattice of small geometrical channels that is thus constructed is used to irrigate the plants, but is also reminiscent of the water channel patterns typical of Islamic cultures. The use of simple streetlamps for illumination highlights the geometrical character of the square.

The second square behind the theatre is also rectangular in shape. A paved footpath cuts across the square diagonally: citrus trees are planted on each side of this path in a lattice formation on a grass surface. The path finishes between the two wings of the building with the C-shaped plan. A well-like fountain has been kept at the centre of the paved axis, recalling the wells formerly used for collecting water.

The complex is separated from the surrounding building fabric by a plastered wall decorated with mural paintings.

Detail of the paving of the square

Shlomo Aronson was born in Haifa in Israel. He studied at the Universities of Berkeley and Cambridge.

From 1963 to 1966 he lived in the U.S.A., where he collaborated with various architecture studios, including Lawrence Halprin's. In 1967 he worked in London. In 1968 he returned to Jerusalem, where he opened an architecture studio, also dealing with urban planning and landscaping. He has taught at various academies and has held seminars at a number of architecture faculties in the U.S.A. and in Germany, as well as in Israel.

THE PIAZZA GIACOMO MATTEOTTI IN CATANZARO (1989-1991)

The Piazza Giacomo Matteotti is the first public space to be encountered by those entering Catanzaro from the north. Historically, it was the access gate to the city; over the years it has been used for different purposes, which have overlapped, to a degree rendering the site's specific character unrecognizable. The square is currently a crossroads where the main road arteries converge, and is surrounded by some of the city's most important buildings: the Court, the High School, the Banca Nazionale del Lavoro and a hotel. The new layout is intended to create a setting abounding in evocative elements. The project is structured around three systems: the promenade, the garden and the square; the latter is characterized by a sundial and the monument to Giacomo Matteotti. The three systems form a sequence designed to establish a relationship with the building fabric, which opens onto the existing road system. The promenade - so typical of southern Italy - runs parallel to the Via Indipendenza; it is bounded on the side of the urban axis by a hedge, a row of Phoenix Dactylifera and a sinusoid-shaped bench, for sitting and resting. The axis faces onto the square across variously-shaped widened areas - which the author calls 'microcosms' - each characterized by a theme: the butterfly, the moon, the fossil, and so on. The ends of the promenade are indicated by two kiosks, where flowers and newspapers are sold. The roofs of these two newsstands take up the paving motif. This motif is an Op-Art design by Vasarely, using travertine and African black granite in alternate polished and flashed stripes. The garden outside the Courthouse, which was created in the thirties, has been revived. Date palms have been planted in the garden, and also in the square and along the promenade, thus becoming a repetitive and unifying element.

The square's position enables it to serve as a 'link' between the promenade and the garden. In the square is a sun clock; this comprises a large sundial with a gnomon that throws its shadow onto the hour lines, which are brass plates on the ground. These lines are intersected by the arcs of the days, which are made of travertine. Stone spheres and shields have been placed at the ends of the arcs of the hour lines. It is always possible to obtain a reading, as there is a digital clock at the base of the gnomon. The square is dedicated to Giacomo Matteotti, and this identity is expressed in the form of a cement, marble and steel sculpture. The monument is shaped like a broad triangular stairway rising from the ground, creating a panoramic viewpoint.

Antonio Uccello, Enzo Amantea and Ferdinando Gabellini collaborated on the project.

Franco Zagari was born in 1945 in Rome, where he lives and works. He is a professor of the Art of Gardens at the Faculty of Architecture at the Università la Sapienza in Rome.

He has taken part in numerous national and international competitions. His works worthy of special mention are: the restructuring and restoration of sections of the Guasco S. Pietro quarter in the historic centre of Ancona (1973-83); the Comprehensive Plan and the Coordinated Plan for the Area for Regeneration in the city of Catanzaro; the restoration and reconstruction of the San Giovanni monumental complex in Catanzaro (from 1989); the 'Italian Garden' at the Garden Festival '88 in Glasgow; the 'Italian Garden' for the Universal EXPO in 1990 in Osaka, now a permanent public garden in the city; the 'DNA '92 Garden' for the Festival des Jardins in Chamont-sur-Loire; 'Le jardin de M. Hulot', an experimental work exhibited at the Niort trade fair in 1993.

He is the author of numerous essays, including 'L'architettura del giardino contemporaneo' (The Architecture of the Contemporary Garden) (1988).

He was responsible for organizing the exhibition 'Beyond the Garden. The Architecture of the Contemporary Garden', which has appeared in many cities both within and outside Europe.

Previous page:
The pedestrian 'promenade' running along the edge of the Via Indipendenza

Opposite:
View of the square, with the sun clock marked on the paving

THREE SQUARES IN THE UNITED STATES OF AMERICA

FRANKLIN COURT IN PHILADELPHIA (1976)

The revering of the past that characterizes American society, which is so youthful where its historical memory is concerned, can create treasures from the most nonmaterial relics. When called upon to design a memorial in honour of Benjamin Franklin as part of the American Bicentennial celebrations of 1976, the Venturi, Scott Brown and Associates studio created a clear demarcation between the seat of study, the museum, which is almost entirely underground, and the space outside, to be used for commemoration; the latter takes the form of an urban public square, in the area where the famous American statesman's house once stood.

The design attitude here is extremely flexible, with the same setting catering for different functional needs and situations. To re-evoke the urban qualities of a small central square from eighteenth-century Philadelphia, five residential units overlooking Market Street have been reconstructed using similar criteria; these are used to house temporary exhibitions and the museum's administrative offices. Respecting its original typological properties, the interior courtyard into which the covered gallery forming the main entrance to the museum complex leads has been preserved as a garden.

A different sort of methodological sensitivity has been shown in the approach to Franklin's house itself; as a mimetic reconstruction of this inside the courtyard would have been a philologically questionable operation, its presence is merely suggested by a metal skeleton discreetly reproducing the lost outline.

Complementary to this, the remaining traces of the original foundations, which were brought to light during the excavation work on the square, are conserved with archaeological care inside display cases. These display cases are located randomly on the paving system, which is a representation of the ground plan of the residential building, a jigsaw puzzle of marble and slate.

Roughly midway along the longitudinal axis connecting the house with the entrance gallery is another 'ghost' structure, this time on a smaller scale; it is a reproduction of the small printing house that in the mid-eighteenth century bordered the courtyard on the northern side.

Concluding the wholly domestic and family-oriented portrait that is offered of Franklin here, mention must be made of the quotations engraved on the ground; these are taken from letters Franklin wrote to his wife during the period the house was built.

WESTERN PLAZA IN WASHINGTON (1980-1984)

Western Plaza is strategically located at the western end of Pennsylvania Avenue, the rectilinear artery that connects the Capitol with the White House, and which forms the main axis of the Federal Triangle where the city's most important government buildings are located.

Although a succession of layout proposals have been made since the plan for the foundation of Washington was drawn up by L'Enfant in 1792, the square has never managed to live up to its responsibilities as a ceremonial location (among others, the triumphal parade when the President takes office takes place here). It arrived at the threshold of the seventies without a recognizable urban identity: a generic, rectangular void, its edges ill-defined and split diagonally by the almost 50-metre-wide Avenue.

Only recently, with the decision by the Federal Government to convert the centre for the city's bicentennial celebrations, were the foundations laid for a definitive transformation, placing the scheme among the priority objectives of the Pennsylvania Avenue Development Corporation (PADC) and fitting it within the more general organization of the surrounding area.

Though it has been impossible to transform the unhomogeneous building curtains forming the backdrop to the square, the project by Venturi, Scott Brown and Associates gives cohesion to the space by affirming unequivocally the priority of the central public and pedestrian zone.

A wide terrace, which is raised with respect to the road level, breaks up the interminable expanse of Pennsylvania Avenue with a carpet of marble, diverting the vehicle traffic along its perimeters.

The terrace is bordered by low walls for use as benches and shaped hedges. At its centre is a parterre which reproduces, on a reduced scale, the road network of the centre of Washington according to

Above:
Detail of the square-based flower-boxes placed at regular intervals in the open layout of Franklin Court in Philadelphia, which once overlooked Benjamin Franklin's house

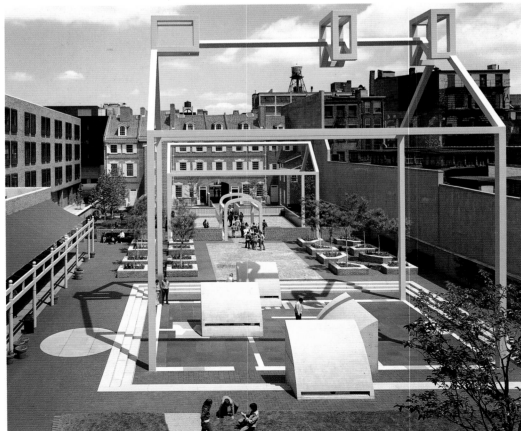

Opposite:
The inner square of Franklin Court with the two 'ghost' structures that allusively reproduce Franklin's house (in the foreground) and the old printing house that in the mid-eighteenth century bounded the courtyard on the northern side

NEW FLOORS

Above:
Detail of the granite paving of the parterre in Western Plaza in Washington. Due to the effect of the perspective distancing, the Capitol and its scale model appear to be the same height.

Opposite:
The scale model of the Capitol is a prelude to the government building located along the focal perspective of Pennsylvania Avenue.

VENTURI, SCOTT BROWN AND ASSOCIATES

L'Enfant's plan. In this planimetric scheme the checked network that is typical of American cities coexists with a system of diagonal axes derived from the tradition of 'French-style' gardens, a very widespread model in newly founded capital cities.

Thus the diagonal lie of Pennsylvania Avenue, denied and interrupted by the creation of the terrace, is represented on the ground as an icon, while the whole square takes on the meaning of a symbolic representation of the city.

Two scale models have been devised to amplify this allusive effect; they portray the Capitol and the White House, but only the former was actually built. The original project also envisaged two panoramic towers, freely inspired by the columns of San Marco in Venice. These were to be faced with white marble and oriented along the directrix of Pennsylvania Avenue; they would have made it possible to frame the White House perspective when viewing long-distance, partially counterbalancing the current predominance of the Capitol in the visual axis of the Avenue.

As the towers were to have been built in real dimensions, and would therefore have been 'out of scale' with the city model in the paving, they would have even suggested more of a sense of disorientation, a subtle conjuring trick where Venturi's hand can be recognized. Ever since his 'Complexity and Contradiction', Venturi has made ambiguity one of the preferential categories of his architectonic poetics.

WELCOME PARK IN PHILADELPHIA (1982)

The evocation of the original planimetric scheme as a metaphorical image of the city is again proposed in the circumscribed space of Welcome Park, a small open-air museum devoted to William Penn in the third centenary of the founding of the city. It was in 1682, in fact, that the English politician disembarked

General view of Welcome Park in Philadelphia, characterized by a graphic pattern reproducing the plan of the city at the time of its foundation. Projecting from the road scheme, which is rigorously orthogonal, are the monument to William Penn (in the square central plaza) and the model of the house where he lived.

from the boat *The Welcome* and founded Philadelphia, using the checked layout suggested to him by the topographer Thomas Holme. The planimetric model - complete with cartouche decoration accentuating the attributes of an old map - lies at the centre of the square, highlighted by the contrast between the white marble road network and the grey brick scheme denoting the blocks. At the barycentre of the system, the meeting point between the main orthogonal axes (High Street and Broad Street), is the monument to Penn, set on a cylindrical plinth, while four saplings represent symbolically the four symmetrical squares positioned at different points in the urban fabric. Isolated on a peripheral lot towards the western edge stands the commemorative cippus of Slate Roof House; this was the residence of Penn and briefly (1700-1701) the city's seat of government. The inscription 'The Slate Roof House was here' - where 'here' precisely identifies the area of Welcome Park - is the magic word allowing a shift in scale and suggesting the ideal comparison between the poetic microscale of the square and the actual macroscale of the city.

Outside a frame which re-evokes in ideal terms the presence of the rivers bounding the city (the River Delaware to the east and the River Schuylkill to the west) and the old route of the railway (the granite and blue stone alley beyond the series of benches to the south), the education programme reaches its peak in the perimeter enclosure wall. Here an illustrated decoration depicts the mythical voyage of foundation, borrowing the impact of its message from the language of commercial strips, and looks back over the key stages in the life of Penn the gentleman and statesman.

G.E. Patton, Inc. Landscape Architect collaborated on the projects.

Detail of the marble and clay brick paving near the cippus commemorating the Slate Roof House where Penn lived. On the perimeter wall behind is a coloured ceramic mural re-evoking the mythical voyage on the boat The Welcome.

Robert Venturi, born in 1925, studied architecture at Princeton University, winning a scholarship for a two-year study period at the American Academy in Rome.

On returning to California, he collaborated with the architect Louis Kahn, and then opened his own professional studio, combining architectonic investigation with energetic theorizing and the dissemination of same that made him one of the major protagonists in contemporary debate.

His writings particular worthy of mention, on account of the interest they aroused, not without polemic, are: *Complexity and Contradiction in Architecture* (1966) and *Learning from Las Vegas* (with Denise Scott Brown and Steven Izenour, 1971). The former constitutes a lively manifesto against the orthodoxy of the International Style movement, in favour of an architecture capable of representing and including different and contradictory stimuli; the latter, which takes its cue from the visual advertising hypercommunication of the contemporary American metropolis, is an invitation to restore a symbolic dimension in architecture, re-evaluating ornamentation as an expressive component that is autonomous and independent of the structural surround.

Denise Scott Brown graduated in 1955 in London, then followed specialization courses in various American universities.
At the Venturi studio she is responsible for urban planning projects and urban design.

THE SQUARE IN SANTA SEVERINA (1980)

Santa Severina, built on a hill, dominates the territory of the Marchesato from the Sila mountain range to the valley of the Neto river as far as the Ionian Sea.

The main square, opening onto the ridge of high ground, is called the 'Campo' by the people of Santa Severina; this, according to Giuseppe Patanè, is in memory of the site's former military use as a parade-ground, as was often the case with outside spaces in historic centres.

The surround consists of long, homogeneous frontages of two-storey houses, arranged very irregularly along the longer sides, with the Norman castle to the south and the cathedral to the north.

Commissioned to design the paving for the square, Anselmi and Patanè have created an arrangement that enhances the character of the location while maintaining the existing form. The result is a square with a renewed external appearance, where the inhabitants can recognize themselves and 'recollect the history of the site'.

At sunset the celestial vault almost becomes the roof of the town, and it is perhaps prompted by this mood, so delicate and penetrating, that the two architects had '... the idea of dropping a piece of that sky onto the ground ...' (V.Barresi, *Il villaggio dimenticato*, 1989).

The square has an irregular, extremely elongated plan, terminating to the south in two widened sections, to the east and to the west.

Taking the surround as it was, the designers concentrated on the paving for the square, choosing a garden as the solution for the glacis to the west. The design is organized with reference to the two main axes: the north-south axis and the one between the castle and the cathedral. Their point of intersection is the centre of a large ellipse, with the larger axis, in a north-south direction, becoming the ordering device of the square. The rest of the paving consists of equidistant concentric circles that are interrupted by the façades of the houses or the garden perimeter. All the connecting points and intersections of the design are indicated by images chosen from a vast symbolic repertoire.

The elliptic area is divided up into twelve sectors, with two main axes and four radials converging in the centre of the figure, highlighted by a compass rose, inside which the 'eye of awareness' is drawn. The directions of the winds are indicated by eight 'triangular needles', at the tips of which are small ellipses, where the winds are shown, and these in turn design a circle.

The intersections of the main axis with the arcs of the circles are indicated by square elements (with 40-centimetre sides) made of travertine; engraved on these are the astrological symbols of the sun and the planets. Circular slabs of travertine (40 centimetres in diameter) are positioned along the north-south axis, at the points of intersection with the arcs of the circles, and engraved on these are the alchemical symbols of the elements of matter.

There are circular slabs at the ends of the two axes; represented on these are the four seasons at the north end and the symbols of the weather at the south end, while the cycle of gold and the 'spirit of metals' are positioned one at each end of the church-castle axis. The lesser axis of the large ellipse is concluded to the east and west by two circles, depicting the sun and moon.

The two belvederes in front of the Norman castle moat, on each side of the square's axial development, form two areas in their own right, and are resolved differently from the square.

The eastern side, paved with bands of porphyry blocks spaced by travertine, is surrounded by a wall built using local stone, shaped to provide seating.

The larger west side is designed as a stone Italian-style garden. The irregularly shaped central area consists of a circular core, emanating from which are eight 'appendices', four pairs, shaped like sinusoidal waves, to be used as seats. Though the overall effect does contain a hint of a 'labyrinth', the shape is actually like a large image of the sun.

Located at the centre of the design is a cube-shaped travertine fountain, with an eye sculpted on its east and west faces; this echoes the central motif inside the compass rose of the large ellipse. Above the fountain is an eighteen-pointed iron star.

Two pairs of parallel axes cross, creating nine delimited areas. The parapet-seating around the outside of the belvedere ends at the points of contact with the sinusoid-shaped seating; spherical iron forms with astronomical images are placed at these points. Orange trees have been planted in the four corner areas, as a reminder of the economic importance of this fruit among the crops grown in the area.

P.Petrucci, E.Rizzuti, M.P.Rizzuti and A.Stefani collaborated on the project.

Alessandro Anselmi was born in 1934 in Rome, where he graduated at the Faculty of Architecture in 1963.

He was among the founder members of the GRAU (Roman Group of Architects and Urban Planners), which was formed in 1964. He has contributed to a number of magazines, including *Itaca* and *Controspazio*, and is currently among the contributors to *Lotus International*.

He has been visiting professor at the ESA (École Spéciale d'Architecture) in Paris and at the ENSP (École Nationale Supérieure de Paysage) in Versailles. He is a lecturer in Architectural Composition at the Faculty of Architecture of the University of Reggio Calabria.

He was a jury member for the Cité de la Musique competition in Paris, and on the organizational committee of the Biennial in Paris.

He works freelance in Rome, where he has an architecture studio. He has participated in various competitions, including the one for the State Archive in Florence (1972) and for the theatre of La Maison de la Culture in Chambéry, Haute Savoie (1982). His projects particularly worthy of mention are the new cemetery in Parabita (1967), the town hall in Rezé-Nantes (1986) and the University of Jurisprudence in Reggio Calabria, which is currently under construction.

Giuseppe Patanè was born in Santa Severina in 1942. He graduated at the Faculty of Architecture of the University of Rome in 1974.

Until 1985 he worked professionally in Rome, gaining his initial experience at Alessandro Anselmi's studio; he has also worked with the architects Alessandro Mariani and Paola Rossetti.

Since 1986 he has lived and worked in Santa Severina.

Besides the projects developed with Anselmi, he has designed the cemetery in Rocca de Neto and the layout of the Municipal Villa in Crotone. He has been responsible for the designing and conversion of public spaces in the Crotone district, the project for the Central Square and La Chiusa del Pozzo, the War Memorial and Peace Monument in Santa Severina, the arrangement of the Piazza della Resistenza in Crotone.

Previous page:
Aerial view of the scheme. The project has concentrated on the paving, retaining the existing surround, which consists of the homogeneous frontage of the two-storey houses, the cathedral and the castle.

ARTISTS' SQUARES

KIKAR LEVANA IN TEL AVIV (1977-1978)

Kikar Levana, which in Hebrew means 'white square', is an 'environmental sculpture' located at the top of the natural mound known as the Edith Wolfson Park, in the south-eastern suburbs of Tel Aviv.

Insulated from any relation with the city's road network, and separated from the continuum of buildings of the urban fabric, Dani Karavan's 'square' is in some ways a paradox.

Can a square stand in the green expanse of a meadow, indifferent to the urban context that generates it and shapes it? For Karavan, the answer is of course yes. He views the square as a place of convergence and meeting, a place for arranging appointments, strolling, relaxing.

And to corroborate this he cites the Campo dei Miracoli in Pisa; this grassy expanse, while apparently anything but urban, attracts social rituals and defines an identity. Kikar Levana's relationship with its own city is nevertheless profound. With its clearly defined geometrical layout and its rigid volumes, Karavan's square presents itself knowingly as the antithesis of the disorder and absence of rationality that characterizes the urbanization of Tel Aviv.

The ideal prototype for an urban civilization that is also idealized, it cannot find space in the real city, chaotic and congested as it is; it can only be achieved in the neutral and experimental space of a garden.

Connected by a slightly sloping flight of steps to the footpath that winds its way up and down across the Edith Wolfson Park, Kikar Levana is a rectangular platform with its sides 30 and 50 metres respectively. Built completely using white cement, it looks like an open-air stage, where a representation of elementary geometrical volumes is being enacted.

The median axis is emphasized by a cut in the paving, running through which is a rivulet of water (symbolizing life). This axis connects the access stairway with a high terraced podium which invites you to walk up and gradually discover the landscape. In actual fact, Dani Karavan's sculptures are not objects to contemplate, but plastic forms to walk over, go round or tread on. The public and their active participation in the experience of the space provide an essential contribution to the unravelling of the profound meaning of the work. For this reason there is no preferential observation point, just as there is no obligatory route to be followed.

The two-part wall septum located in the geometrical centre of the platform interrupts the rectilinear trajectory between the flight of steps and the terraced podium, and invites you to circulate freely between the other elements of the system.

The north-west corner of the square is occupied by a pyramid with a huge section cut out of its eastern face.

Almost a symbol of passing time, the sun's rays reach the ground at exactly midday, illuminating a line engraved in the paving. Near the pyramid, in the north-east corner, there stands a square-shaped sunken court, the stepped sides of which bring to mind the image of a truncated, upside-down pyramid. A similar dialectic between concave and convex space governs the relationship between the hemisphere and the semicircular amphitheatre located in the southern area of the square.

Broken in two by a rectilinear axis that allows the strip of grass under the paving to emerge, the hemisphere is the connecting element with the surrounding natural environment.

In the circular cavity at the centre there is an olive tree (calling to mind the Bible), which is reflected specularly in a second olive tree planted in the park, at the continuation of the bisectrix. On the same axis, in a symmetrical position with respect to the hemisphere, is a tall square tower; this structure actually covers a pre-existing watchtower.

The multiplicity of levels on which Kikar Levana is articulated offers various possibilities for relations with the city and the surrounding landscape. The sea, for example, which is practically invisible at the height of the dais, looks like a thin strip cut up by the skyscrapers if you go up the terraced podium, and becomes the dominant element in the panorama if you look at it from the top of the tower. On the other hand, if you go down to the level of the sunken court, the paving of the square disappears and its huge geometrical volumes seem to hover in a void.

Previous page:
Aerial view of the square in the middle of the Edith Wolfson Park, located in the south-east suburbs of Tel Aviv. The precise geometry that pervades the composition is a polemical response to the disorder of the city's building development.

MA'ALOT IN COLOGNE (1979-1986)

Ma'alot, an ancient Hebrew term from the Book of Psalms, which literally means 'footsteps', is the name Dani Karavan has given to the square outside the Ludwig and Wallraf-Richartz Museums in Köln.

The modern museum complex - created by the architects Peter Busmann and Godfried Haberer, the competition winner in 1975 - is fitted into the densely stratified area between the bank of the Rhine (to the east), the Cathedral (to the west) and the lie of the railways converging on the Hohenzollern Bridge (to the north). The two buildings - the Ludwig Museum for Contemporary Art and the Wallraf-Richartz Museum for historical collections - stand parallel to each other, occupying the western area facing the river and the narrow strip of land adjacent to the railway.

The architectural language used here is strictly functional and is articulated in a series of parallel structures; each of these has zinc roofing with a rounded outline. As part of the organization of the

View of the project in the urban context

NEW FLOORS

exterior space the architects had initially envisaged a sculpture by Barnett Newman (firstly a split obelisk, then a steel screen), but in 1979 the future director of the Ludwig Museum, Karl Ruhrberg, suggested a more ambitious project, and invited Dani Karavan to become involved in designing it.

Ma'alot is structured around two episodes, which are formally distinct yet dialectically related.

The first is a pathway, located in the narrow corridor separating the two buildings. The second is a slightly concave elliptical space that occupies the vast area between the south wing of the museum complex and the river embankments. The unifying element here is the clay brick paving that forms the neutral background on which the Israeli artist's geometrical plots take shape. According to an often tested artistic code, Karavan's compositions are based on the use of pure forms and volumes linked by a system of numerical relationships.

The path between the two museum buildings is approximately 100 metres long and begins at the foot of the Cathedral, heading with a rectilinear trajectory towards a panoramic tower; this can be scaled, thanks to an interior staircase. In the centre of the paving system, consisting of light-coloured granite slabs, is a metal track, which echoes the nearby railway structures. At the beginning of the path is a square metal plaque with an ambiguous number engraved on it - it can be read as a 6 or a 9 - which provides the key to the numerical symbolism of the whole complex. There were six days in the Creation, there are six working days in a week, while nine and multiples of three represent the measurement of perfection. The panoramic tower comprises six blocks, alternately made of granite or cast steel; each of these blocks is six feet high (about 1.8 metres), which is man's approximate height. The outline of the tower is vertical on the path side, but terraced on the side facing the river, with 18-inch recesses at each floor.

The number 6 also governs the series of steps at the western entrance to the tower, as well as the row of trees flanking the northern wing of the museum, adjacent to the railway.

A slightly sloping elliptical space has been created in the esplanade that looks onto the river, the embankments of which can be reached via a gradatory system. The outline of this ellipse is shown by white markings in the clay brick paving. Near one of the focuses is a disk consisting of six concentric circles of steel and granite; this reproduces the tower's two-coloured system on the horizontal plane.

A rectilinear line of white granite, beginning at one end of the ellipse, highlights the solar axis with a north-south orientation, and extends to intersect with the path on the northern side. A metal track traces a different path, heading from the centre of the disk towards the eastern stairway leading down to the river, till it comes to an end in a hollow in the ground near the benches.

With an effect similar to that achieved in the Campo in Siena - an explicit design model for the creation of the Ma'alot - the slight inclination of the elliptical square gives a sensation of concavity to those who walk in it, while the outline of the surrounding buildings seems to disappear into the distance.

The disk and the panoramic tower from the museum's exhibition spaces

The son of a landscape engineer, **Dani Karavan** was born in 1930 in Tel Aviv. He embarked upon artistic studies in his city of birth (under the painters Avni, Stematsky, Streichman and Paul Levy), and then enrolled at the Bezalel Academy in Jerusalem. In 1956 he moved to Florence, in order to learn fresco technique.

From 1960 to 1973 he was active primarily as a scenographer, and was responsible for the sets for the Martha Graham Dance Company.

With his participation in the 38th Venice Biennale (1976) and in the exhibition Documenta 6 in Kassel (1977), he met with international success, earning him numerous commissions in Europe and the U.S.A. In particular, two Italian realizations - the

temporary structures for the Forte Belvedere in Florence and for the Castello dell'Imperatore in Prato (1978) - conditioned the subsequent course of his work, directing him towards minimal-concept sculpture that is highly charged with symbolism. His interest in landscape and his monumental vocation have led Karavan into direct contact with architecture.

Of his recent projects, particular mention should be made of the following: the arrangement outside the Ludwig Museum in Cologne (1979-86), Kikar Levana (the White Square) in Tel Aviv (1977-88), the 'Path of Light' at the Olympic Park in Seoul (1987-88) and the entrance to the Shiba Hospital in Tel Hashomer (Israel, 1992).

THE PLAÇA DE LA CONSTITUÇIÓ IN GERONA (1992)

The Plaça de la Constituçió, in Gerona, is situated between the Gran Via De Jaume and the Calle Acequia, in the city's inner suburbs. It occupies an irregularly shaped area demarcated by important road axes and surrounded by buildings that are heterogeneous as regards their architectural forms and functions. The pedestrian zone has been created above an underground car park and is higher than the street level. The area is delimited by a concrete wall with a discontinuous perimeter, giving the impression of 'containing' the surface of the square. This is the effect sought by the designers, who have conceived the Plaça de la Constituçió as a garden in the city, a natural oasis in the urban fabric, 'una maceta en la ciudad' (a pot of flowers in the city), living according to its own rules, independent of its setting. The trees are arranged in parallel rows, alternating with sculptures and items of ornamentation that make ironic reference to the city or the surrounding buildings, giving the square a playful, surreal appearance.

Opposite the Banco de España, whose convex façade faces onto the square, some enlarged Spanish coins have been embedded in the perimeter wall of the Plaça. *Moscas* (flies) have been inserted into the paving around the trees, because they are 'narcissistic' insects (St. Narcissus is Gerona's patron saint), while gargoyles shaped like the heads of carps from the Rio Onyar (one of the city's rivers) protrude from the concrete perimeter wall. Anthropomorphic forms are used for the benches and other decorative elements. Marble sculptures resembling Japanese *origami* shapes created with paper have been placed amongst the trees; in the midst of these sculptures is a fountain that spurts water into the city's four rivers. In front of the fountain is a sculpture by Francisco Lopez, the figure of a young girl, symbolizing the Constitution.

A new sculpture is to be added every five or ten years, on the anniversary of the promulgation of the Constitution. This, according to the designer, will enable the square to go on living and changing as time goes by.

Head collaborator on the project: Carlos Lloret.

Juli Esteban y Noguera was born in Gerona in 1944. After graduating in architecture, he taught urban planning for a few years at the ETSAB.

He has been responsible for urban planning and participated in the drafting of the Plan General Metropolitano (1976) for Barcelona. He is currently director of Urban Services for the metropolitan area of the Catalan city, and is the author of the book *Elementos de Ordenación Urbana* (Elements of Urban Ordering), published in 1980.

Antonio Font Arellano was born in Palencia in 1944. After graduating in architecture, he devoted his time prevalently to teaching. He has taught in Barcelona, in Valledolid, at the ETSAV (Escuela Técnica Superior de Arquitectura del Vallés), and at the Institute for Metropolitan Studies in Barcelona.

He founded the Laboratorio de Urbanismo de Barcelona (Barcelona Urban Planning Laboratory - LUB), and has been the director of the school and urban and regional planning department of the Universitat Politècnica de Catalunya. He currently teaches urban planning at the UPC, and has published numerous articles and critical essays.

José Antonio Martinez Lapeña was born in Tarragona in 1941. He graduated in architecture in 1968 at the ETSAB. He has taught planning at the ETSAB, and is currently a lecturer in planning at the ETSA in Vallés.

Jon Montero Madariaga was born in Barcelona in 1944. He is the author of articles and essays published in specialist magazines. He is a member of the TAU (Taller de Arquitectura y Urbanismo) in Barcelona with the architects Esteban and Font, and has been responsible for the planning of public spaces.

Since 1980 he has been the head of the Asociación de Municipios de la Area Metropolitana de Barcelona.

Elias Torres Tur was born in Ibiza in 1944. After gaining his degree in architecture in 1968, he devoted himself to teaching; he has taught composition and planning at the ETSAB, where he is currently a lecturer in Landscape Architecture. He has held courses and seminars at the UCLA in Los Angeles, at Harvard University and at the Accademia di Spagna in Rome. In 1980 he published a guide to the architecture of Ibiza and Formentera.

In 1986, with the architect Martinez, he founded an architecture studio in Barcelona.

Previous page:
Aerial view of the square

Opposite:
The image of the Constitution, created by Francisco Lopez

THE SQUARE IN FUORIGROTTA (1987-1990)

In the Fuorigrotta quarter, bordering on the San Paolo Stadium in Naples, the Piazza dei Campi Flegrei, which in the early fifties became Piazzale Tecchio, has now been redesigned as Piazza di Fuorigrotta, and is a nodal point for the mobility of Campania's principal city, it being the point of confluence of the underground railway, the Cumana railway, the Rapid Tramline, the Fuorigrotta intersection of the Naples bypass and the road axes coming from the west.

The project by the Pica Ciamarra Associati studio is part of the 'dream of transformation' of the whole western area of the city, conceived as a system of places of urban aggregation. The large tree-lined open square, initially intended for parked cars, has been transformed into a square serving the quarter, in a pedestrian area connecting the buildings around it - the Polytechnic, the Mostra d'Oltremare exhibition hall, the CNR Technological Pole, the San Paolo Stadium - while the car park has been housed in the floor underground.

The project could be defined as 'a square within a square': the area, tree-lined and for pedestrian use, covers a surface of over five hectares. One part of the area is defined by three 'lookout towers', which create a secluded triangular space; here, according to the authors, 'nonmaterial' sensations should hold sway. The three modern obelisks, each approximately 40 metres high, are reminders of the 'macchine da festa' (festival machines) from Neapolitan eighteenth-century tradition, which are still present in many of the city's piazzas. These three towers are all different, and decidedly technological.

The Tower of Time and Fluids, made of laminated wood, designs a sundial on the ground; if it is stirred by the north-east or sirocco winds, it produces sounds through a 'sound machine', while a 'rigid sail' forms the screen for the laser rays emitted by the Tower of Memory.

The aluminium Tower of Information represents the evolution of information systems. The Tower of Memory is equipped with a large periscope that allows you to see images of the city and the gulf.

Outside the triangular piazza, a flight of brick steps serves a dual purpose, as a place to sit and as ornamentation: on one side stands a fountain, the jets of which are driven by photovoltaic cells that are sensitive to atmospheric variations. The rivulets of water create designs in the square and intertwine with the lines of the sundial. It provides an ideal link between the atomized water fountain of the CNR building and the fountain (yet to be built) outside the Faculty of Engineering. An 'olfactory garden' and a 'space to sit down' characterize the zone surrounding the triangular piazza. The predominant use of brick, wood and stone is intended to present the character of the historic city in reinterpreted form. The waterworks of the fountain, based on the principle of the saving of rainwater, create sensations that allow a diversified appropriation of the square. This theme of the *piazza d'acqua* has also been used by the Pica Chiamarra studio for the Cavalleggeri d'Aosta Quarter and for Bagnoli.

P. Gargiulo and M. Russo collaborated on the project.

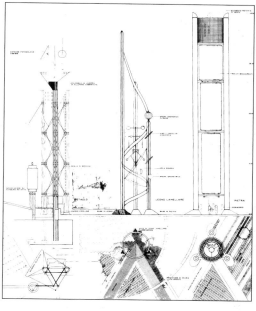

Plans and view drawings of the three 'lookout towers' that emphasize the triangular structure of the square

Previous page:
Aerial view of the square in the urban context

Below left:
General ground plan of the Fuorigrotta area

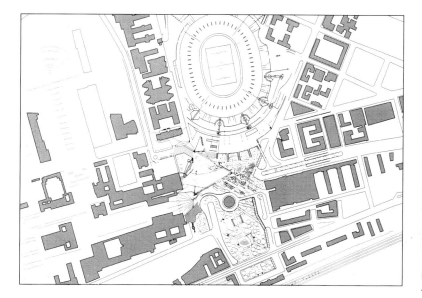

Massimo Pica Ciamarra, born in 1937, is lecturer in Architectural Composition at the University of Naples.

The Pica Ciamarra Associati studio began its activities in the seventies, and currently De Martino, De Rosa and Rocereto work there. They have been responsible for various projects, from the planning of university poles in Messina, Naples, in Basilicata and Molise, to the restructuring of the Royal Palace and the Palazzo Mascobruno in Portici, of the Theatre of the Four Horses in Pavia, of the Palazzo Corigliano in Naples, as well as designing urban layouts such as the Mergellina area.

In *L'Héritage des CIAM 1958-1988* Schimmerling and Tzonis defined the work of the Pica Ciamarra Associati studio as an example of the continuation of the theses of Team X. The studio has participated in competitions, both nationally and internationally, such as those for the Piazzale Roma in Venice, the Piazza dell'Isola in Vicenza, Les Halles and La Villette in Paris, the universities of Lattakya, Amman and Yarmouk.

A monographic exhibition devoted to the studio's designs and research was promoted by the Istituto Nazionale di Architettura in 1986, and shown in Rome, Paris, Dublin, Bruges, in Brazil and in Lanciano in 1989 on the occasion of the Premio Terras.

The studio expresses a policy of design research that is poised between utopia and reality, and is multidisciplinary and complemented by multiple cultural stimuli.

THREE ARCHISCULPTURAL SQUARES

THE PLAZA OF THE THREE POWERS IN BRASILIA (1959-1960)

The city of Brasilia is an artificial aggregate, built in less than four years in accordance with an urban planning scheme that was defined in detail 'around the table'. It came in for severe criticism on the social level ('a poor country like Brazil cannot afford the luxury of a city dictated solely by architects', wrote G. Freyre vehemently), yet the formal solutions adopted for it also met with enthusiastic support ('there is invention here', Le Corbusier said). Today's Brazilian capital is in any case one of the most fertile laboratories of experimentation of the theories and urban models of the late postwar period.

In contrast to what is generally thought, the construction of Brasilia did not come about because of a sudden decision fostered by the celebrative ambitions of President Juscelino Kubitschek, but was the result of a long process of national self-acknowledgement, which - beginning with the independence movement of the Inconfidentes Mineiros of 1789 - aimed at the creation of a capital city on the central high plain, intentionally set in opposition to 'Portuguese' Rio de Janeiro. The idea of a new federal capital was in fact provided for in both the constitution of 1891 and the renewed one of 1946, while with the law of 5th January 1953 the forming of a commission to choose the definitive site had been authorized. This does not alter the fact that, with the election of Kubitschek in 1956 to the Presidency of the Republic, the project acquired a new boost, fitting within a broader economic programme of the populating and exploitation of the desert regions of the interior.

The urbanization programme for the new capital - organized according to a highly symbolic design suggesting the flight of an aeroplane - was drafted by the Brazilian architect Lúcio Costa (one of the best-known of Le Corbusier's collaborators), the winner of the competition of ideas promoted by Novacap (Companhia Urbanizadora da Nova Capital do Brasil) in September 1956. Curvilinear in

Previous page:
The butterfly-winged outline of the Pantheon Tancredo Neves terminates the vast eastern esplanade. In the foreground, the mosaic paving with irregularly cut brown stone.

Below:
The Planalto Building, suspended on pilotis, is conceived as a 'box' of glass supported by a structural cage of reinforced concrete posts. In the background, the National Congress Building, with the twin towers of the administration offices.

shape and 12.5 kilometres long, the area for residential use is intersected by a rectilinear axis with an east-west orientation that begins at the railway station outside the urban core and culminates, at the eastern end, in the Plaza of the Three Powers, which is the city's municipal and ceremonial centre. The most important public and administrative buildings (the ministries, the cathedral, the National Theatre, the shopping centre, the Radio and Television Tower, headquarters of banks and offices, etc.) are located along the rectilinear axis, while the President's residence (the Palace of the Alvorada) and the Hotel Brasilia Palace occupy an area away from the centre, close by Lake Paranoa.

Circulation is characterized by rigid criteria of separation between vehicle and pedestrian traffic and is articulated around routes on different levels. Within this urban planning scheme - which is explicitly indebted to the culture of 'zoning' - the architectonic and spatial definition of the new capital is inextricably linked with the personality of Oscar Niemeyer, who was 'discovered' by Kubitschek at the time of his early activities in Pampulha (Belo Horizonte) and named chief architect of Novacap.

Within the space of four years - from 1956 to 1960, the date set for the inauguration of the new capital - Niemeyer constructed the city's most prestigious buildings (the Hotel Brasilia Palace, the University Planning Centre, the Chapel of Our Lady of Fatima, the Dominican Monastery), created eleven residential blocks with over four hundred apartments and completed the Plaza of the Three Powers administrative complex. In the years that immediately followed, despite attempts at boycott by the government brought about by the coup d'état in 1964, he designed the City Stadium (1961), the head office of the Touring Club (1962), the Ministry of Foreign Affairs (Itamaraty Palace), the Ministry of Justice (1963) and the Ministry of Defence Building (1968).

Positioned at the geometrical and symbolic head of the whole core of construction (a perhaps intentional analogy with the Capitol in Chandigarh), the Plaza of the Three Powers (legislative, executive and judicial) occupies a broad pedestrian esplanade to the east looking over Lake Paranoa. The western end of the square is occupied by the terrace of the National Congress Building, in a lower position with respect to the road arteries running parallel to the parallelepipedal volume of the building. Projecting from the terrace level, which can be reached via a double flight of stairs, are

The raised square of the Planalto Building, the pedestrian access ramp of which can be seen to the right. The Supreme Court Building is flanked by the stereometric volume of the Museum of Foundation.

the strongly plastic geometries of two domes - one the usual way up and the other inverted - which accommodate the halls of session of the Chamber and the Senate respectively. According to a compositional principle that makes different plastic forms correspond to different functions, the offices of the central administration are grouped into two rigidly stereometric tower buildings; because of their verticality, these contrast with the horizontal directrix of the long pool of water at the lower level. At the eastern end beyond the pool stands a raised platform, paved with stone fragments with a warm, brown colour; this acts as a connecting element between the two symbolic projections of state authority, the Supreme Court Building and the Planalto Building, the latter housing the presidential offices. The formal cohesion between the buildings, located symmetrically at opposite ends of the broad central esplanade, is obtained by recourse to the same construction motif for both. Each creation is in fact proposed as a 'box of glass', enclosed in a structural cage formed by thin reinforced concrete 'columns'. Standing out, as if to reinforce the dynamic attraction between the two buildings, at almost a third of their distance, is the prismatic volume of the Museum of Foundation; this consists of two parallel septa projecting over a wide pier which contains the access stairway.

The final episode in the design of the Plaza of the Three Powers, the Pantheon dedicated to Tancredo Neves, is a recent addition (1987), and was Oscar Niemeyer's homage, when the military regime ended, to all those who fought for freedom and democracy. Positioned parallel to the raised east platform, to which it is connected by means of a raised walkway, the Pantheon Tancredo Neves building opens out like a fan that is structured on three levels: at ground level is an auditorium for one hundred people, and the entrance hall is by the access ramp. The main hall is in a slightly raised position, and is decorated with a mural by Joao Camara. The lateral façades are animated respectively by a large window by Marianne Peretti and a bas-relief by Attros Bulcao, while the butterfly-winged outline standing out against the sky synthesizes Niemeyer's poetics and the free play of plastic forms that encapsulates his architecture.

LA MAISON DE LA CULTURE IN LE HAVRE (1972-1983)

The House of Culture in Le Havre stands in the middle of the Place Gambetta, a rectangular esplanade generated by Auguste Perret's roads plan, and terminates the view along the vast Bassin du Commerce. To guarantee it conditions of spatial autonomy, differentiating it from the rigid geometries of the surrounding buildings, Niemeyer has organized the municipal complex around an internal square, sinking this three meters below street level and surrounding it with an irregular cantilever. The square area thus takes on the appearance of 'an open-air hall, sheltered from the wind and rain' and becomes the connecting element between the building's different spatial units.

The various functions to be performed by a modern 'machine of culture' are in fact distributed over two distinct structures which project from the horizontal plane, each with an outline like a truncated cone, yet each different in terms of its height and inclination.

The lower building, structured over three levels, houses the cultural centre and includes a vast entrance hall, a double-height multi-purpose hall to seat approximately 1,100 people, a 300-seat cinema projection hall, an audiovisual studio, a recording studio, an 80-seat auditorium, a documentation room, rooms for exhibitions, meeting halls and offices.

In the more slanting building is a theatre for 1,150 people. In the ground floor area, with direct access from the square, are the entrance hall and rooms with various facilities, including a projection hall and a 300-seat conference hall.

The two truncated cones created by Niemeyer in Le Havre are unmistakable evidence of his mature language, which refuses all a priori functionalisms for the sake of the inventive freedom of architecture. In neither of the two buildings does form automatically follow function; rather, it pursues an aesthetic dimension that develops the expressive potential of reinforced concrete to its extreme consequences.

The centre of distribution and symbolism of the House of Culture remains the semi-covered space of the internal square. 'In the presence of two architectures', Niemeyer has written, 'you cannot ignore the space separating them.' Connected to street level by a gently sloping ring-shaped ramp, the lowered square of Le Havre is animated by the presence of a restaurant, a café and a couple of shops, sheltered by the overhang that forms the perimeter outline. In a central position, sheltered by the concave wall of the theatre building, is a bronze fountain in the shape of a large open hand of solidarity.

Plastic model of the project for La Maison de la Culture in Le Havre

NEW FLOORS

THE MEMORIAL OF LATIN AMERICA IN SÃO PAOLO IN BRAZIL (1988-1989)

The Memorial of Latin America is a vast cultural complex placed within an urban context that is disorderly and fragmentary, without monumental projections of impact. The site on which it is built in fact includes two pedestrian islands with undefined outlines, situated close to the railway and separated by a very busy road axis. To confer a monumental scale upon it - the Memorial in fact represents a call for faith and solidarity for all the peoples of Latin America - Niemeyer has distributed the different functional units over an unbroken horizontal esplanade, intentionally without the trees or the green areas which characterize the open spaces of Brazilian cities. 'A square with Mediterranean characteristics', as Niemeyer has defined it, 'which, if it is to host political events, cannot have elements that obstruct visibility and prevent escape.' Uniformly paved, the vast esplanade of the Memorial has no element to provide geometrical rhythm and no ordering graphic motif. Its function as a powerful catalyst for the disorder of the surrounding buildings is entrusted solely to the strong plastic projection of the architectures, the value of which is enhanced by the rigorous horizontality of the ground. In actual fact, the buildings forming the Memorial complex seem to act as independent objects, distributed in an open order that eludes the thin thread of formal analogies. Located on the smaller of the two pedestrian islands, by the southern access point directly connected to the underground railway line, are the Hall of Acts, the library and the restaurant. The Hall of Acts - so called because it was intended as the seat of the solemn ceremonies and major decisions of the state - is a structurally very daring building consisting of a huge barrel vault supported by a 60-metre beam. The beam rests on two large vertical towers, forming an H-shaped structural element that acts as a porticoed space by the entrance. The interior hall, measuring 3,240 square metres, extends outside with a truncated pyramid-shaped tribune of honour which is reflected in the two pools of water at the foot of the building.

The library, containing 50,000 volumes on the history and culture of Latin America, has a curvilinear covering coupled onto a 90-metre prestressed reinforced concrete beam, which is supported at the sides by two monumental columns. Less cohesive is the spatial articulation of the

The vast esplanade of the Memorial in São Paolo in Brazil, with, at the centre, the 'open hand' inspired by Le Corbusier

interior, where the distribution of facilities does not correspond directly with the sequence of bays defined by the vaulted roof. In contrast with the quadrangular ground plan of the Hall and the library, the restaurant is a circular construction that is structurally resolved by a single central pier supporting the roofing slabs. The small information pavilion positioned opposite this, immediately to the right of the main entrance, is also round in shape. Located on the larger island, connected to the previous one by a curvilinear bridge suspended from a pier that is bent into an arch to form a symbolic portal, are the Pavilion of Creativity, the Centre of Latin American Studies and the Auditorium.

The Pavilion is a building with a convex outline located at the northern end of the square. Designed to house folk craft exhibitions, it has a porticoed front with modular metrical structure and is the only building of the Memorial using prefabricated elements. In its 700 square metres the Study Centre, a building situated near the bridge, houses a research centre on the culture and art of the South American continent and includes the administrative buildings of the whole cultural centre. Its rigidly parallelepipedal volume is suspended from the roofing beams by a spider's web of metal stay bolts that accentuate the impression of structural lightness. Finally, the Auditorium, in a dominant position at the eastern head of the square, has a sequence of three parallel domes resting on a 40-metre-span intermediate beam. The interior space includes a foyer and two sets of stalls

The Hall of Acts dominates the vast southern esplanade of the Memorial. In the foreground, an overhang protecting the lighting equipment. To the left, the Open Hand monument.

NEW FLOORS

separated by a stage positioned near the ceiling beam. There are few ornamental elements or facilities spread over the surface of the esplanade: one or two benches with linear outlines, a metal sculpture by Alexander Calder and one or two booths providing toilet facilities. Looming over the vast dimensions of the space is the presence of a white cement hand with a deep blood-red wound cut into it. This is a citation of the Open Hand placed by Le Corbusier as the emblem of Chandigarh, but with all the dramatic force of the history of Latin America.

    M.C. Scharlach, M.A. Mello Galvao, F. Andrade, H. Ponteado, J. Soares Brandao collaborated on the project.

The Hall of Acts seen from the pool of water in front

Oscar Niemeyer was born in Rio de Janeiro in 1907, and graduated in architecture at the Escola Nacional de Belas-Artes in 1934. He met Le Corbusier at Lúcio Costa's studio in Rio, and was given the opportunity to work on his project for the Brazilian Ministry of Education and Health. With the completion of Pampulha in 1940-42, he embarked upon a personal path of investigation based on a radical critique of orthodox functionalism, in favour of an aesthetics of free form capable of exploiting to the utmost the structural potential of reinforced concrete.

Following the military coup d'état in 1964, after concluding his experience in Brasilia, he was forced to leave the university where he was head of the Faculty of Architecture. Obstructed for political reasons in his own country, he began to travel abroad, where his work met with considerable and increasing appreciation.

Of his many well-known works, particular mention must be made of: the headquarters of the French Communist Party in Paris (1967), the Universities of Algiers and Constantine in Algeria (1968-78), the head offices of the publishers Mondadori in Segrate, near Milan (1975), and of Fata Engineering in Turin (1976), and the Bourse du Travail in Bobigny, near Paris (1978).

He lives and works in Rio de Janeiro.

LEVI'S PLAZA IN SAN FRANCISCO (1982)

In the glass and concrete setting that forms the fabric of American metropolises, Lawrence Halprin's schemes are a natural oasis. Yet there is nothing mimetic in the scenographic compositions that perhaps America's most famous environmental designer stages by decomposing and reassembling materials taken from the biological world.

Indeed, what would be the point of reproducing fragments of the High Sierra or a museum-sized portion of the Grand Canyon in the heart of a city such as San Francisco? Aware of its own artificial origins, accustomed to the frenetic pace of American life, Halprin's 'nature' does, however, seem more real than the sort that is usually imprisoned within the fences of a public garden. Levi's Plaza in San Francisco - built for the leading American jeans manufacturers, with the collaboration of the architects Hellmuth, Obata & Kasselbaum and Gensler & Associates - does not conceal its ambivalent nature, as a square and a garden. The large rectangular esplanade lying at the foot of the terraced blocks that form the administrative complex is given over to the square. The garden winds around and continues onto the eastern wing, beyond a street that divides it from the buildings. The paving of the plaza has a geometrical design of interwoven coloured bands (created using red and white tiles) which stand out from a uniform background of light-grey granite. The horizontal sequence is suddenly broken up, interrupted by an imposing fountain; in an articulated interplay of gradually descending terraces, this fountain constitutes the element of connection with the garden area. Here the marriage between nature and artifice reaches a moment of tension. Yet Halprin is able to obtain new equilibria from this dissonance. In the middle of the large rectangular pool looking onto the plaza stands a huge block of granite which introduces a clashing note of decontextualized nature. The vortex of pools, wells and waterfalls that begins here actually has a rigorously geometrical profile and blatantly expresses the artificiality of its own composition, of blocks of cement. The surviving natural element is the water; in flowing whirlpools, darting streams and rapid falls, it re-evokes the sounds and light effects of the wild American sierras. The surrounding park is more tranquil, reconciling the taste for the multi-coloured effects of the English garden with the placid rhythm of the great prairies. A stream winds its way through, surrounded by grassy knolls and piles of stone, where only the volumetric regularity of one or two cylindrical blocks reveals the artificial nature of the representation.

The reinterpretation which Halprin gives to evocation of the natural world goes beyond the logic of the 'green in the city', arriving at compositions which are highly charged figuratively, capable of standing up in comparison with the macroscale of the surrounding buildings.

'I introduce nature, but strongly, decisively', Halprin declared when presenting his work at the San Francisco Museum of Modern Art. 'I do not seek to copy it, of course, but transform it, creating places where people can be happy.' The direct involvement of the community of 'users and enjoyers', invited to climb up onto the rocks and ford the streams, is in fact one of the indispensable ingredients - along with the water, the paths, the rocks and shrubs - for the creation of Lawrence Halprin's three-dimensional environmental experiences.

Lawrence Halprin was born in 1916 in New York of Jewish parents. He studied agriculture at Cornell University and Botany at the University of Wisconsin, and then attended the Graduate School of Design at Harvard, working with Tunnard and Walter Gropius.

In 1949 he founded Lawrence Halprin & Associates, specializing in environmental design. The activities of the early years - some private gardens and the Old Orchard Shopping Center in Skokie, which in the fifties launched the fashion of garden-shops - quickly brought him international success. Of his subsequent projects, particularly worthy of mention are Sproul Plaza in Berkeley, the Nicollet Mall in Minneapolis, the Lovejoy Plaza and the Transit Mall in Portland Oregon, the Freeway Park in Seattle, the Franklin Delano Roosevelt Memorial, the ecological plan for the Sea Ranch in California, the Embracadero Plaza and Market Street in San Francisco.

Alongside his design activities, he has promoted seminars in participatory planning (Experiments in Environment 1966-68) and written numerous books: *Cities* (1963), *Freeways* (1966), *New York New York* (1968) and *Taking Part: a Workshop Approach to Collective Creativity* (with Jim Burns, 1974).

Previous page:
Natural and artificial elements coexist in the representation of the American landscape, staged in the garden.

Opposite:
One of the points for walking across the fountain pools

FIVE URBAN PROJECTS IN NORTH AMERICA

Paul Friedberg fits within the tradition of American landscape architecture that was begun by Frederick Law Olmsted midway through the last century. In line with his training as a landscapist, the urban schemes we present here constantly highlight the introduction of the natural world into the tightly woven fabric of the contemporary metropolis. The result is not, however, an anachronistic biological oasis, but a park plaza where the eternal dialectic between nature and architecture is given form. Indeed, the biological element is enhanced in the contrast with its opposite, the geometrically defined artificial form.

Created to respond to the manifold desires of the continually changing masses, Friedberg's squares use flexibility as their organizational principle. They are squares for walking, sitting, relaxing, squares for reading and eating that quick lunch. They are squares for sporting activity and for cultural events, squares for large entertainment events and to attract people with spontaneous performances by jugglers, mime artists, musicians. They are multi-purpose plazas, organized three-dimensionally to enable each activity to find its own appropriate setting within the macro-scale of the overall design.

Many elements frequently recur:
- artificial terracing with an amphitheatre layout, the archetypal form for large mass meetings;
- large swimming pools, which can easily be transformed into skating rinks or stages;
- waterfalls, with their continuous gurgling of water helping to animate the square with sound.

And, of course, an abundant variety of plants and flowers, entrusted with the task of reawakening the biological and climatic *genius loci* of each creation.

Previous page:
View of Peavy Plaza in Minneapolis

Below:
Image of the fountain-sculpture located at the edge of the large pool

PEAVY PLAZA IN MINNEAPOLIS (1973)

Positioned beside Nicollet Mall, the main artery of Minneapolis, and adjacent to the new Concert Hall, Peavy Plaza is a favorite stopping-off point along the footpath linking the city centre with the green system comprising Loring Greenway and Loring Park (Friedberg was responsible for designing the general layout of this in 1974). This large area with an elongated outline (a surface area of approximately 8,000 square metres) is structured around a rectangular swimming pool; a water drainage system enables this to be transformed into an esplanade to host the city's large public events. The swimming pool is supplied with water by a fountain-sculpture located on the western corner facing onto Nicollet Mall. Consisting of a complex system of terracing, pools and monumental flights of steps, emerging from which are water jets and 'organ pipe' effects, created by a group of metal rods, the fountain is the dominant element of the whole complex.

Arranged around the swimming pool are gradually descending terraces, partly paved, partly left to grass. Emerging here and there are thickets of vegetation, consisting of juniper bushes and different varieties of flowers.

There is a refreshment area in the northern zone, separated from vehicle traffic by a regular grid of trees.

PERSHING PARK IN WASHINGTON (1979)

Pershing Park, the very name of which brings out its character of a garden-square, is located along Pennsylvania Avenue, in a specular position with respect to Western Plaza, realized by Venturi, Scott Brown and Associates.

The central area is occupied by a large rectangular pool, bordered on two adjoining sides by a flight of steps studded with tubs of planted greenery. On the west side the steps are interrupted by a granite block which protrudes into the water, forming the support for a waterfall. The interior of this is partly hollow, and includes a service room for the equipment that enables the swimming pool to be transformed into a skating rink during the winter months.

Opening onto the eastern side is a terrace that in the summer months offers a refreshment area leading to a circular kiosk. The toilet facilities, the changing rooms for the skating rink and a

Aerial view of Pershing Park in Washington

NEW FLOORS

storeroom are all located underground. Beside the terrace is a small rectangular square, with a monument to General Pershing in the middle.

The green perimeter ring offers a large number of places to sit down (flights of steps, semicircular enclosures, etc.) and provides a filter zone between the square and the large surrounding road arteries.

PARK PLACE IN VANCOUVER (1982)

In a central position, alongside the Christ Church Cathedral, Park Place is the product of the organization of a marginal space, which came about as the covering for a four-level underground garage.

The most meaningful element in the project is the 'cascade' faced with clay brick, which delimits the area on the north side and masks a pre-existing blind wall. The stair-like arrangement of the baked brick tiles - of different shapes and sizes - offers a rough surface for the water to run down and permits the creation of pools with vegetation, from which lush thickets of laurel and rhododendron emerge.

An area for sitting and relaxing has been created opposite the waterfall, in the open space looking onto Burrand Street, with benches and flower-boxes spread about randomly around the modular scheme established by the planted birch trees.

BATTERY PARK CITY PLAZA IN NEW YORK (1982)

The waterfront plaza that constitutes the administrative heart of Battery Park City - a financial stronghold situated on the left bank of the Hudson - is a public space with a highly articulated design.

Opposite the administrative buildings with their L-shaped ground plans, two rectangular terraces converge towards the area in front of the Winter Garden (a shopping arcade designed by architect Cesar Pelli) with a checked paving design. Both terraces have a double row of plants, regularly arranged inside the granite paving, and terminate with a linear fountain that produces a lightly cascading effect.

On the lower level, beyond the fountains, a gradually descending series of benches and steps spills water onto the narrow promenade that runs across the whole expanse of Battery City Park like a linear park.

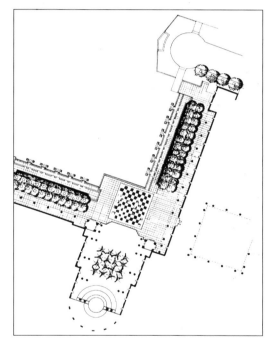

Ground plan of Battery Park City Plaza in New York

OLYMPIC PLAZA IN CALGARY (1987)

Designed to host the medal presentations at the Olympiad in 1988, Olympic Plaza is still the venue for important open-air public events. It occupies a strategic position between the City Hall and the Calgary Center for the Performing Arts, and there is direct access to it from Eighth Street Mall, the city's most important pedestrian street.

The central core is occupied by a large square pool of water that can be quickly transformed into an esplanade capable of containing over 10,000 people. In the winter months it can become a large skating rink. Arranged along the north-eastern edge is a monumental structure, part stage, part fountain, which contributes to masking the service structure positioned below (toilet facilities, water supply and drainage system, equipment for ice formation, etc.).

On the other side of a dais for open-air performances is a *frons scenae*, consisting of a classically-inspired colonnade, while unravelling all around is an interplay of small cascades, pools and fountains providing the visual focus for the complex.

The fountain and the colonnade are at a 45-degree angle with respect to the city's orthogonal road network, so as to grab the attention of the traffic coming from Eighth Street Mall.

At the sides of the pool, rows of terracing, covered with grass and with vegetation in certain sections, create a large terraced surface for sitting; in the western corner, a semicircular amphitheatre is thereby created, overlooking the water. Uniform curtains of trees establish the perimeters of the area, while the southern access is defined by a metal arcade which - for occasions such as fairs and exhibitions - provides the structure to support the stalls.

Opposite:
Park Place in Vancouver: the garden area looking onto Burrard Street

Below:
Battery Park City Plaza in New York: detail of the spaces for sitting

NEW FLOORS

Above:
A theatre performance beside the large pool of Olympic Plaza in Calgary

Opposite:
The metal arcade which forms the southern access to the plaza

M. Paul Friedberg was born in 1931 and graduated in natural sciences at Cornell University in 1954.

In 1958 he launched the M. Paul Friedberg and Partners studio, specializing in urban design and environmental planning. His most memorable works are the U.S.A. pavilion at the international exposition in Osaka, the Moscow Trade Centre in the Russian capital, the City Hall Fountain in New York, the Fulton County Government Complex in Atlanta, the Transpotomac Canal Center in Alexandria in Virginia and (in the process of preparation) the Seiko Project for Tokyo and MacArthur Place in Santa Ana in California. Besides his professional activities, he has also taught at the major American universities and founded the Urban Landscape Architecture Program at City College in New York.

The author of numerous articles and of three books devoted to urban planning (*Playground for City Children, Play and Interplay, Handicrafted Playgrounds*), he received the gold medal of the American Institute of Architects in 1980.

FIVE 'ARTIFICIAL GARDENS'

In the tradition of American landscape architecture, the urban planning schemes by Peter Walker and Martha Schwartz - partners in life and sometimes in their work - can be recognized by their accentuated graphic characterization of paved surfaces.

Modular compositions and intersections of axial directrices form the regular layout into which decontextualized naturalistic elements are inserted, while objects spread around in geometrical conformations evoke a surreal landscape, now rendered completely artificial.

CAMBRIDGE CENTER ROOF GARDEN IN CAMBRIDGE, MASSACHUSETTS
PETER WALKER & PARTNERS (1979)

Though this is the roof of a multi-storey car park, and not automatically recognizable as an urban square, the Cambridge Center Roof Garden is emblematic of the above design approach and acts as a prologue to subsequent schemes.

Its quality as a public space is derived from the direct access gained to it from the multi-purpose spaces of the Cambridge Center, which houses commercial, service sector and reception facilities.

The reduction in surface area and the regular metrical structure obtained by working principally on the floor surface are in this case a formal response to difficulties of a technical nature.

The prefabricated structure of the car park below would not in fact have borne the weight of a garden with vegetation, while the drainage system located below the surface meant that the floor had to be highly permeable. The image of a traditional hanging garden is evoked with a maze-like ornamental flower bed created using juniper hedges, while the presence of tall-stemmed plants is simulated by metal structures covered with climbing plants projecting from the floor. Perennially shady 'green rooms' are created inside the larger metal structures.

Previous page:
Cambridge Center Roof Garden in Cambridge, Massachusetts: detail of the tubular metal structures which act as supports for the climbing plants

Below:
General view of the square-garden created on the roof of the multi-storey car park

The central area is different; it is in contact with the entrance, and acts as a counterpoint to the naturalistic metaphor enacted by the parterre: the repetitive paving of white tiles on a brown background reveals the geometrical pattern governing the whole composition.

MARAGUME PLAZA IN MARAGUME, JAPAN
PETER WALKER & PARTNERS (1983)

A clearly recognizable formal graphic pattern also determines the design of Maragume Plaza, located on a strategic site between the municipal museum and the railway station.

A paving motif with a powerful visual impact was chosen in order to emphasize the spatial continuity of the plaza beyond the caesura caused by the many road axes running across its surface, and this motif is repeated homogeneously on each pedestrian island, connecting the public space outside the station on an ideal plane with the series of shops on the opposite side and with the museum building on the southern side.

The paving motif, a grid with parallel black and white bands, is reminiscent of the two-coloured striped material of which traditional kimonos are made, and is a homage to Japanese engineering tradition, bringing out the material qualities of the asphalt and cement, which are used to build the broader section bands. A dark stone similar to basalt, used for the thin black lines that divide the white bands lengthwise, is the same material as is employed to face the museum, highlighting the spatial relationship between the different component parts of the square.

Opposite the station, inside a circular disk of water, there is a fountain symbolizing a triumphal gate, positioned to welcome the thousands of commuters who pour into Maragume every day from the nearby suburbs.

Four steel frames with a thin veil of water running over them offer a visual screen, affording increasingly out-of-focus and allusive views, depending on whether the gaze passes through one, two, or all of them. A little way on, at the corner between two very busy avenues of traffic, a row of stones arranged in a spiral simultaneously acts as a transenna and a bench. In the nocturnal light

Maragume Plaza in Maragume: view of the pedestrian area outside the railway station

NEW FLOORS

Opposite:
South Coast Plaza in Costa Mesa: the paving design opposite the
Plaza Tower

Below:
Splice Garden in Cambridge, Massachusetts: a blend of a Japanese
garden with a French-style geometrical garden

PETER WALKER AND MARTHA SCHWARTZ

it shines with an internal luminosity, making it look like an unreal bed of lava. Water and fire do indeed constitute the two poles of the Japanese symbolic universe, enacting a small cosmological representation in the domestic space of Maragume Plaza.

SOUTH COAST PLAZA IN COSTA MESA, CALIFORNIA
PETER WALKER & PARTNERS (1991)

The South Coast Plaza Complex is an enormous multi-purpose centre, which was built in the mid-sixties to meet the urban requirements of a district - Orange County - with a prevalently agricultural economy. Numerous administrative buildings, a hotel, some restaurants, one or two banks and two theatres (the Plaza Theater and the South Coast Repertory Theater) have been progressively added to the elegant shopping mall that forms the original core. The area's cultural potential has recently been expanded with the creation of the Orange County Performing Arts Center, from a project by the Causill, Rowlett, Scott studio and the Blurock Partnership, while Isamu Noguchi was responsible for the building of 'California Scenario', a public court near the large southern car park.

As from 1974, the designing of the layout of the Town Center Park (which occupies the central area of South Coast Plaza) and of certain public spaces outside the buildings was entrusted to Peter Walker.

To be specific, a small square was obtained opposite the Plaza Tower, an IBM administration building designed by Cesar Pelli and Associates (1991); with its extremely rarified language, this is representative of Walker's typical style. On the directrix of a rectilinear avenue planted with poplar trees is a granite slab with parallel steel beams running across it; these reflect the orthogonal pattern governing the orientation of South Coast Plaza. By the entrance to the building the rectilinear beams intersect with a different geometry introduced by two disks of concentric circles, where the mediation between the square and the green area surrounding it is concentrated.

A similar structure with tangent circles also appears in the space outside the Orange County Performing Arts Center, breaking up the orthogonality of an area of triangular ornamental hedges. The circular shape of the furthest disk is in turn broken by an imposing cement portal, underlining the ambiguity of the geometrical forms upon which the whole composition is based.

SPLICE GARDEN IN CAMBRIDGE, MASSACHUSETTS
PETER WALKER AND MARTHA SCHWARTZ (1986)

Located at the top of the White Head Institute for Biochemical Research, Peter Walker and Martha Schwartz's Splice Garden is an ironical response to the bioengineering research carried out in AI (Artificial Intelligence) Alley in Cambridge.

Indeed, to correspond to the blending of genes obtained artificially in the laboratories of the building, on the roof there is an artificial mixture of green spaces, consisting of the union between a Japanese garden and a French-style geometrical garden. The point of intersection occurs on a straight metal line - the splice line whence the project takes its name - which continues straight up the perimeter wall. Both of the green areas are created using artificial and indestructible materials, a solution which the two American architects found congenial, though static requirements nevertheless made it necessary (the roof would not in fact have borne the weight of real planted vegetation), as did economic ones.

The rarified atmosphere of a Japanese garden is re-evoked with a floor surface of raked gravel, projecting from which there are the perfectly smooth spheres of plastic trees and shrubs.

In contrast, the meticulous geometry of a French garden is reproduced with a maze-like pattern of shaped hedges, these again made of plastic materials, which can be used for seating.

The joint presence of flower species from profoundly different climatic conditions - ferns, tulips and bougainvillea - betrays in an apparently insignificant detail the intentional artificiality of the whole scheme.

KING COUNTY JAIL PLAZA IN SEATTLE, WASHINGTON
MARTHA SCHWARTZ (1983) WITH KEN SMITH AND DAVID MEYER

In the space in front of the new prison building in Seattle, Martha Schwartz has created a pedestrian courtyard which presents itself as a formal garden of stone. The mosaic paving design, created using fragments of coloured ceramic (grey, yellow, violet and light blue), forms an orthogonal grid that suggests the existence of a latticework of linear paths.

At the centre of the space a circular structure reflecting blue-green simulates the presence of a fountain, while the geometrically shaped elements distributed freely over the paved surface evoke the shaped foliage of trees and hedges. On the back wall a mural of blue ceramic tiles depicts a glimpse of sky, against which there stands out a grey gate that gives the impression of an imaginary way out. Despite the naturalistic illusion offered by the reference to the 'French-style' geometrical garden, Martha Schwartz's project does not intend to eschew the social dimension of the scheme; it is after all a prison area, and this must not be forgotten.

King County Jail Plaza in Seattle: general view of the project

Peter Walker graduated at the University of California in 1957, and gained a masters degree in Landscape Architecture at the Graduate School of Design of the University of Harvard.

In 1957 he founded Sasaki, Walker and Associates (named SWA Group in 1975), specializing in urban and environmental design. In 1983 he launched his own studio (Peter Walker and Associates), though he continued to collaborate actively with William J. Johnson Associates, a fact which led to the two groups amalgamating in 1992.

Granted the Honor Award of the American Institute of Architects, he is professor at the Harvard University Graduate School of Design, where for some time he headed the Landscape Architecture Department.

He was joint author of the volume *Invisible Gardens, the Search for Modernism in the American Landscape*, devoted to

the recent history of American landscape art, and is preparing a book on his minimalist approach to environmental archtecture.

His projects particularly worthy of mention are: the landscape design for the Kempinski Hotel and for Munich Airport (with Murphy Jahn Architects), the redesigning of the Todos Santos Plaza in Concord (California), the renovation of the Martin Luther King Jr. Promenade in San Diego, the Cultural Arts Center in Fremont in California (with BOOR/A Architects) and Disney City in Orlando, Florida.

Among the projects realized in collaboration with William Johnson: the master plan for the Nishi Harima Science Garden City in Japan (with Arata Isozaki); the Euralille Park in San Diego (with Rem Koolhass) and the layout design of the Exposition Park in Los Angeles (with Zimmer, Gunsul, Frasca, Architects).

Martha Schwartz graduated at the University of Michigan in

1977, and then gained her diploma in Landscape Architecture at Harvard University Graduate School of Design, where she currently works as Associate Professor of Environmental Architecture.

After collaborating with Peter Walker (first at the SWA Group im Boston, then at the Walker-Schwartz Office in New York), with Ken Smith and David Meyer, she recently opened a studio (Martha Schwartz Inc.), with offices in Cambridge, Mass., and San Francisco.

Alongside her professional activities (projects worthy of mention are the competition project for Todos Santos Plaza in Concord and for the Marina Linear Park in San Diego, the 'Limed Parterre' of Radcliffe College, Cambridge and the project for Candlestick Park in San Francisco), she has participated in numerous art exhibitions, obtaining extensive and increasing international recognition.

Costantino Nivola: sketch of the project for the Piazza Sebastiano Satta, in Nuoro

LANDSCAPES
OF
SCULPTURE

THE PIAZZA SEBASTIANO SATTA IN NUORO, SARDINIA (1966)

The Piazza Sebastiano Satta lies within the old core of Nuoro: a compact fabric of construction intersected by narrow, irregular streets, without historic squares. The only public spaces are the widened areas at crossroads, otherwise they have formed at the edges of the historic centre. The Piazza Satta is the fruit of urban planning decisions from the later postwar period.

In 1965 the Municipal Administration, aware of the need to create a square in the older fabric, allowed the demolition of a block of unsafe buildings located between the Via Marconi, the Via Baccarini and the Via Satta. The square is dedicated to the poet from Nuoro, Sebastiano Satta (1867-1914).

Costantino Nivola was commissioned to create the monument to the poet (1966), and also to devise the layout for the square. The artist conceived the piazza as a venue for town life, as a place for meditation between the past and the present, where people can sit and meet, recalling the culture of the Sardinian people.

In actual fact the square is a large widened area, without any obligatory routes through it, where seven streets of the historic centre converge. The houses surrounding it stand alongside each other at irregular angles and partly conceal the roads leading into the square. These characteristics prompted Nivola to order the façades of houses to be painted white, in order to give the square chromatic unity.

The artist's project is then restricted to certain characterizing elements. The paving consists of hewn slabs of stone. Their arrangement into orthogonal rows forms a measuring grid that continues all the way up to the irregular edges of the square. The paved surface is broken up by groups of cobblestones, projecting from which are large lumps of granite from the quarry at Monte Ortobene, overlooking Nuoro.

'Rocks, moved from their natural and familiar environment, separated and divided, arranged thus, form a gathering, a meeting of mythical personalities, in contrast with the geometry of the paving and the architecture of the houses.... That way, as well as better revealing their characteristics and fantastic shapes, the rocks in this context also have a didactic purpose, as they invite the observer to evaluate and, finally, to contemplate...' (from *Appunti dell'artista* (Artist's Notes), a private collection belonging to S. Congiu).

The arrangement of the rocks is in relation to the shape of the piazza: they are concentrated at the widest point, while being in an isolated position they act as an optical focus for the roads entering the square.

Positioned in the niches, either natural or created artificially, are small bronze statues of the poet Satta portrayed at various times of day: working as a lawyer or as the father of a family, while riding or writing poetry. The decision to avoid unnatural poses or symbolic forms prompted the elimination of the pedestals.

Protruding from the ground are seats arranged in parallel rows transversal to the axis of the square, consisting of blocks of stone of the same dimensions as the paving slabs; these are devised by Nivola to be 'a portion of the paving that has risen from the ground to meet us half way in our search for a place to rest'.

Previous page:
General view of the square

Costantino Nivola, the son of a builder who was an expert at construction using stone, was born in Orani (Nuoro) in 1911. In 1931 he was granted a scholarship from the Nuoro Economic Council to attend the Higher Institute for Industry in Monza, where he gained his diploma in 1935. Pagano and Persico were his teachers.

In 1937 he was named Director of Graphics at Olivetti. During a stay in Paris (1938) he met Giorgio de Chirico; he subsequently moved to New York, where he met De Kooning, Sterne, Vincente, Klein, Léger and Calder.

The memory of Sardinian tradition in arts and crafts, combined with the expressive freedom enriched by the relationships with the artists he met in America, characterizes his sculpture, where abstract forms overlap in a severe linearism.

From the late forties come the first bas-reliefs created with the sand-casting technique, invented by him: pouring cement onto a sand base. These bas-reliefs are housed in both public and private buildings.

His first solo exhibition was held at the Galleria Tibor de Nagy in New York in 1950; this was followed by numerous exhibitions in various American and Italian cities.

He created mural graffiti for the façade of the Church of the Madonna d'Itria in Orani and for Hurley House in Boston, and he taught at schools and universities in America, Rome and The Hague.

Among the many acknowledgements he received, he was named an Honorary Member of the Royal Academy of Fine Arts in The Hague. He died in May 1988.

CALIFORNIA SCENARIO IN COSTA MESA (1983)

California Scenario is the name given to an urban revival project carried out in a residual space in the centre of the town of Costa Mesa, in southern California. This approximately rectangular area is surrounded on three sides by tall administrative buildings, and borders on an open-air car park, from which it is separated by a simple white-painted curtain wall. Despite the smallness of its dimensions, Isamu Noguchi's scheme has managed radically to transform the space, suggesting - with a rarefied language that is reminiscent of Japanese gardens - the multiform appearance of the Californian landscape.

As in a theatrical representation - the reference is implicit in the term 'scenario' - the elements constituting the project, juxtaposed according to a paratactic compositional order, appear in their dimension as semantic objects. A vertical cut in the back wall reveals the presence of a spring, from which there originates a water course that finds itself a river-bed with a winding outline, forcibly breaking up the arid paving of large irregular-shaped stone slabs. Monolithic blocks or heaps of stones emerge here and there, recalling the variations in altitude of the great American canyons.

Along the borders, the bare, stony hill that stands against the perimeter wall acts as a counterpoint to the spots of grass and vegetation which, at the foot of the transparent curtains of the buildings, allude to the Californian forests. There is no sentimental attitude to nature here, no direct imitation of its forms. Noguchi's artistic approach consists in the capacity to construct a landscape with avowedly artificial elements. Sculpture, for him, is something more than the creation of art objects to be offered up to gain admiration. It is a much broader experience, involving the human environment in its entirety.

Fuller Sado collaborated on the project.

Isamu Noguchi was born in Los Angeles in 1904, and grew up between Japan, where he lived for some years, and New York.

In 1927, during a stay in Paris, he worked as an assistant to Constantin Brancusi.

In the thirties he developed an interest in environmental art, perfecting his own language, which draws from both Japanese tradition and the heritage of surrealism. He worked with various architects, including Arata Isozaki and Louis Kahn.

His works particularly worthy of mention are the project for the two bridges in Hiroshima (1952), the garden of the Unesco Headquarters in Paris (1956-58), the organization of Hart Plaza in Detroit (1972-78).

He died in 1988, at the age of eighty-four.

Previous page:
General view of the square

Opposite:
Detail of the 'stream' in the paving of large irregular-shaped stone slabs

THE CAMPO DEL SOLE IN TUORO SUL TRASIMENO, ITALY (1985-1987)

The Campo del Sole, conceived as an architecture of sculptures, stands in Punta Navaccia, in the municipality of Tuoro sul Trasimeno, a few kilometres from the centre of population. Far from the road network, without any relationship with the buildings of Tuoro, Campo del Sole is an anomalous square, considering the usual meaning given to the term. It is a public space conceived of as a place for meeting, meditation, recollection, relaxation and contemplation of the natural environment. It is steeped in history (nearby, in 217 B.C., the battle was fought in which Hannibal defeated the Roman army led by consul Gaius Flaminius). Pietro Cascella's project is a work 'in progress', built in three years with the contribution of sculptors of various nationalities. The first nine sculptures were put in place in August-September 1985, another nine during the same period the following year, the last in summer 1987. The Campo del Sole consists of 27 columns, each four and a half metres high and approximately 90 centimetres in diameter, aligned along a route that sketches a large spiral (the simplest shape in perpetual progress) that is 45 metres in diameter. The central core consists of a work by Pietro Cascella, called *Desco collettivo* (Collective Dinner-Table), since the site is intended to provide a place for 'meeting and familiarity'. All the sculptures are made from grey sandstone extracted from the local quarries, and the area's craftsmen contributed to working the stone.

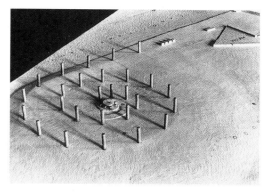

View of the model with the spiral arrangement of the sculptures

The theme of the column was developed according to various interpretations, the fruit of the cultural background of the artists invited to collaborate on the realization of the sculpture-square. Works by African artists have been positioned alongside those of Italian, American, European and Asian masters, without any attempt at continuity of themes.

Campo del Sole is not a monument dedicated to the celebration of a personality or an event, but is a site of joint presence, a place to bear witness, an invitation to come together and enter into a dialogue with the natural surroundings and the different cultural panoramas.

Mauro Berrettini and Cordelia von den Steinen collaborated on the project.

Previous page:
The Dinner-Table with a solar symbol on top, conceived by Pietro Cascella as the symbolic barycentre of Campo del Sole

Opposite:
Overall view of the scheme, from the access point to the tailed spiral

Pietro Cascella was born in Pescara in 1921. He began his artistic training as a painter at his father's school, and completed his studies at the Academy of Fine Arts in Rome.

In 1943 he exhibited at the Quadriennial in Rome. His activity in the late forties and early fifties was characterized by works in polychromatic ceramics, but with clear echoes of Picasso and surrealism. This period produced the sketch for the War Memorial in Albissola.

He subsequently devoted himself to working with bronze; one of such works that is particularly worthy of mention is *Le Tavole della Legge* (The Tablets of the Law). In 1958, with his brother Andrea and the architect Lafuente, he designed the Monument to Auschwitz, realized in 1967 in stone. In the early sixties he worked on his 'Intonaci' (Plasters), works using crushed earthenware, bitumen or coal on a canvas support; these are evidence of the influence of his meetings with the painter Sebastian Motta.

In 1960 he worked on the fountain for the Piazza di Pescia Romana.

Ever since the seventies Cascella has devoted himself predominantly to stone sculpture. Since 1977, when he moved to Verrucola, he has moved his field of investigation into larger-scale works. From 1979 to 1983 he worked on the 'Monument to Every Day' for the Silonian Study Centre of Pescia Romana; at the same time he created the monument dedicated to the Fallen Members of the Resistance in Massa Carrara and the Monument to the Carabinieri in Monteroni d'Arbia. One of the characteristics of his work from this period is that it can be scaled; sculpture is conceived of here as an environment to be lived in.

The works of smaller dimensions propose the anthropological theme, expressed through scenes of birth and motherhood.

Of his most recent works, two particularly worthy of mention are *La Nave* (The Ship; 1986-87), made of Carrara marble, situated on the Lungomare in Pescara, and *Blocco verticale* (Vertical Block; 1990) for Farmitalia in Ascoli Piceno.

THREE URBAN PROJECTS

The relationship between square and sculpture is one of the themes that characterize the planning of contemporary urban spaces. In numerous situations the task of furnishing a site with meaning is entrusted to sculpture. The works by Arnaldo Pomodoro, which are highly charged figuratively, with allusive references, repetitiveness and diversity, seem particularly suitable for this purpose. There are a large number of these, but we present here those created for the Amaliehaven Garden in Copenhagen, for the Piazza in Lampedusa and for City Hall Square in Brisbane.

THE AMALIEHAVEN GARDEN IN COPENHAGEN (1981-1983)

The Amaliehaven Garden is situated between the octagonal Amalienborg courtyard, surrounded by the buildings of the Royal Palace, and the Inderhaven, the internal port, or canal port. It occupies a rectangular area beside the road connecting the medieval core with the Kastellet and the canal.

Pomodoro and Delogne designed the site to relate to both the historical Amalienborg court and the large waterway.

In his design for the green area, Jean Delogne was inspired by the richness and harmony of the gardens of the eighteenth century. He has created a location to sit and rest, to observe the port activities and to contemplate the sea.

The sculptures by Pomodoro represent the ideal point of contact between past and present, as well as a concrete mediation between the different functions that characterize the area. Four square-based pilasters with 80-centimetre sides, of which two are seven metres tall and the others nine metres, highlight the vertices of an imaginary square shape that circumscribes a fountain with a circular basin.

Though they all have similar shapes, each of these obelisks expresses its own individuality through

certain distinctive elements differentiating its surface. Their shapes recall those of the 'mainmasts', hence they take on a symbolic function of unusual berths for ships. The positioning of these obelisks and their differentiated physiognomies are used to form a rudimentary setting, oriented towards the equestrian statue of Frederick V which stands in the centre of Amalienborg, reproducing the tradition of French royal squares.

The decision to create these 'obelisks' using a combination of burnished bronze and the verdigris produced by corrosion over time is designed to echo the character of the dome of the Royal Palace, where 'the ribs gleam and the copper is reflected in the reliefs'.

At the extremities of the Amaliehaven Garden stand two fountains, with which Pomodoro expresses in an overall image the vitality and destiny of the country.

The water is conceived of as a characteristic element of the Copenhagen cityscape and as an instrument of reflection into the origins of life.

A PIAZZA IN LAMPEDUSA (1987)

The idea of an obelisk-sculpture was taken up again in Lampedusa in 1987. The Municipal Administration commissioned Arnaldo Pomodoro to build a War Memorial to be placed in the town square. The study was drafted in collaboration with Dialmo Ferrari and Ermanno Casasco.

The rectangular surface of the Piazza in Lampedusa is bounded on two adjacent sides by residential buildings and on the other two sides it opens onto the road. Emerging from the cobblestone of the floor surface are groups of boulders, chosen from among the rocks of the island, arranged in such a way as to create places to sit down and talk: a setting where people can feel they are protagonists and express their sense of belonging to the place. Pomodoro's large bronze obelisk, similar in shape to the four masts in Copenhagen, is positioned near the corner of the square that opens onto the two roads.

Arnaldo Pomodoro's obelisk in the small square in Lampedusa

CITY HALL SQUARE IN BRISBANE (1983)

The 'Shapes of Myth', sculptures created by Isgrò for the *Oresteia* by Aeschylus, staged in the ruins of Gibellina in summer 1983, testify to a different relationship between square and sculpture. In the 'Shapes of Myth', the work of art is transformed from a symbol of the culture and history of a people into a 'large figure' in a dialectic relationship with the square. These sculptures are similar in shape to geometrical bodies: the square-based pyramid, the cone, the parallelepiped. They can be transported by means of bars which, as Pomodoro affirms, 'contain the actors coming out of the doors of the sculptures themselves, which in their form define and clothe them; they appear to perform as actors and as men of today'.

They currently stand in City Hall Square in Brisbane. The Studio Gregotti e Associati was responsible for designing the ornamentation for this square, in collaboration with Ermanno Casasco. The square occupies a vast quadrangular surface. Along one of its long sides stands a platform that surrounds a rectangular pool of water on three sides. The structure has the appearance of a stage, on which the 'Shapes of Myth' are positioned. The position of the sculptures is the result of an attempt to make them visible from every point in the square. A double row of trees around the platform creates green stage wings which partly conceal the buildings around the public space.

J. Delogne, E. Casasco, D. Ferrari, Gregotti e Associati collaborated on the project.

The 'Shapes of Myth', positioned at different points, as though on a stage, in City Hall Square in Brisbane

Arnaldo Pomodoro was born in 1926 in Morciano in Romagna, but lived the years of his youth and professional training in Pesaro. He studied architecture, scenography, goldsmithery, and only subsequently sculpture. This enabled him to enrich his works with the contributions acquired from his previous experiences.

In 1954 he moved to Milan. He has received numerous awards: in São Paolo in Brazil in 1963, in Venice in 1964, one of the six international awards from the Carnegie Institute in 1967, the Grand Prix Henry Moore in Japan in 1981, and, in 1990, the Japan Art Association awarded him the Imperial Praemium for sculpture. In 1992 Trinity College Dublin awarded him an Honorary Degree in Letters. His exhibitions have been plentiful: at the Rotonda della Besana in Milan in 1974, at the Musée d'Art Moderne de la Ville de Paris in 1976, at the Forte di Belvedere in Florence in 1984, as well as travelling exhibitions in museums all over the world.

His works stand in many squares in Italy and abroad, in the Pepsi Cola Park, outside Trinity College Dublin, at Mills College in California, at the Department of Water and Power in Los Angeles, in the Cortile della Pigna at the Vatican Museums and in major public collections.

He has taught at a number of American universities.

He has been responsible for designing the stage sets for certain Italian theatre productions: for Rossini's *Semiramide* at the Opera in Rome in 1982, for Gluck's *Alceste* at the Opera in Genoa in 1987, for Stravinski's *Oedipus Rex* in Siena in 1988, for *The Passion of Cleopatra* in 1989, and for Eugene O'Neill's *More Stately Mansions* in 1993.

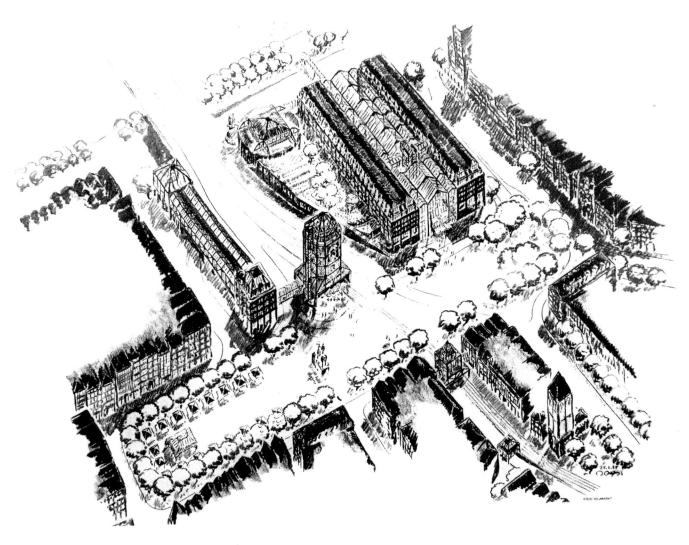

Gottfried Böhm, project for the Prager Platz in Berlin

THREE SAMPLE CITIES

THE PLATEAU BEAUBOURG IN PARIS (1971-1977)

Strategically placed in the heart of the historic centre of Paris, less than a kilometre away from Notre-Dame, the Plateau Beaubourg has enjoyed popularity without compare in the French capital, at least ever since the creation of the Centre Culturel Georges Pompidou by Renzo Piano and Richard Rogers. If it may appear barren at first sight as far as formal attractions are concerned - especially if you compare it with the figuratively highly charged architectural device overlooking it - it cannot be denied that, of all the public spaces in Paris, it is the one that most uninhibitedly welcomes and promotes the public and social rituals that are traditionally staged in a square.

The definition of the external space is resolved with a small number of elementary ingredients: a slightly sloping parvis which seems to convey the crowds of passers-by into the voracious mouths of the great cultural machine; a 'cut' in the parvis, the start of a second slope, inclined in the other direction, which gives access to the underground rooms; a granite paved surface bridled within the geometries of a cross-banded grid of blue and white stone. And in the background, beyond the three pairs of hatchways (serving as air intakes for the underground areas) which reproduce the blatantly technological language of the Centre Pompidou, the continuous wings formed by the well-aligned outlines of Parisian residential buildings. If truth be told, the space outside the cultural centre is one of the elements that have most changed its configuration during the various development phases of the project from which today's Beaubourg was generated.

In the project presented at the competition in 1971, which was awarded first prize by an international jury headed by Jean Prouvé, a lowered pedestrian square was envisaged (approximately 3.20 metres below street level) as a direct continuation of the broad forum located below the building, made possible by the structural solution on *pilotis*.

Previous page:
Aerial view of the Plateau Beaubourg, the centre of gravity for Parisian social life on the rive droite

Below:
The frontage of the Centre Culturel Georges Pompidou facing the square. The building is conceived as a tectonic mechanism that draws its figurative power from the blatant externalization of its technological and structural components.

Commencing with the second version, of May 1972, the square began to be populated with episodes, housing artificial terraced hillocks with planted vegetation, gigantic screens for TV projections, igloo-shaped pavilions and tall flagpoles anchored to the ground by metal stays.

In the general ground plan that accompanied the executive project dated 1974, the sloping solution, which was later realized, finally involved a subdivision of the space on the basis of activities: a performance area equipped with steps and a small podium; a series of square-moduled pavilions for cultural and commercial activities; a play area for children; a large pentagonal marquee to house a bar; a small exhibition centre and a garden corner.

Beyond the different possibilities of formal configuration, the esplanade outside the cultural centre has nonetheless always remained faithful to its initial premise: to be a flexible and open space serving communication. That is to say, borrowing an expression dear to Renzo Piano, 'a Parisian Hyde Park Corner'. Flexibility is in fact the leitmotif that has guided the designing of the whole of the Plateau Beaubourg.

Conceived as a large multi-purpose machine, the Centre Pompidou is built in such a way as to provide the whole supporting structure and the service equipment along the external perimeter, thereby obtaining an interior space (with a surface area of 50 x 170 metres on each floor) that is completely free from space restrictions.

The decision to 'externalize' all the functional components also guided the figurative choice, to the extent that the Beaubourg has the appearance of an organism with its insides open, where the different construction components can be recognized by all simply on the basis of colour (the supporting structure is white, the air-conditioning system blue, the vertical circulation system red, the water system green, the electrical one yellow, etc.).

Perfectly consistent with its multi-purpose vocation, the version of the Place Georges Pompidou that was actually built contains nothing but its own inclusiveness. An inclusiveness that is realized in the simplest, most immediate way, with a sloping level that gathers and distinguishes (is it legitimate, here, to suspect an implicit citation of the Campo in Siena?).

The absence of any preliminary spatial subdivision actually allows the space to be filled on each occasion, according to requirements, using provisional structures and stage wings for the succession of performances, parades, fairs and concerts.

The animated sculptures by Jean Tinguely and Niki de Saint-Phalle for the fountain in the Place Igor Stravinsky

THREE SAMPLE CITIES

'A square is what happens in a square' was said of Gio Ponti's creation in Eindhoven. Yet this appears truer than ever if referred to the Plateau Beaubourg.

The tiny Place Igor Stravinsky, which opens along the southern side of the Centre Pompidou, has been resolved in a totally different manner. Here the concern was not to convey a heterogeneous crowd of 'users', but to give an urban configuration to the uniform terrace covering the underground spaces of the IRCAM (Institut de Recherche et Coordination Acoustique/Musique).

Using a more traditional approach, recourse was made to a large fountain, designed jointly by Jean Tinguely (creator of the metal robots that spurt out jets of water in all directions) and Niki de Saint-Phalle (author of the coloured plastic forms).

Image of the groups of people around the spontaneous performances that enliven the square every day

Renzo Piano was born in Genoa on 14 September 1937 and graduated in architecture at the Milan Politecnico in 1964. In his years at university he combined an apprenticeship at Franco Albini's studio with on-site experience in his father's construction company. He subsequently worked with Louis Kahn in Philadelphia and with Makowski in London.

A key influence in his training was his friendship with the French engineer Jean Prouvé. His association with Richard Rogers dates back to 1971, when their victory in the competition for the Centre Georges Pompidou brought them international fame. In 1977 he began a partnership with Peter Rice; in 1980 with Richard Fitzgerald in Houston.

He has received numerous awards (worthy of mention here are the Compasso d'Oro - Gold Compass - and the Honorary Fellowship in the United States), and has taught as visiting professor at a number of U.S. and European universities.

His most renowned works are: the IRCAM in Paris (1973-77), the Menil Museum in Houston (1983-84), the Olivetti offices in Naples (1984) and the Bari stadium (1988-89). Among those in the process of completion: the restructuring of the Lingotto in Turin, the Museum of American Art in Los Angeles and the Kansai Airport in Osaka.

The Renzo Piano Building Workshop is based in Genoa, Paris and Osaka.

Richard Rogers was born in Florence on 23 July 1933. Since 1939 he has lived in London, where he gained his diploma at the Architectural Association in 1959.

In 1963 he founded Team 4 with his wife Sue Brumwell and the architects Norman and Wendy Foster, designing the Reliance Controls Factory in Swindon (1967). In 1971 he became partners with Renzo Piano; in 1977 with John Young and Marco Goldschmied, launching the Richard Rogers Partnership.

This studio is responsible for the Lloyd's Building in London (1978-86), the Inmos plant in Newport (1982) and the reconversion of the Royal Docks in London (1986) and the Fujisawa Shopping Centre in Tokyo (1987).

He has received countless international awards; those worthy of specific mention here are his nomination as Fellow of the American Institute of Architects (1984), the Gold Medal for Architecture from Yale (1985) and the title of Chevalier de l'Ordre National de la Légion d'Honneur (1986). He has also been visiting professor in Europe, the United States and Canada.

THE PLACE DE STALINGRAD IN PARIS (1986-1989)

The context into which Bernard Huet situated his Place de Stalingrad is a site replete with historical memory.

   Located at the edge of the city centre, approximately one kilometre from the park of culture and leisure, La Villette, the former Place de la Rotonde at one time formed one of the sections of the Parisian customs barrier, erected on the eve of the Revolution to separate the city from its *faubourgs*. Evidence of this former functional use remains today in the shape of the neat geometrical volume of La Rotonde, built in 1789 by Claude-Nicolas Ledoux as lodgings for the customs officers. The two toll-houses which initially stood beside it, positioned to control the main accesses to the city from the north-east, the road for Flanders and the one for Germany, are now gone, however.

   In the early nineteenth century, the original radiocentric configuration created by Ledoux, which included a double row of poplars arranged in a hemicycle around the Rotonde to balance the curvilinear course imposed by the surrounding residential building, was denied by the strong axial directrix of the dock of La Villette, which Napoleon ordered to be built there to strengthen river links with the capital.

   Finally, in 1905, in line with the process of functional decommissioning that invested the area, turning it into a storage warehouse (the abolition of the toll-house dates back to the mid-nineteenth century), the raised lie of the city Métro definitively broke off any spatial relationship between La Rotonde and the curvilinear frame formed by the crossroads between the boulevards.

   The redesigning of the layout only began in the early eighties, when restoring the area outside Ledoux's Rotonde for public use was included among the key points of Chirac's programme for converting the north-east sector of the city. It was significant that Bernard Huet was chosen for the project, as he was the architect who from the pages of the magazine *Architecture d'aujourd'hui* had

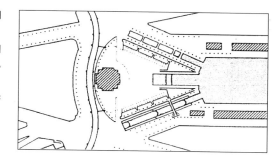

Above:
Ground plan at the level of the esplanade

Previous page:
The circular shape of La Rotonde de la Porte de la Villette, built by Claude-Nicolas Ledoux as lodgings for the customs officers, is reinforced by the fountain forming the element of mediation between the Place de Stalingrad and the stretch of water of the canal.

Below:
Detail of the grass glacises bordering the square on each side. The higher terrace forms a tree-lined promenade joining up with a belvedere overlooking the canal.

on more than one occasion called people's attention to the unavoidable need to get to grips - in design rather than mimetic terms - with the architectural heritage of the past.

In the case of the Place de la Rotonde, this getting to grips required a flexible approach. It was a matter of reconciling Ledoux's bare, abstract language with the late eclectic decorative profusion of the Métro (a mixture of 'Greek' and 'Assyrian' in the cast-iron columns, an unlikely 'Neo-baroque' in the stone piers), at the same time employing the technical language of the iron viaduct and the hydraulic tradition of French engineering. And all this should give form to an unquestionably contemporary work, where citations of historical origin were not to be resolved in a pastiche.

Having defined the purpose (public and pedestrian) of the area once and for all, the project choice was to take the Rotunda to be the focus of the composition, re-establishing a relationship - which had never really existed - with the Napoleonic dock of La Villette.

After ruling out, for obvious reasons, the idea of reproducing a circular-shaped square, Huet opted for a triangular scheme tapering significantly in the direction of the dock, almost as though he wished to create a spyglass-like frame for the vista of the canal. Needless to say, a part may have been played in the genesis of the project - more or less knowingly - by a formal reference to the Place Dauphine, with which the western head of the Ile de la Cité had been resolved more than two centuries before. Presenting itself as an element generating the symmetrical plan governing the whole composition, La Rotonde forms the ideal pivotal point between the square and the city, partly denying the western limit constituted by the convex lie of the Métro.

Bordering the triangular space on the sides are two new constructions; these, significantly, are shaped like two 'bastions' (obviously a reference to the city's old customs barrier) facing - with two sloping glacises covered with grass - towards the tamped earth central esplanade. The terraces at the top of the bastions, which are accessible via flights of steps, are conceived as two tree-lined promenades which terminate in the belvedere-promontories overlooking the docks of La Villette. Located below these, in the rooms facing directly onto the water's edge, is some of the service equipment (supply pumps, filtering apparatus, maintenance systems), screened from the outside by a colonnade, the intentionally elementary language of which begs comparison with the simplified Doric adopted by Ledoux.

The two colonnades that converge in the direction of the canal frame the view of the La Villette docks. Inspired by the bare and essential language of Ledoux, the colonnades conceal the service rooms located below the belvedere. terraces.

THREE SAMPLE CITIES

The stone walkway that divides the fountain from the canal conceals the presence of a water filtering system.

A fountain is placed at the caesura between the grassy glacises and the colonnades; this acts as a link between the square and the stretch of water of the canal. Framed by small water spouts positioned around it, the central rosette - for which an obelisk dedicated to Ledoux was planned - cleverly disguises the presence of the ventilating shaft of the underground railway below. In the same way as the sequence of stone slabs that separates the canal basin is an artifice to conceal the water filtering mechanism.

Finally, the character of the central esplanade as a tree-lined square is underlined by placing a double row of maple trees with stone benches between them inside square-shaped lawns at the foot of the glacises. Completing the ornamentation is an enfilade of streetlamps in the style of the Second Empire, still in production at the behest of the City of Paris Lighting Department.

Consistent with its symbolically defensive function, the external view of the bastions has an austere outline. An unbroken facing of decorative strips of bossage forms an ideal continuation of the more austere component of Ledoux's architecture, while the frieze of engraved characters on the parapet is an overt homage to the 'revolutionary' architect, running through the complete list of the toll-houses he built.

Outside flow the two lateral canals which branch off on oblique trajectories from the waters of La Villette docks. The southern arm is the link with the underground tract that flows into the canal of Saint-Martin and is equipped with a lock to regulate the different water levels. The northern arm is used as a reservoir and has a pedestrian walkway in the centre, framed by four fluted cast-iron columns with an unusual capital. These are four of the Formigé-style columns that support the raised lie of line two (Formigé was the head architect of the city of Paris who ordered the Métro's structures to be embellished in the *beaux-arts* style). They were repositioned here to form propylaea when the decision to open the area below the viaduct to vehicle traffic made it necessary to replace them with more functional supporting structures.

Bernard Huet was born in 1936 in Quinhon, in Vietnam. He attended high school in Toulon, and subsequently, pursuing his passion for classical culture, he made trips to Greece and Italy.

After gaining his diploma he studied law, but he immediately broke off these studies to devote himself to architecture. He studied with Georges Gromort in Paris, then with Ernesto Nathan Rogers at the Milan Politecnico.

In 1963, in Philadelphia, he worked in Louis Kahn's studio. Two years later, on his return to France, he began teaching.

A fervent opponent of the *beaux-arts* method, he was one of the leaders of the 1968 students' movement, founding L'Unité Pédagogique n. 8 in Paris. In 1974 he joined the editorial staff of the magazine *Architecture d'aujourd'hui*, of which he was editor-in-chief until December 1976. In the mid-sixties, with David Bigelman, Bernard Leroy and Serge Santelli, he formed the TAU Group (Théorie-Architecture-Urbanisme), whose projects for the Parque de la Villette (1976) and for the town of Rochefort (1977) are particularly worthy of mention.

Professor at the École d'Architecture n. 8, he has his own professional studio in Paris. A collection of critical and theoretical writings is published in his book *Anachroniques d'Architecture* (AAM, Brussels).

LES DEUX PLATEAUX AT THE PALAIS ROYAL (1986)

The expanse of columns Daniel Buren has used to reclaim the court of honour of the Palais Royal for use by the public as a contemporary urban square is not merely to be considered a work of sculpture, more or less intrusively qualifying and decorating a space that is predefined architecturally.

Consistent with other works undertaken on location by the French artist - though he gives the impression of installing his objects provisionally, as if on display temporarily - he endows them with a symbolic resonance, conferring a radical new meaning on the context within which they are located. The 'otherness' that all everyday spaces possess potentially if their appearance is altered for occasions of celebration or mourning is in fact one of the basic themes of Buren's artistic quest, stemming from a profound questioning of the role - and the possible purpose - of contemporary art. In this particular project at the Palais Royal, which Buren conceived in close cooperation with the architect Patrick Bouchain, he has had to take on a site with a powerful character of its own.

Situated between the entrance façade and the double colonnade separating it from the garden, the court of honour of the Palais Royal is in fact a closed space with a rectangular plan, delimited on three sides by a homogeneous porticoed screen of architraved Doric columns. The presence of the portico of columns, explicitly inspired by compositional forms from the classical tradition, infuses the enclosed space with a linear and repetitive rhythm.

With his design explicitly superimposed on the pre-existing compositional structure, Daniel Buren's first concern has been to provide a geometrically based key to interpreting this space, amplifying the visual perception of the columns in a multiplication that we could define as kaleidoscopic. The paved surface has been subdivided into a geometric orthogonal grid consisting of basic square forms (13 x 20 in total), the 319-centimetre sides of which are equal to the distance

Previous page:
Detail of a sequence of cylindrical pillars, aligned with the colonnade dividing the court of the Palais Royal from the garden behind

Below:
Overall view of the scheme. The variation in height that characterizes Daniel Buren's pillar-columns generates a contrast between the sequence of horizontal planes, all parallel with the base level, and the oblique plane determined by the gradually increasing heights of the central columns.

between the centres of the columns of the northern arcade facing the garden (in fact, the only alignment with the side porticoes is with the central fornix of the atrium, located on the western side). At the centre of each square is a circular pillar, always on an axis with the western arcade; the height of these pillar can vary from the 'zero level' constituted by the planimetric representation up to the virtual height of the columns. A sequence of spatial planes is thus created, each defined by the alignment of pillars (ideally column drums) of the same height, all parallel and all horizontal, which amplify and confirm the horizontal plateau that the composition develops.

At this point, however, an element of disturbance can be perceived. In certain spots the perspective vista of the columns highlights a second oblique plateau, the inclination of which 'unveils' the basement below. Through three cuts made in the orthogonal mesh of the paving, looking like a metal grating on the plan, the underlying floor in fact materializes, along with the watercourse that provides the true impost level for the pillars. At this point the whole spatial organism clouds into ambiguity, leaving one to presuppose an ideal - and theoretically infinite - continuation of all the pillars below the plane represented by the paving.

The decorative treatment of the pillar surfaces also contributes to the general effect of alienation. The multiple repetition of the alternating black-and-white stripe motif (given concrete form here by inserting bands of black marble into light-coloured concrete) is a stylistic code which characterizes all of Daniel Buren's recent work and which provides an effective interpretation of some key points of his poetics.

In the first place, in many Oriental cultures alternating two-coloured strips are one of the most immediate systems for transforming everyday reality into a ritual space. Secondly, repeating two tones in alternating strips holds considerable possibilities for negating the traditional concept of a work of art.

Generally, if developed on a flat surface, alternating strips can be considered to be a painting, yet they depart from the concept of the painting as a field of figurative limitation.

Applied to three-dimensional objects, as in the case of the Palais Royal, the bands can be considered to be a work of sculpture; yet this sculpture does not respect the rules of construction of plastic bodies, obeying instead the principle of extension by repetition. Their theoretically

The decorative treatment of the pillars with alternating black and white bands obeys the principle of extension by repetition. In Buren's poetics, this is an instrument to combat the traditional image of the work of art.

limitless multiplication finally abolishes any possibility of finiteness, eliminating the aura of perfection that traditionally accompanies any definition of a 'work of art'.

In the apparent continuity that has guided the designing of the Deux Plateaux at the Palais Royal, there is therefore a hidden conflict between the artist's activity and the pre-existing spatial configuration.

It is almost as though Buren's columns - potentially infinitely multipliable and theoretically limitless - wished to negate the reassuringly measurable and replete framework of representation as staged by the architecture of classicism.

The orthogonal lines that divide up the floor surface into square-based modules are differentiated by different graphic markings.

Diagram of the ground-plan layout. The square-based modular grid is broken by three 'cuts', which reveal the impost level of the pillars on the underlying floor through the grating of the covering.

Daniel Buren was born in Boulogne-Billancourt (Hauts-de-Seine) in 1938. He studied at the School of Applied Arts and at the École Nationale Supérieure des Beaux-Arts (ENSBA) in Paris.

The maturing of his personal language dates back to the mid-sixties, when he discovered in the motif of two-coloured bands (grey and white or black and white) the possibility of a radical critique on the work of art based on an automatic and impersonal pictorial output. For Buren these two-coloured bands represent a means of exploring the constituent elements of painting and of investigating the relationships between the objects that make up our sensory reality.

This path of development has led to his becoming involved directly with architecture, creating numerous provisional on-site projects.

A tireless creator, he has participated in more than 250 solo exhibitions and has received a number of acknowledgements, including an award from the Biennale des Jeunes in Paris (1965), the Leone d'Oro at the Biennial in Venice (1986) and the international Grand Prix for painting and sculpture (Stuttgart, 1991).

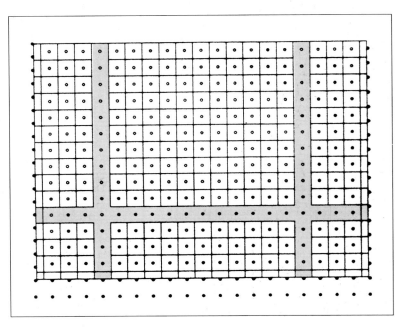

LES ECHELLES DU BAROQUE (1979-1985) &
LE CREUSET DU TEMPS IN PARIS (1987-1988)

Placing a building alongside another formally similar one does not produce the sum of two buildings. The result is the compositional principle that generates the street or the square.

Ricardo Bofill's Taller de Arquitectura are well aware of this, and ever since their projects from the early sixties the revision of the modern tradition that they have promoted has been orientated towards reproducing the compact and planned urban environment of seventeenth- and eighteenth-century cities. They have recognized baroque urban planning theory's merit of knowing how to reconcile the rigorous sequence of homogeneous façades with the varied and unpredictable effects of a monumental and scenographic spatiality.

Involvement with the French context, which has absorbed most of Bofill's design activities since the sixties, has only amplified this latent tendency. From the Versailles 'trident' to the elegant Places Royales in Paris, there is in fact a vast repertoire of models capable of demonstrating the enduring attractiveness of formally defined and complete urban spaces.

Bofill's historicist premise has found a surprising terrain for experimentation in the rigid prefabricated systems imposed by the building requirements of low-cost housing. From the orthogonal grid project for Les Arcades du Lac near Versailles to the surreal geometries of the Palacio in Les Espaces d'Abraxas in Marne-la-Vallée, the Catalan architect has progressively developed his own classicism, epitomized by macroscopic out-of-scale constructions and a totally new functional use of individual components.

The project for a low-cost social housing complex in a block of the Zac Guilleminot-Vercingétorix, in the fourteenth Parisian *arrondissement*, represents the culmination of this series of creations. Facing on the east side onto a broad circular square, defined by the pre-existing urban fabric (the

Previous page:
Detail of the hemicycle-shaped northern square. The perimeter curtain of buildings, the regularity of its layout marked by a gigantic order of pairs of parastades, is a transcription into contemporary terms of the monumental classicism of the baroque age.

Below:
View of the hemicycle from the entrance towards the Rue Vercingétorix. The arrangement of the open space reproduces in synthetic form the spatial structure of a baroque garden, defined by the perspective alignment of balustrades, cippi and flower beds.

Place de Catalogne), Les Echelles du Baroque - the name given to the project - houses 274 flats organized into two distinct blocks, each of which is articulated around an inner square. Inserted between the two cores is a rectilinear pathway that terminates in a monumental arch facing onto the Place de Catalogne, bringing out the central symmetry of the curvilinear frontage.

The north block forms a hemicycle-shaped square, defined at the edges by a homogeneous curtain of monumental paired pilaster strips, which are placed in the spaces between the regular sequence of openings. With a plinth that rises to the level of the first floor and extends to cover another four residential floors, the parastades are surmounted by a Doric frieze with triglyphs whose repetitive metrical structure establishes the position of the windows of the sixth floor. The inner space is in the style of a French eighteenth-century garden, with rectangular flower beds connected in the perspective by rows of *cippi* and alignments of balustrades.

The south core includes a similar central concave space (later named the Place de Seul), with an elliptically shaped ground plan. If we exclude the enormous portal and the entrance with propylaea that define the accesses positioned asymmetrically, the square is entirely circumscribed by an unbroken sequence of huge Doric semicolumns faced with reflective glass panels. Only at the top-floor level does a prefabricated cornice openly state the residential function of the whole complex with its regular series of windows. In the interior the geometry of the space covered with lawns is controlled by a classical-style balustrade; this changes shape in certain sections, creating semicircular balconies.

Bofill's project thus employs the square as the generating element of the residential complex, subordinating the constructed spaces to the rigid uniformity of the perimeter curtains. This attitude is consistent with the Catalan architect's design philosophy, whereby he aims to transfer the monumentality and urban quality that characterize the compact pattern of the historic city onto the formless townscape of the suburbs.

The predominant role assigned to the open spaces of interconnection meant that it was subsequently also decided to redefine the shape of the Place de Catalogne, which acts as the main access point to the whole complex. The sculptor Shamaï Haber was commissioned to design this; he

The amphitheatre-shaped south square. The residential building that defines it appears as a Doric colonnade of reflective glass, broken at the centre by a monumental portal which opens in the direction of the south entrance.

devised a fountain to confirm the centripetal spatial layout of the square, at the same time suggesting a metaphorical image of the universe.

Le Creuset du Temps - as the design has been called - consists of a large circular disk (with a 50-metre diameter) comprising 300,000 blocks of partially dressed granite. The disk, which has the appearance of a huge monolithic block emerging from the ground, is on an incline, with a difference in level of 2.4 metres between the upper and lower parts, and has a continuous thin layer of water running down it, becoming a cascade at the edges. The lighting at night, which comes from apertures inside the perimeter fosse, arouses the sensation that the disk is weightless and is floating freely on the water.

The façade of the residential complex looking onto the Place de Catalogne. In the middle of the square Shamaï Haber's design suggests a metaphorical image of the universe, with a huge granite disk that seems to hover in mid-air.

Born in Barcelona in 1939, **Ricardo Bofill** gained his diploma in 1956 at the Technical High School of Architecture in his city of birth, and then continued his studies at the University of Geneva.

In 1963, with a group of collaborators, he formed the 'Taller de Arquitectura', the combined methodology of whom resulted firstly in the projects for the Barrio Gaudí in Reus near Terragona (1964-68) and for the 'Walden 7' on the outskirts of Barcelona.

Bofill's success in the 1975 competition for the redesigning of the layout of the Les Halles area in Paris marked his passage to activity at international level.

His projects completed in various European countries - France, Spain, Belgium and Sweden - as well as in Algeria and in the U.S.A. are characterized by an architecture which also reinterprets the monumental characteristics of classical architecture in the low-cost residential building projects completed using prefabricated systems.

Shamaï Haber is a French sculptor of Israeli origin who, since the sixties, has been engaged in a personal investigation centred on the relationship between the plastic form (generally compact stone or slate masses) and the space, whether urban or natural, into which the work is placed. Particularly worthy of mention here are: the granite monument of the Atomic Centre in Rehovot in Israel (in 1962, alongside Philip Johnson's functionalist building), the fountain in the Vondelpark in Amsterdam (1964), the exterior layout of the Faculty of Science in Reims (1961), the landscaping-scale project for the Municipality of Vitrolles in the Bouches-du-Rhône region (1982) and the layout design (currently in progress) for the Carrefour de la Plaine de France, north of Paris.

THREE SAMPLE CITIES

THE PUBLIC SPACES OF LA DÉFENSE IN PARIS

The service industry pole of La Défense, located in the western suburbs of Paris, was developed in the mid-fifties as an administrative stronghold as part of a programme of decongestion of the old city centre.

Thirty years on - thanks also to its easy accessibility and the policy of patronage promoted by the EPAD (Établissement Public d'Aménagement de la Région de la Défense) - the new quarter has acquired many of the characteristics of a central urban area, adding residential and commercial functions, cultural and recreational activities and considerable potential as a tourist attraction to its original service-sector uses.

The large rectilinear *parterre* exclusively for pedestrian circulation that forms the backbone of the complex, an axis that is located on the historic directrix of Paris linking the Louvre with the Place de l'Étoile, in fact provides the backcloth to the view of an extensive series of urban layout design projects which make La Défense a privileged laboratory for experiences of contemporary *ars publica*.

The western end of the *parterre*, by the exits to the Regional Metropolitan Railway (RER) and State Railway (SNCF), is the most representative nucleus of the new administrative 'city'. It is here, in fact, that the two most architectonically interesting buildings in the whole complex are located: the CNIT, with its characteristic aerial vault on three points of support, which came about with the very idea of La Défense as proof of the ambitious urban planning programmes of those years, and La Grande Arche, built in 1989 from a design by the Danish architect Otto von Spreckelsen, which has become one of the symbols of Paris today. The huge parvis that stretches out at their feet is identified by a graphic pattern of large squares, cut by a white diagonal, which with its offset orientation dynamically accentuates the perspective in the direction of the capital.

Previous page:
The western end of the huge parterre *of La Défense, conceived as an open-air sculptural walkway*

Below:
View of the parterre *from the Grande Arche. The white diagonal that breaks up the orthogonal grid of the paving dynamically accentuates the vista towards Paris.*

Standing at the foot of the Arche, in a northerly direction, are 25 cylindrical pillars, grouped in six different constellations by filiform connections waving in the air. Created in 1989 by the Japanese sculptress Aiko Miyawaki, the work belongs to the series of *Utsurohi* (a word which in Japanese expresses the concept of mutation) that was launched in the town of Ichinomiya and has evolved - through thirteen imperceptible metamorphoses - as far as the very recent creation sited beside the Olympic Stadium in Barcelona.

With a constant height of four metres, each pillar consists of a galvanized steel column covered in a vitreous material with a smooth, shiny unalterable surface. Welded to the metal heads are stainless steel cables of different thicknesses and lengths, which seem to issue forth from inside the columns. The cables wave in the air, giving an idea of freedom, lightness and elasticity, and sketch ethereal designs on the surface of the sky.

At the edge of the central parvis, near the south gate, is the Place des Degrés (or the Place Pascal), the result of a competition promoted by the EPAD in 1982, and won by the Polish artist Piotr Kowalski. To overcome a difference in levels of ten metres, structured around three different terraces, Kowalski has created two wide stairways that operate as keys to the interpreting of the geometries subtending the spatial structure. The rising sequence of steps - made dynamic by the presumed movement of a wave made of granite that emerges from the lower stairway - is in fact the visible sign of two pyramids, the vertex of which is synthesized by a metal rod positioned at the top, while the base is represented by luminous lines impressed on the paving. The paving of the upper terrace is characterized by an orthogonal grid of white bands subdividing the space into square nuclei - partly paved, partly grassed - from which there project the blind prisms that conceal the technical volumes of the warehouses located on the level below. Among these is an iceberg-shaped sculpture, covered in grey ceramic tiles and consisting of a lively succession of differently sloping pyramids.

Continuing along the axial directrix that links the administrative centre with Paris, the parvis of squared paving gives way to the Place de la Défense, which has conserved in its name the memory of the widened area of the quarter that formerly stood there.

The sculpture by Alexander Calder, in the middle of the parterre

THREE SAMPLE CITIES

In actual fact, the bronze sculpture by Louis-Ernest Barrias depicting the Defence of Paris in 1870 (whence the name of the whole quarter) used to stand in the middle of that space; it was moved here in 1983.

Utsurohi, a work by the Japanese sculptress Aiko Miyawaki

Two modern sculptures now act as counterpoint to the above; one of the *Stabiles* by Alexander Calder opposite the police station, and two fantastic figures by Joan Miró, placed at the entrance to the Le Quatre Temps shopping centre.

In a dominant position, crosswise in relation to the central *parterre*, stands a large fountain designed by Yaacov Agam, spurting from which are 66 water jets in synchronization with a musical programme.

The rectilinear perspective then continues with the Esplanade du Général de Gaulle, a wide tree-lined avenue flanked by shops which concludes at the eastern end of La Défense, opposite the Pont-de-Neuilly. Here stands a welcome sign by the Greek artist Takis, devised for the 1974 competition by invitation and built in the mid-eighties. Projecting from a rectangular basin of over 2,500 square metres in size are 49 luminous signs, each composed of a black-painted steel pole with an aluminium sheet head at the top fitted with a light source.

The different shapes of the heads and the varying heights of the metal supports (from 3.5 to 9 metres) create an effect of mobility that is amplified with the undulating brought about by the wind and the different coloured lights. Takis' large surreal flowers are in fact the silent messengers of a modern polytheism that refuses all monopolies of culture and power in its pursuit of the Platonic utopia of good government.

The roof covering of the Grande Arche positioned at the western end of the *parterre* has also been used to form a square.

Based on a design by Jean-Pierre Raynaud, a Map of the Sky has recently been realized, inscribed on the four 400-metre-square patios on the top floor. Projecting in fragments from the paving of large white marble slabs is the representation of the zodiac circle; the symbols of the different signs are made of black granite.

THE SANTS STATION SQUARE IN BARCELONA

The layout designed for the Plaça deis Paisos Catalans, better known as the Sants Station Square, fits into the vast programme of conversion of urban public spaces promoted by Barcelona's municipal administration since 1980. At the time that Piñon and Viaplana were commissioned to redesign it, the area of the project, in a zone of residential expansion at the western edge of the city, was a formless, undifferentiated open space, bombarded by the traffic flowing in the direction of the Sants station.

The presence of railway tracks in the underground level below the square excluded both the possibility of planting greenery and also any recourse to large volumes, suggesting rather a 'light' scheme. With this premise, the designers have succeeded in developing an original solution that finds consistency and cohesion in the relationship - and sometimes in the contrast - between independent and differentiated metal manufactured items.

At the centre of the square a pedestrian walkway with a corrugated roof gives a longitudinal directrix and acts as an element of separation between the two differently characterized sectors.

Dominating the side facing the sea is a square pavilion, supported by sixteen thin metal supports and covered with a translucent shelter roof receiving light from below, from a large reflector inclined at 30 degrees.

On the opposite side, starting from the marble wall curtain which, like a triumphal arch, defines the entrance to the covered walkway, a winding sequence of benches circumscribes an area set aside explicitly for sitting and relaxing. The slight alterations in height of the pink granite paving follow the uneven ground level, allowing the geometrical layout underlying the project to appear; this creates a slight slope, down which flows the water from low spouts protruding directly from the ground.

Eric Miralles collaborated on the project.

Helio Piñon and **Albert Viaplana**, born respectively in 1942 and 1933, gained their diplomas at the Barcelona School of Architecture (ETSAB) in 1966. In their university period, both were assistants to Rafael Moneo; they formed a partnership in 1963. Beginning with the designing of the layout for the Sants Station Square - a project which earned them the FAD award for architecture and the Ciutat di Barcelona award for 1983 - they have been involved predominantly in the designing of urban spaces, defining a strategy of action that is far removed from both historicist evolcations and green solutions.

Within an ordering scheme that establishes the directrices of the project in planimetric terms, they place an abundant repertoire of technical objects and ornamental elements (metal screens, cantilevers, benches, fountains, light beams, etc.), tending to suggest, as Ignasi de Solá Morales has acutely observed, a space abstracted by the ritualization of objects.

Previous page:
View of the square in the urban context. In the foreground is the winding row of benches that defines the western side. Visible in the background, to the right, are the pavilion and the pedestrian walkway, covered with a corrugated outlined 'pergola'.

Opposite:
Modular metal elements mark the regular rhythm of the open space outside the Sants Station. In the background, beyond the broken-line screen, the square pavilion facing in the direction of the sea is visible.

THE CLOT PARK IN BARCELONA (1984)

The Clot Park is located in the Sant Martí quarter, one of the suburban districts of Barcelona built in the latter postwar period at the edge of the Ensanche (the urban development planned by Idelfonso Cerdá at the turn of the century).

The park extends over a surface of approximately three hectares occupied by the depots of the RENFE (Spanish state railway) until 1976, the year these were decommissioned following the approval of the Plan General Metropolitano.

Freixes and Miranda, winners of the competition announced in 1982 for the conversion of the area, have devised a multi-purpose arrangement where the characteristics of an urban park and a civic square are both present, deeming it necessary to once again provide the city with a public space capable of offering varied and diversified possibilities for use. The ground surface covered by the scheme, which is rectangular in shape, is divided into two areas: to the south the square, to the north the park.

The square is paved, and is articulated in two bands: the outer one forms the element of mediation between the Clot Park and the quarter. The rows of trees and the remains of the pre-existing railway depot in the south-west corner emphasize the boundaries of the scheme. The inner band is surrounded on two sides, to the west and south, by a gradatory that links the square to the floor level of the outer band and thus to the block. The resulting area is more secluded, and is intended to host sporting activities. A multi-purpose hall has been built to the east of the square.

The north area of Clot Park is conceived as a 'natural island' in the city. The earth excavated to lower the ground level of the paved part has been used to create knolls surrounded by trees, chosen from the typical Mediterranean flora.

As in the area serving as a square, the park area has also kept part of the structure of the decommissioned building. Indeed, the limits of the park are highlighted by maintaining the old arched perimeter wall of the disused depots. A section of the west side is re-used as a waterfall, the water from which is collected in a small artificial lake at the foot of the hill.

The site is given identity by maintaining some of the elements of the pre-existing construction, conserving the memory of the past. Two elevated walkways cross the park diagonally with respect to the geometry of the space. As well as serving as points for observing the urban layout, these raised walkways connect the garden area to the square and thence to the city.

The carefully studied lighting system brings out the different characteristics of the public space. Four triangular-based towers, with reflective surfaces, bound the civic square. The raised pathways are highlighted by luminous arches transversal to the course of the axis. Groups of tall, thin cylinders light up the various areas of the park.

Eulalia Gonzales, Chechu Sanz, Dolors Andreu and Manuel Rui Sanchez collaborated on the project.

Previous page:
Detail of the waterfall at the western end of the park

Below left:
Ground plan of the square

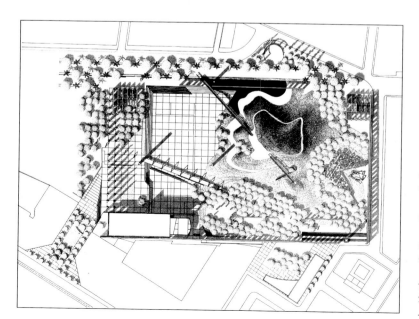

Daniel Freixes Melero was born in Barcelona in 1946. He studied at the Escuela Técnica Superior de Arquitectura de Barcelona (ETSAB), where he graduated in 1971. In 1975 he followed a doctorate course.

After his degree he devoted himself predominantly to teaching activities; he has been professor of Design and Composition and currently teaches Planning at the Technical High School for Architecture in Vallés in Barcelona.

He has been a member of a number of juries for competitions on public works, interior architecture and restoration.

He has held conferences and seminars in Spanish schools and universities. For the Clot Park project, developed with Vincente Miranda Blanco, he won the FAD prize in 1987 and the Prince of Wales award for urban design in 1990.

Vincente Miranda Blanco was born in Logroño, in Old Castille, in 1940. He gained his diploma in 1963 at the Technical School of Architecture in Barcelona and in 1973 at the Escuela Técnica Superior de Arquitectura.

His professional activities span various sectors, from the fitting out of exhibitions and sets for performances to architectural design and the planning of public spaces, as well as interior decoration.

He has received numerous awards, particularly for his project for the Zsa Zsa Cocktail Bar and for the set design for performances such as *Tierra*, held at the Pavilion of Navigation at the EXPO in Seville in 1992.

THE PLAÇA D'ANGEL PESTAÑA AND
THE PLAÇA FRANCESC LAYRET IN BARCELONA (1986)

The Plaça D'Angel Pestaña and the Plaça Francesc Layret are in the Nou Barrio (New Quarter), one of the housing schemes in the suburbs of Barcelona outside the nineteenth-century Ensanche. They occupy part of an area of approximately 8,000 square metres allocated for the creation of a series of public spaces, which are sadly lacking in a quarter characterized by condominium buildings. The project is part of the programme of conversion of the city's public spaces, and provides for the rearrangement of four areas to form a large L shape. The western end and the point where the two arms join are organized as squares, respectively the Plaça Francesc Layret and the Plaça D'Angel Pestaña, while the connections between the two squares and the termination to the north are designed as pedestrian axes (not yet realized).

The Plaça Francesc Layret occupies a square-shaped surface separating the dense mass of building fabric between the Carrer de Casals Cuberó and the Vía Julia, an important axis of communication for the city. The Plaça D'Angel Pestaña occupies the end of a block delimited by one of the quarter's internal roadways.

Enric Pericas y Bosch has conceived the Plaça Francesc Layret as an oasis in the city, modifying the topography of the site and creating embankments where the lawns alternate with flowers and trees typical of Mediterranean flora.

The different levels are connected by kerbs, designing geometrical paths, and forming a pedestrian link between the two roads facing onto the square. The huge sculptures by Jaune Plensa, similar to erratic boulders, placed along the side beside the Vía Julia, lead into the pedestrian axis that is to connect the two squares. In the Plaça D'Angel Pestaña artificial and natural elements merge, generating a multi-purpose space.

The centre of the surface, at the point where future pedestrian axes are to intersect, is highlighted by a stretch of water, usable also - once the water is removed - as a multi-purpose platform. Located on the edge of the pool is a bronze sculpture by Enric Pladevall, with the appearance of tree bark. To the south of the small lake there extends an esplanade surrounded by trees of various species which recreate a natural setting, while to the north a multi-purpose hall has been built, partially sunk below ground level, for sporting activities. The roof is designed at a higher level than the square, and is also to be used as a space for sports, such as skating.

The square is linked to the pedestrian axis that is to form the northern end of the system of public spaces via a tree-lined path, the paving of which is designed with geometrical shapes.

Pere Camps collaborated on the project.

Enric Pericas y Bosch was born in Barcelona in 1957. He attended the Escuela Técnica Superior de Arquitectura de Barcelona (ETSAB), where he graduated in 1982. He followed specialization courses in landscape architecture, and in 1989 he gained his masters degree at the Universitat Politecnica de Catalunya (UPC).

He has held courses at the Barcelona Agriculture School and at the ETSAB.

He has been responsible for designing residential buildings and sports and hospital structures; in particular he has been active in planning public spaces, both in Barcelona and throughout the region.

Since 1992 he has directed the Servei d'Elementos Urbans at the city hall of the Catalan capital.

Previous page:
The central pool near the terraced roof of the multi-purpose hall of the Plaça D'Angel Pestaña

Opposite:
Plastic model of the project for the Plaça Francesc Layret

Above:
View of the Plaça Trilla

Above right:
The Plaça de la Virreina, opposite the church of St. John

Opposite:
The majolica decoration of the access ramp to the underground car park, with the raised pedestrian walkway of the Plaça del Sol

THREE SAMPLE CITIES

THE SQUARES OF GRACIA (1981-1985)

Gracia was an urban core independent from Barcelona. Through the process begun with the nineteenth-century expansion of the Catalan city, it has been transformed into a residential district.

This incorporation has upset the balance of the small centre of population. Multi-storey buildings have been erected alongside the characteristic dwellings, with their two floors above ground, suffocating the narrow streets. Cars have invaded the roads and the squares.

The Municipality of Barcelona decided to commission a single studio to convert the squares of Gracia, considering that the homogeneity of the various projects would also contribute to restoring the unity and identity of the quarter.

The architects Bach and Mora were given the job of converting the following squares: Rius and Taulet, Sol, Diamant, Virreina, Trilla, Raspall, Nord, Unificació and Rovira. These were anti-monumental squares, surrounded by often inferior, unhomogeneous architectures. The elimination of the car parks, the careful designing of the urban ornamentation and the paving materials have made it possible to highlight their specific qualities and embellish their character.

THE PLAÇA TRILLA

This has been designed as a 'small oasis'. Freed from traffic, it has trees planted in a geometrical grid. The road leading to the square, pedestrianized and paved with the same material, seems to perform the double role of main entrance and link between the two blocks that border it.

THE PLAÇA DE LA VIRREINA

This square is delimited to the east by the façade of the church of St. John. The decision to also forbid indiscriminate parking in the streets flanking the church has the purpose of expanding the square, thereby creating the idea of a 'square with a church in the middle', as the paving and the rows of trees emphasize.

The double row of trees has been designed to throw shade on the benches, envisaged as places to sit and chat.

The focal point of the urban space in this case is constituted by the façade of St. John's, embellished by the trees, the paving and the flagpoles.

THE PLAÇA DEL SOL

The largest of Gracia's squares, this is the covering for an underground car park.

The lighting system, studied to the smallest detail - just as the other decorative elements - by Bach and Mora, uses reflected light, obtained with a 1.2-metre diameter white disk. This, along with the benches and a row of plane trees, defines the south side. To the east, the access ramp to the car park is hidden by a portico decorated with coloured majolicas. A raised pedestrian walkway joins the square to the footpath, crossing the obstacle formed by the ramp. The north side is characterized by magnolias and semi-spherical terracotta flower-boxes, on which bronze coats of arms of the city are shown.

To the west, beyond the two pedestrian accesses to the car park, bounded by wrought-iron railings, there is a sundial showing the signs of the zodiac, a bronze sculpture by Joaquim Camps.

The paving serves the purpose of unifying the different levels and linking the different elements of the square.

Born in 1943, **Jaume Bach Nuñez** graduated at the Escuela de Arquitectura de Barcelona (ETSAB) in 1970. In the same year he began working professionally at the Dols-Millet-Páez architectural studio, and taught the composition course at the ETSAB.

In 1978 the University of Urbino gave him the professorship of the International Laboratory of Architecture and Urban Design.

Gabriel Mora Gramunt, born in 1941 in Barcelona, obtained his diploma as an architect in 1966. From 1966 to 1974 he worked with the Piñon and Viaplana studio; since 1973 he has taught composition at the ETSAB. In 1976 he established a studio with Jaume Bach.

Bach and Mora have dealt predominantly with the conversion of urban spaces. In 1978 they won first prize in the competition to revitalize the historic centre of Badalona, in 1988 for redesigning the layout of the Bospolder Place in Rotterdam. They have participated in many exhibitions, including the XIII Biennial in Paris (1985).

In 1992 they were present at the exhibition held in Florence on 'Barcelona 1981-1992. Urban Transformation as Urban Planning Project'.

JAUME BACH AND GABRIEL MORA

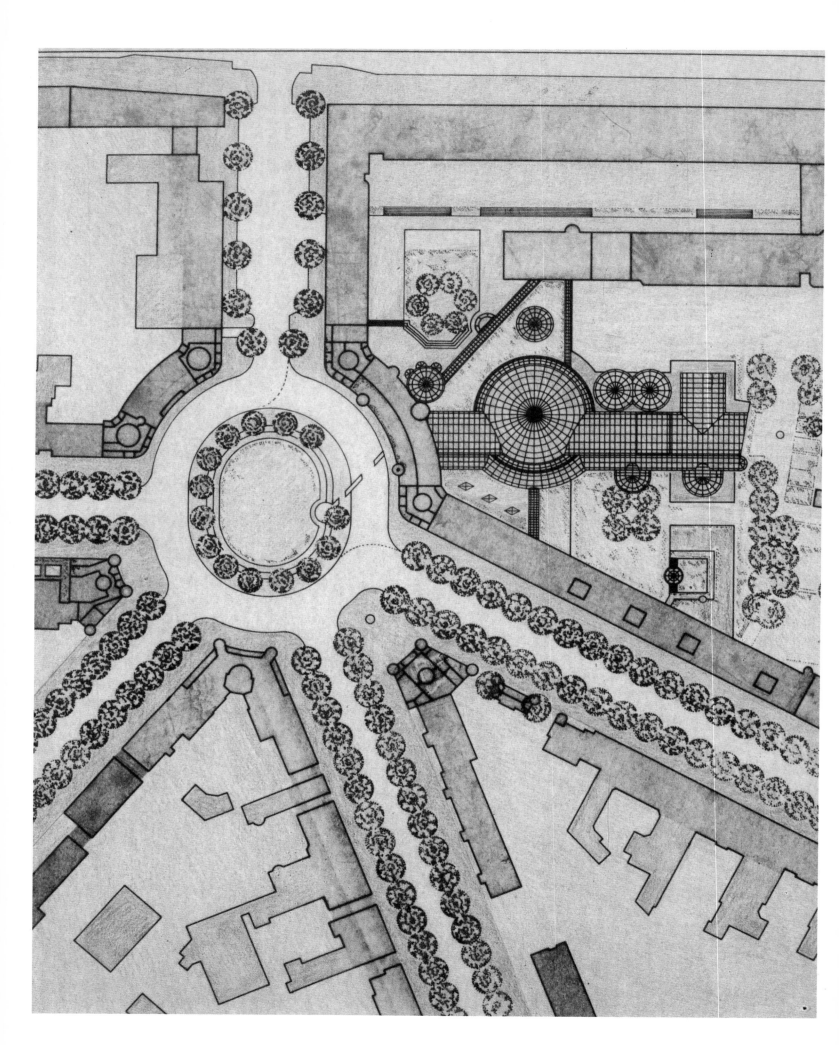

THREE SAMPLE CITIES

BERLIN - CITY OF TOMORROW

Berlin developed chiefly in the second half of the nineteenth century, in little more than seventy years. The plan drafted by James Hobrecht in 1862, the year in which the city's expansion was reaching its highest levels, contributed to consolidating and accelerating the process of 'industrialization and building construction at all costs'.

Like all German cities, at the end of the Second World War Berlin appeared very seriously damaged, and entire areas were reduced to piles of rubble. Aggravating the situation, after the war there was a strong desire to remove memories of the past, to suppress any residue of the culture of *Nationalsozialismus*.

The Marshall Plan once again proposed the idea of unbridled industrialization, paving the way for reconstruction that was fast, to the point of being wild, and based on hurried planning. The Wall built in 1961 divided Berlin into two parts, truncating important axes of communication and inflicting deep wounds on the urban structure. In the meantime avant-garde urban planning culture was on the retreat compared with the position of the Modern Movement, which had set the problem of design on a lower plane with respect to the crucial points of the urban problem. An attempt to regain space in the city was undertaken in the seventies at international level, yet the desire to put this into practice in Berlin began only in the eighties, with the Internationale Bauausstellung Berlin (IBA).

The IBA set itself the task of restoring Berlin's lost urban identity, yet limited its actions to only one of the two parts of the city. The knocking down of the Wall (1989) brought the debate on the future of this metropolis to the fore.

The case of Berlin reflects and amplifies difficulties present in other contexts and poses questions of urban design that are of general interest.

Within the debate on the redesigning and the critical reconstruction of the city, the theme of the square has certainly been an important point, inasmuch as the will clearly emerged to reaffirm the traditional framework of urban architecture constituted by the system of roadways-squares-blocks. Yet the problem of the square in particular has so far remained for the most part unresolved. Only one of the IBA competitions has set as its specific objective the redesigning of the layout of a square: Prager Platz.

In another competition announced by the IBA in 1983, concerning the organization of the area of the Kulturforum, the proposal was made by the architect Hans Hollein to open up a large pedestrian square articulated across two levels, outside the church of St. Matthai. Having once again proposed the nineteenth-century housing model of the block as the one to be adopted, the IBA has brought about the creation of numerous semi-public spaces inside blocks, rather than full-blown squares; these spaces are a continuation of the tradition of the Hof.

Courts, small courtyards and gardens were understood as places for collective gathering, relaxation, and as such they were designed.

With the falling of the Wall, the central theme of the international debate is now the redesigning of the heart of the city, the reconstruction of the centre of a large metropolis which, for totally exceptional reasons, is studded with large, still empty spaces.

THE MEHRING PLATZ (1968-1975)
WERNER DÜTTMANN

The Mehring Platz is in Kreuzberg, one of the quarters of Berlin seriously damaged by the destruction of the Second World War. Cut in two by the Wall, to the 'west' it became home to Turkish emigrants, avant-garde artists and students, thus transforming itself into a suburban area of the city rich in cultural and political ferment. The problem of its re-use has been one of the main themes in the postwar reconstruction of Berlin, and with the fall of the Wall it has become a nodal point in the redesigning of the heart of the capital city.

At the southern end of the Friedrichstrasse, the Mehring Platz has been built where before the war the Belle-Alliance-Platz was situated.

Below:
The circular fountain at the centre of the Prager Platz, with
the residential building designed by Gottfried Böhm in the
background

THREE SAMPLE CITIES

The project by Werner Düttmann has once again proposed the traditional round shape and a design consistent with the theme of the ornamental Berlin square. A curtain of houses with five floors above ground delimits the circular space of the square. Now free of traffic, it has been transformed into a garden, with lawns, trees and benches.

Thus a multi-purpose space, an area to sit and relax, has been designed. The paving design has been formed by the pedestrian footpaths, which emanate like rays from the centre, causing the area to be partitioned into eight zones of planted greenery.

The extension of the Friedrichstrasse, which cuts the square diametrically from north to south, is the main pedestrian footpath, and is considerably larger than the others. A winged Victory on a column by the sculptor Raich (1843) has been placed at the centre of the Mehring Platz. A second curtain of houses, semi-circular in shape, bounds a large pedestrian walkway with shops that runs around the square.

J. Burtin, E. Grassow, C.A. von Halle, S. Hein and R. Scheper collaborated on the project.

THE PRAGER PLATZ
GOTTFRIED BÖHM

The project for the Prager Platz is the result of a competition by invitation announced by the IBA. The initial premise was the need to revive the memory of the historic city by taking into consideration the lie of the road network and conceiving the city in the traditional terms of the street and the square. The competition envisaged the redesigning of the layout of the Prager Platz, in an attempt to confer upon it a precise function of reference for the surrounding quarters. The following architects participated in the competition: Gottfried Böhm (Cologne), Rob Krier (Vienna), Carlo Ajmonino (Rome) and Aldo van Eyck (Amsterdam).

The Prager Platz is located at the intersection of five roads and is one of those urban spaces that until the nineteenth century broke up in a rather haphazard manner the thin road layout at the points where the traffic converged.

A 'simple hole in the plan' Werner Hegemann defined it, in a polemic against the new urban planning arrangement given the city by James Holbrecht (1862-81), the author of the new plan that was to have led to the more unrestrained urban expansion and property speculation. From the turn of the century until the Second World War, the Prager Platz was surrounded by beautiful houses in eclectic style, on the ground floor there were shops and restaurants, the pavements were broad, an open invitation to go for a stroll. It was a typical ornamental Berlin square, with a green central reserve, simple and unpretentious, but not without a certain ceremonial quality.

During the Second World War, the houses on the Prager Platz were completely destroyed and to date these 'wings' to the square have only partially been reconstructed. The IBA competition was won by the architect Gottfried Böhm, who in his project for the general redesigning of the layout for the area took account of the square's particular charm, due to the irregularity and individuality of the streets converging on it.

The constructions have been designed by a number of different architects, and once they have been built they should form a unitary whole. The square has maintained its original regular oval shape, surrounded by buildings with a green central reserve; at one time this was cut in half by the rails of the tramway, but today it is brightened by the presence of a fountain.

In 1981 the IBA announced a second competition for the designing of the central space of the square; this was won by Holm Becher, Klans Baesler and Bernard Schnidt.

THE AUGSBURGER PLATZ (1981-1982)
URS MÜLLER AND THOMAS RHODE

The Augsburger Platz is a stone's throw away from the Breitscheidplatz, the main square in West Berlin, dominated by the broken spire of the Kaiser-Wilhelm-Gedächtniskirche, in the new barycentre that the 'city of the West' had to invent for itself, once deprived of those areas that had always been the centre of the historic capital.

In 1978 a competition was announced for the reconstruction of the Augsburger Platz, which had been reduced to a pile of rubble during the Second World War, and this was won by the architects Urs Müller and Thomas Rhode.

The project deals with the theme of the city square understood as a multi-purpose space in which

Opposite:
The rectangular stretch of water at the centre of the space
with facilities of the Augsburger Platz

Below:
The circular flower bed of the Mariannenplatz, with the broad
flight of steps leading to the Künstlerhaus Bethanien

THREE SAMPLE CITIES

the natural element alternates with the constructed one of urban ornamentation, giving rise to a new pedestrian area with facilities, a place to relax, to meet and enjoy yourself.

The square has been rebuilt over an underground garage and occupies a richly designed rectangular-shaped surface. The area is subdivided into four parts, all resolved in different ways, and developed at different levels, while rows of trees and hedges define their outlines.

To the east is a square-shaped garden with a brick and wood pergola along its four sides. In the centre, a children's recreation park has been created, facing onto the Augsburger Strasse, with slides, swings and sandpits with brickwork surrounds, and a sort of fun castle.

Two tall rows of trees enclose the space where there is an elongated regtangular-shaped stretch of water. The water source is a fountain, shaped like a small church, located at the northern end of the pool, while benches have been located along the east and west sides.

It would seem that the designer wished to identify a sort of square within a square.

A semicircular theatre concludes the designed space to the west. The pedestrian footpaths along the perimeter and the rays of the semicircle identify four green flower beds and a central stage.

THE MARIANNENPLATZ (1979-1980)
DIETMAR GROTZEBACH, GUNIER PLESSOW, REINHOLD EHLERS

The Mariannenplatz is in the Kreuzberg district and is dominated by the façade of the Künstlerhaus Bethanien: a Neo-Gothic hospital currently used as an alternative meeting place, where a number of artists' studios and craftmen's workshops are situated. Completely destroyed during the war, when the square was first rebuilt, it entirely disrupted the original structure of the site.

A second reconstruction, in 1979-80, attempted to reproduce in general terms the design of the project from before the wartime destruction; realized by Peter Josf Lunné in 1953, it reaffirmed the typical Berlin theme of the ornamental square.

Raised with respect to street level, since it was built on top of the rubble from the war and distributed over different levels, it is prevalently a space of planted greenery, used as a full-fledged urban garden.

Blocks of porphyry have been used for the paving of the non-green area, while strips of basalt mark the edges of the steps linking the different levels.

A circular flower bed stands in the middle of the square, and is highlighted by three concentric circles of basalt set at three different heights. A wide pavement goes around the flower bed, taking you to the flight of steps that leads to the Künstlerhaus Bethanien.

At the sides of the paved area, six layers of grass terracing mark the start of the green areas.

Werner Düttmann was born in Berlin in 1921. In 1939 he began his studies at the Technische Hochschule in Berlin. In 1948 he graduated at the Technical University (T.U.) in Berlin. In 1950 and 1951 he attended the Institute for Town & Country Planning at Kings College, the University of Durham in England. From 1956 to 1966 he worked freelance. From 1960 to 1970 he was full professor at the T.U. in Berlin. From 1971 to 1983 he was president of the Academy of Art in Berlin. He died in 1983.

Gottfried Böhm, born in Offenbach am Main in 1920, is one of the most important exponents of Post-Bauhaus architecture in Germany. While still devoted to certain of the Bauhaus' ethical principles, he has developed a method of research and design of his own, honed over years of professional practice. During the course of his career Böhm has shown an increasing interest in urban planning and has developed his thought, attempting to grasp the link that exists between the forms of private and public space. All his public spaces seem in fact to guarantee continuity between the constructed work and the urban surroundings and give particular importance to the configuration and design of

roads and squares. These characteristics appear particularly in some of his projects, such as for the area around the Cathedral and for the Heumarkt area in Cologne; for the Friedrichplatz in Kassel and for the area around the castle of Saarbrücken. As regards the evolution of his professional career, Böhm studied architecture from 1942 to 1947 at the Technical University in Munich.

From 1947 to 1955 he worked at the studio of his father, Dominikus Böhm, in Cologne. In 1950 he collaborated with the Society for the Reconstruction of Cologne under the directorship of Rudolf Schwarz. In 1951 he worked with the Cajetzn Baumann architectural studio in New York. In 1963 he began his university career at the Technical University of Rhineland-Westphalia, in Aachen, with a professorship in Urban Planning.

Urs Müller was born in 1923 in Zürich, where he graduated in Architecture and Urban Planning. He studies and works at the University of Zürich, and with various companies in Stockholm, London and Berlin.

Thomas Rhode was born in 1944 in Brilon, in Westphalia. He

graduated in architecture. He studies and works in New York, Düsseldorf and Berlin. Since 1978 he has worked with an associate studio.

Dietmar Grotzebach, born in 1937, studied from 1955 to 1960 at the Technische Hochschule in Braunschweig and at the Technical University in Berlin. From 1962 to 1965 he was assistant at the latter university, where he became a lecturer in 1972. A freelance professional since 1965, he died in 1985.

Gunier Plessow was born in 1934 in Berlin. From 1954 to 1960 he studied at the T.U. in Berlin. In 1961 he attended the Royal College of Art in London, and from 1962 to 1964 he was an assistant at the T.U. in Berlin under the professorship of Prof. Hermikes. Since 1964 he has been a freelance professional.

Dino Buzzati: design for the Piazza del Duomo in Milan

AN EPILOGUE

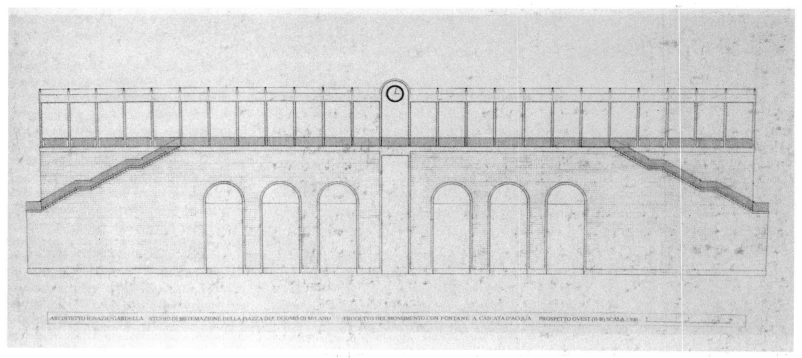

ARCHITETTO IGNAZIO GARDELLA   STUDIO DI SISTEMAZIONE DELLA PIAZZA DEL DUOMO DI MILANO   PROGETTO DEL MONUMENTO CON FONTANE A CASCATA D'ACQUA   PROSPETTO OVEST (B-B) SCALA 1:100

Above:
The project for the Piazza del Duomo by the architect Ignazio
Gardella

Opposite:
View of the model for the reshaping of the Piazza del Duomo,
designed by Ignazio Gardella

MILAN: THE MISSED OPPORTUNITIES

Paolo Favole - Giovanni Terzi

In Milan the problems of the urban design and layout of areas and settings, including central ones, have not been resolved; these have remained in their postwar condition. Indeed, many current debates, such as over the Piazza del Duomo or the Piazza Fontana, are taking up problems from that time. All this means that the Milan of today must still answer questions from forty years ago, within a framework to take account of all the elements involved, with a view to its new role in present and future society.

The various administrations have only pursued 'large-scale urban strategies', so we can well understand that a problem such as how to give back value and meaning to urban squares, even if important, is never felt to be a decisive objective in the reshaping of the city. It must be borne in mind that the projects for Milan are concerned with central areas, of prime importance in city life, such as the Piazza del Duomo and the Piazza Fontana or the *sagrati* (church squares). This is because if, as in other cities, we set ourselves the goal of converting the squares in the suburban areas, the subject would be postponed even further.

Only marginally, and in very recent years, have these approaches seemed to alter, with a public company - MM (Metropolitana Milanese) - announcing a series of competitions to regenerate Milan's piazzas and *sagrati*. The Milanese administration would seem to have understood how, since in the short term the 'large-scale urban strategies' had failed, important transformations in the urban fabric could also be brought about through precisely targeted schemes.

In reality the reshaping of certain squares was only an expedient to formally conceal a technological imperative, the construction of the third underground railway network and of Milan's Through Rail Link.

With these words the reasoning behind the introduction of the various architecture competitions is presented by an MM manager: 'The MM company, in close cooperation with the Municipal Administration, has seen fit to take the opportunity to convert the surfaces tampered with by these works, to overcome a conception of minimum repair, and to act in a systematic manner through more general and organic planning.'

Already from this declaration of intent it can be understood that these competitions came about to put right a situation compromised by the passage of Line Three and the Through Rail Link.

The opportunity has therefore been lost to build a priori an integrated system where the functional part (Line Three and the Through Rail Link) and the formal part (the piazzas and church squares) could come about together within a single intent of supplying the city with a service. Consequently Metropolitana Milanese have announced a series of competitions to commission work on the following squares: the Piazzas Duca d'Aosta/Repubblica, Cavour, Missori and the squares of the churches of San Gioachimo, Santa Francesca Romana and San Carlo al Lazzaretto in Largo Fra' Bellintani. Alternatively, professionals have been directly commissioned to carry out certain other works without there being any competition announcement.

Examples of this are the monument to Sandro Pertini in the Via Croce Rossa by Aldo Rossi or the project by Ignazio Gardella for the Piazza del Duomo, assigned after the Tognoli administration had previously commissioned and paid Enzo Mari to draw up as many as three projects. Metropolitana Milanese have also assigned to Achille Castiglioni the project for the Largo Richini, to Lodovico and Alberico Belgioioso the project for the Piazza Velasca, to Umberto Riva that for the Piazzetta San Nazaro and to Guido Canella that for La Crocetta.

Of all these competitions announced and all these commissions - apart from those for the Via Croce Rossa and the Piazzetta San Nazaro - none is in the construction or completion stage. Yet other competitions have also met with the same fate: this is the case with Garibaldi/Repubblica, won by Pierluigi Nicolin, and today invalidated, or the competition to regenerate the area and the piazza of the columns of San Lorenzo, won by the architects Tintori and Calzavara, still stuck in the second phase, or the double competition for the Piazza Fontana.

All these competitions, though part of a single approach, have not succeeded in formulating a set of prerequisites capable of generating one single large project of architecture, rather than simply of urban ornamentation. Typical of this is the project by the architects Chambry-Zanuso-Pascoe, in the

Piazza della Repubblica, they have designed a raised green platform attached to the gardens of the Porta Venezia in an attempt to generate a continuous system of parks, cutting the city in two. This objective would have been possible if it had become the project theme for the Garibaldi/Repubblica competition. Only the architect Paolo Favole's group considered this an opportunity to also modify this area through a unitary treatment.

A paradox thus occurs: the city that is the unquestionable capital of design worldwide has not been capable of giving itself an urban design through public initiative. Over 1,000 projects produced for these commissions or competitions, far from resolving the priority themes, have only resulted in very insignificant realizations; as though the abundance of project production and the vast eclecticism that has characterized this had suffocated any possibility of decision-making supported by a widespread consensus as to the choices.

Moreover, it can be said that for fifteen years the Tognoli and Pillitteri administrations have not been able to come to grips with any problem of urban layout (not to mention those for squares); this is because they in their turn have been conditioned by a political and administrative debate that has been at one and the same time widespread, derided and inconclusive. Indeed, the only important works, public or private, have been the result of very anomalous and forced procedures (we need only think of the new stadium as a case in point).

Now everything still remains to be done: the speculations over the city have fortunately left this great opportunity intact: let us hope that it is not once again ignored or, the opposite, wasted in a short time with makeshift projects.

THE PIAZZA DEL DUOMO
IGNAZIO GARDELLA (with J. Gardella, F. Nonis, G. Peia)
The long career of Ignazio Gardella began in 1934 with the competition for the Torre Littoria in the Piazza del Duomo in Milan.

After half a century, architect Gardella finds himself once again coming to grips with this piazza that is the symbol of Milan. Thus the idea of a square understood as an open and, at the same time, complete place returns: a space emblematic of the civil value of a whole city. The project finds its constructional theme in the very history of the square, a history of demolitions and reconstructions.

The intention in Gardella's project is for it to be an element of caesura, re-establishing a new order, regulating histories that were at one time unitary. It is the desire to be the instrument of knowledge, carrying with it, in memory, themes of projects never realized, such as those by Pistocchi and Caimi.

Gardella's venture therefore aims to recompose the square in a unitary space through a project that confirms its theoretical basis in the proper relationship with its context. Subsequently the new construction finds its natural home on the west side, precisely where the architect Mengoni had placed a building closing off the square, which was never realized, called the Palazzo dell'Indipendenza.

Of this building Gardella says: '... it fitted between the south and north porticoes and overlapped them for a section: the fact that it overlapped rather than stood beside gives a greater sense of closure, like a lid closing a box.' Hence the idea of placing a new element between the monument to Victor Emanuel and the Palazzo Carminati; a monument with fountains and cascades of water consisting of a gallery, or rather of a 'civic tribune', positioned on a huge plinth marked by the shadow of six apertures arranged in two sets of three antae and symmetrically with respect to the central passage.

THE PIAZZA DEL DUOMO (1983)
ENZO MARI
The debate that took place in the eighties around the problem of the Piazza del Duomo must not be understood to set into question the latter's significance as the focal point of the city, but as a recognition of the inadequacy of the nineteenth-century layout for current social and political requirements.

Called upon to give a response in terms of 'urban ornamentation', Enzo Mari proposes three alternatives that can be interpreted as progressive variants on a single design approach. The area of the scheme covers the public spaces surrounding the Cathedral and goes as far as the threshold of the Piazza Reale, including the Piazza della Scala; these are seen as a pedestrian island that needs to be regenerated and embellished.

The first hypothesis was borne of the consideration of the square as a stage for collective events and is resolved in the redesigning of the paving of the whole pedestrian island in a homogeneous and uniform manner. The decorative motif that Mari proposes for this unitary surface is a mesh of large squares, each of which having the distance between the centres of Mengoni's porticoes as its sole reference point.

The second hypothesis has as its title 'The square as the institutional centre of two fundamental civic functions', and proposes the construction of the so-called 'city café' and the use of a floor below the church square to house the Metropolitan Museum of the Lombardy Region.

In his third proposal Mari uses an axis in the direction of the Palazzo Reale to cut a piece of the Arengario, reconstructing the course of the 'Manica-Lunga' (Long Sleeve) demolished in 1936 and establishing an improved connection between the Piazzetta and the Piazza del Duomo. A mirror-glass façade should plug the 'wound' inflicted on the building from the thirties. The Café and the Museum, as in the second solution, are the two poles that must support the quality of civil participation in the square.

THE PIAZZA DEL DUOMO
GIORGIO MADINI MORETTI, EMILIO SALA, ANDREA MADINI MORETTI

In March 1984 forty-seven studies were put on display at the San Fedele gallery as a contribution to the debate under way on the future of the Piazza del Duomo in Milan. At the meeting organized by Padre Bruno, the man responsible in the Diocese of Milan for running the San Fedele cultural centre, it was envisaged that a mention of merit would be awarded to the first three projects chosen by a jury composed of both architects and citizens who had been involved with the exhibition.

The project by the architects Madini Moretti received a mention for the impact of its forceful modification of the square's layout.

The point of departure of the architects' design thesis is the presence of two negative characteristics of the square: the first being the overlarge dimensions of the square itself, which thus removes value from the cathedral, and the second being the lack of a standpoint from which to observe the Duomo.

The response given in this project to the problems is the creation of two zones: one contemplative, obtained through the construction of a gradatory which, shortening the proportions of the piazza, makes the Duomo visible frontally by compressing the perspective, which today is too long; the other

The project by the architects Madini Moretti for designing the layout of the Piazza del Duomo

an active zone, made possible by the construction of an iron and glass building (in an attempt to establish relations with Mengoni's Galleria) to house commercial functions, including a full-blown covered 'market'.

THE PIAZZA SANTA FRANCESCA ROMANA
FRANCO DELL'ORTO, MARINA BASSO, MARIA VITTORIA BOCCONI, GIOVANNI TERZI

The project sets itself the task of reviving the meaning of *sagrato* as 'a sacred space standing before the Church', identifying it through a rotation of the plan and its paving.

Through the paving design, the project aims to identify certain layouts or marks that are capable of both weaving together a context marked by unplanned schemes and establishing new hierarchies between the spaces.

The extension on an ideal plane of the Via Spallanzani, which is envisaged as being pedestrianized, terminates within the new church square; the latter serves, and not only formally, to underline the old perspective relationship between street and church, which has today been obliterated.

The aim is to create the impression that this piazza, which is the product of the intersecting of the traditional routes with the nineteenth-century orthogonal grid, provides an opportunity not only to cross but also to sit and rest.

Finally a third mechanism establishes the mediation between the street and the piazza-*sagrato*, qualifying itself as a different element upon which different materials are placed (porphyry), and upon which collateral functions rest (parking areas). Thus the three exits from the Through Rail Link line become the functional and architectonic elements that formally reshape the sites; these sites, in the unitariness of their decorative elements and the materials used for them (trachyte and beola gneiss), seek specific identity in relation to history and today's presences.

THE PIAZZA SANTA FRANCESCA ROMANA
LUIGI MARIA GUFFANTI, PIERGIUSEPPE DIODATO, GIORGIO REBOLI

The project in the empty urban area that provides the competition theme has been carried out with a certain 'lightness of touch', implying the coming to terms with a reality characterized by the historical stratification of constructions.

Defined by multiple actions that are interconnected yet easily interpreted, the project seeks an image that is ordered and at the same time articulated and flexible. A square-shaped copse of *acer saccharinum* filters the traffic coming from the Viale Regina Giovanna, while a row of these trees along the Via Cadamosto stands in relation to the building opposite like the wings of a stage, delimiting its contents.

The covering of the moving stairway, made of arched methacrylate plates, is supported by pink quartzite columns, the rhythm of which is taken up in the balustrade of the nearby stairway and in the double row of pillars surmounted by tubular streetlamps that draw attention to the modular grid of the pedestrian square.

This project too sets itself the goal of marking, through a rotation of the plan, two moments in the same square: the *sagrato* and the piazza proper. The paving design of the pedestrian square, modules comprising squares of red porphyry and white granite from Baveno, is broken up by the rectangular carpet that defines the space of the *sagrato*, following the orientation of the church façade.

The dynamic rhythmic structure of the white granite geometrical lines on the 'carpet' matches the cadence of the lines forming the outline of Santa Francesca Romana.

THE PIAZZA DUCA D'AOSTA / THE VIA VITTOR PISANI / THE PIAZZA DELLA REPUBBLICA
CARLO CHAMBRY, ANTONIO ZANUSO, WILLIAM PASCOE

Redesigning the Repubblica/Duca d'Aosta axis provides a great opportunity to weave back together the fracture created in the quarters between the Corso Buenos Aires and the Via Melchiorre Gioia. Indeed, this was the objective sought by the project, together with the redefinition of the identity of a sequence of spaces situated along the Via Vittor Pisani.

In the intentions of the project, the Piazza della Repubblica thus becomes the gate to a new urban system, housing a two-hectare garden that restores form and unity to the 'square of hotels'.

The reduced dimensions of this square piazza (90 x 90 metres) is intended to amplify the presence of the Bacciocchi tower and the Soncini-Mattioni skyscraper; two broad pedestrian walkways lead into the porticoes of the Via Vittor Pisani, the 'virtual centre' of the new system. The channeling of the traffic to the centre and the large pavements move the sides of the street closer, both perceptively and physically, giving it an appearance that is more in keeping with its function, to welcome those coming out of the station to the city. The Piazza Duca d'Aosta, bound to the station's system of relationships, free from constructions and completely pedestrianized, becomes the *sagrato* of the building, which reappropriates the 'gallery of carriages'. Freed from the vehicle pollution and brightened up by the restoration, the latter goes back, in the best Milanese tradition, to being a place for interrelating and for facilities on an urban scale, hosting a series of functions that are currently crammed inside the old ticket offices and acting as a pedestrian link to the system of adjacent squares. The Piazza IV Novembre is reserved for public transport, and is divided up into a tree-lined island with a kiosk and two long benches at right angles for the urban bus terminus, together with a large taxi-rank.

THE PIAZZA FONTANA (1989)
GINO POLLINI, GIULIO MARINI, GIACOMO POLIN

The project that won the second competition for the reconstruction of the Piazza Fontana starts out with the consideration that in the centre of Milan there are few usable green spaces and that this competition could provide the opportunity to create a garden near the Duomo.

The square proposed is in fact entirely planted with greenery, following an order that can be read through the paving design; a proper pedestrian square thus takes shape, connected to the system of the Piazza del Duomo and the Corso Vittorio Emanuele.

A new building is envisaged in the part still undeveloped following the demolition of the Commerce Hotel. This is to house commercial activities on the ground floor, hotel and reception facilities on the upper floors and spaces for congresses on the floor below ground level.

The Piermarini fountain, kept in its current position, will stand off-centre in the new square, and will be decorated with benches and enhanced by the addition of a statue. To resolve the traffic flow problem, in the last section of the Corso Europa the traffic should be diverted, shifting the tram terminus to between the former court building and the Verziere gardens.

THE BASILICA DI SAN LORENZO COMPETITION
SILVANO TINTORI, MAURIZIO CALZAVARA

There are two themes in the project to redesign the layout of the area, which can be summed up in the need to recompose the urban fabric along the axis of the Corso di Porta Ticinese and in the desire to consider the Parco delle Basiliche as an element in the context of San Lorenzo.

The succession of historical events and the haphazard process of decay have determined the current conditions of unhomogeneity that the designers propose to resolve through the regeneration of the networks and buildings of the historic fabric.

It being utopian to reproduce the layout of the inner city walls, the project envisages a re-evaluation of the areas of the old *sostre* transformed into welcoming terraces, in the shade of trees. Yet the axis of the Corso di Porta Ticinese is recognizable; there are plans for this to be pedestrianized to give greater impact to the project.

The *stradicula* (little street) serving the walls has remained intact by the Via Pioppete, and a 'gate-house' is planned to close off to the east, while a covered street and porticoes created in the middle of a square lead this back to the Via Mora.

The regenerating of the buildings in the eastern lot is understood as a recomposition of the site where the new construction continues and completes the existing one. In contrast, a more unitary architectural solution has been sought in the western lot, providing for a building constructed in accordance with the alignments and heights of the 1953 city planning scheme.

The space around San Lorenzo is organized in such a way that the green area of the Basiliche reaches the sides of the church and a 'mirror' wall identifies a civic space towards the columns and a religious space in front of San Lorenzo. With the creation of the wall, the designers wish to open up new vistas which can be reached thanks to the 'promenade' stairway that is located between the wall diaphragms. In the second-degree project a stairway and a lift have been introduced; these lead underground, where three potential museum buildings are planned.

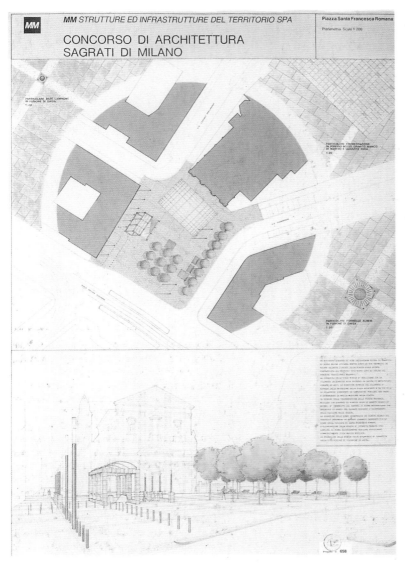

Above:
Winning project in the competition for the Piazza della Repubblica-Via Vittor Pisani, by the architects Chambry-Zanuso-Pascoe

Opposite:
Project redesigning the layout of the Piazza Santa Francesca Romana, by the architects Guffanti-Diodato-Reboli, winners of the competition 'The sagrati in Milan'

THE BASILICA DI SAN LORENZO COMPETITION
UGO LA PIETRA (head of group), LUIGI MACHERONI
Betti Arienti, Giuseppe Gaviraghi, Giuseppe Habe, Cristina Pallini collaborated on the project

In the project for conversion of the area certain fundamental choices can be inferred, through schemes which on each occasion give specific answers to the problem areas identified, and which prove to be emblematic and therefore extendible to the whole city.

The project foresees the construction of a homogeneously paved, rectangular piazza, with organic 'fractures' at intervals and a stretch of water in which the columns, a purely scenographic

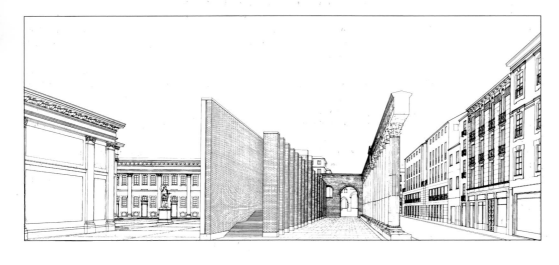

Project by the architects Tintori-Calzavara for the redesigning of the layout of the Basilica di San Lorenzo area

device, are reflected.

The project envisages the realization of a series of 'strong points', indicator elements, along the axis of the Via De Amicis. These take the form of eight towers and serve the purpose of resolving the sudden setback positionings and architectonic and visual voids along the street frontage. An important aspect of the project is the realization of a construction along the Corso di Porta Ticinese, a space compromised by the presence of buildings of limited architectural value.

This building has a mixture of uses: commercial on the ground floor, residential on the upper floors, with services on the top floor. It faces the square, and has a large opening that leads to a gallery at right angles to the square itself; the desire to give continuity to the frontage along the Corso di Porta Ticinese, rendered impossible by recent construction in the Via dei Fabbri, is expressed through a 'scenographic cutaway' and a small square with its colonnade broken up.

The project proposes a series of small operations that are intended to characterize the broken heads and blind frontages of the Via Pioppette and the Via Molino delle Armi. These operations are not intended to resolve the problem created by the blind frontages, but rather to highlight the limitations of these.

Ignazio Gardella was born in Milan in 1905 to a family from Genoa, where the profession of architect has been a tradition for four generations. He studied civil engineering at the Milan Politecnico and at the same time gained practical experience at his father Arnaldo's studio.

In 1931 he graduated and began his independent professional career. In 1949 he graduated in architecture at the IUAV in Venice, where in 1962 he taught with a professorship in Elements of Composition.

His works are among the most significant in Italian rationalism. Particularly worthy of mention among his early architectural work are the layout of Villa Borletti in Milan (1935-36) and the antitubercular dispensary in Alessandria (1938).

In 1955 he was awarded the Olivetti National Prize for Architecture. Between 1953 and 1959 he was involved in the project for the Olivetti recreation centre, a large-scale scheme where the attention to detail that had characterized his previous architecture is perhaps less evident.

He has been a member of the most important cultural associations, from the MSA to the INU to the CIAMs. His professional activities range across all the architectural disciplines.

His most significant works are: Alessandria, competition for the livestock market (first prize 1938); Ischia, Terme Regina Isabella (1950); Cesate, accommodation in the INA quarter-houses (1952); Milan, Gallery of Modern Art (1953, in reconstruction); Florence, redesigning of layout of certain rooms in the Uffizi Galleries (in collaboration with G. Michelucci and C. Scarpa, 1956); Venice, the Casa delle Zitelle (1957); Arenzano, general plan for the pinewood (in collaboration with L. Caccia Dominioni).

Enzo Mari was born in Novara in 1932. He works in Milan. Since the early fifties he has been engaged in research into the psychology of vision, concerning himself in particular with the perception of three-dimensional space and the programming of perceptive structures. He is interested in the problems inherent in production relationships and techniques, the ideologies and methodologies of projects.

He has taught at the Study Centre for Visual Communication at the University of Parma, the Academy of Fine Arts in Carrara, and the Faculty of Architecture at the Milan Politecnico. He has been awarded numerous prizes for his research and design work, and his works are exhibited in fourteen museums.

Franco Dell'Orto was born on 11 June 1948 in Seregno, and graduated in 1974 at the Politecnico in Milan, where he has lived and worked since 1976, dealing with architectural planning, with particular attention to urban and green ornamentation.

Marina Basso, born in Treviso in 1953, graduated in architecture at the Milan Politecnico in 1980. She works in the fields of building design, urban planning and environmental impact evaluation studies. A registered member of the Order of Journalists as a freelance journalist, she has been involved in various publishing activities. She is a member of In/Arch.

Maria Vittoria Bocconi was born in Milan in 1962 and graduated in architecture at the Milan Politecnico in 1988. She is involved in building design and regeneration and urban planning studies. She is a consultant to the Municipality of Milan for the revision of Building Regulations.

Giovanni Terzi was born in Milan in 1964 and graduated at the Milan Politecnico in 1990; he is involved in building design and regeneration. An assistant at the Politecnico in the department of Design and Surveying under Professor Arnaboldi, he contributes to a number of magazines in the sector, including *Arca*, *Lighting Design* and *Milano '90*.

The architects **Luigi Maria Guffanti**, **Piergiuseppe Diodato** and **Giorgio Reboli**, who all graduated at the Milan Politecnico, now work together in the field of architecture, urban planning and interior design. Their partnership began in 1972 with the opening of their studio in Milan.

Their most recent and significant projects in the field of architecture and urban planning concern the restorations to the churches of San Protaso (1986) and San Cristoforo (1990) in Milan, the designing of the tourist housing development in Piazzatorre (1987), the urban and environmental planning study for the Via Calatafimi and Santa Croce in Milan (1989) and the project for the San Donato interchange for Metropolitana Milanese (in collaboration with others).

The architect **Carlo Chambry** was born in Milan on 11 October 1945. He graduated in architecture at the Milan Politecnico in 1970 after collaborating with the architect Ignazio Gardella (1967-69). He began his professional activities in 1970 in Milan, and is involved in planning and works management in the field of construction and restructuring, urban design and industrial design.

His works most worthy of mention are: Milan, Architectural competition for the designing of the urban system of the Piazza Duca d'Aosta-Via V. Pisani-Piazza della Repubblica (with the architect Antonio Zanuso). First prize, work commissioned by the Metropolitana Milanese: Work in progress (1988); Milan, MM competition by invitation for the designing of the Piazza Missori (with the architect Antonio Zanuso). Prize-winning project (1988). He also collaborated with architect Antonio Zanuso's studio on certain projects, including the special planning scheme for the area of the 'Mario Negri' Research Institute.

The architect **Antonio Zanuso** was born in Milan on 16 June

1949; he began his professional activities in 1971 and in 1974 he graduated at the Milan Politecnico. He has worked with the architect Renzo Piano in Genoa and Paris.

The architect **William Pascoe** was born in Ann Arbor, Mich., on 10 April 1954. He collaborated with various architecture studios in New York and Chicago between 1977 and 1982.

His most significant works are: the project for didactic decor for Olivetti Synthesis; Milan, restructuring of the former Stelline building and courtyards, the Corso Magenta; Milan, MM national competition - Piazza della Repubblica/Piazza Duca d'Aosta - first prize. Work in progress (with the architect Carlo Chambry); Milan, MM national competition for the Piazza Missori - prize-winning project (with the architect Carlo Chambry); Milan, restructuring of the third courtyard of the former Stelline building; Milan, AIM urban planning competition - for the Garibaldi/Repubblica area (with the architect Carlo Teoldi). Prize-winning project (1992).

Gino Pollini was born in Rovereto in 1903. For many years he worked alongside Luigi Figini, and was one of the promoters of Group 7.

His most significant works are: the recreational building at the III Biennial of the Figurative Arts in Monza (1927); Monza, Electrical House (1930); study of an artist's villa at the V Biennial in Milan (1933); Milan, Church of the Madonna dei Poveri (1952-54); Ivrea, Olivetti social services zone (1954-57); Sparanise (Caserta), industrial complex for Manifattura Ceramica Pozzi (1960-63); Milan, Chiesa Rossa quarter (1960).

Silvano Tintori (Novara, 1929) and **Maurizio Calzavara** (Milan, 1931-93) were trained at Ernesto Rogers' school and worked together in Milan since 1958. Many civic and public buildings have been built in Milan and in Italy from their designs.

Calzavara, a scholar of Milanese Modern, was a lecturer in Architectonic Composition; Tintori is a full professor of Urban Planning Theory at the Faculty of Architecture at the Milan Politecnico.

Ugo La Pietra was born in Bussi sul Tirino on 16 November 1938. He graduated in architecture at the Politecnico in Milan, where he carries out his professional activities.

His production cuts right across the world of architecture, from interior design to planning, also embracing the publishing world.

Of his construction works should be mentioned the Gescal residential complex in Vimodrone; he is currently involved in designing the layout of the Stadera complex for the IACP in Milan.

Printed in Italy